THE CULTIVATION OF READING

Teaching in a Language/Communication Context

THE CULTIVATION OF READING

Teaching in a Language/Communication Context

HORST G. TASCHOW

TEACHERS COLLEGE PRESS

Teachers College, Columbia University
New York and London

Published by Teachers College Press, 1234 Amsterdam Avenue, New York, N.Y. 10027

Copyright © 1985 by Teachers College, Columbia University

All rights reserved. No part of this publication may be reproduced or transmitted in any form or by any means, electronic or mechanical, including photocopy, or any information storage and retrieval system, without permission from the publisher.

Grateful acknowledgment for the preparation of Figures 2.1, 3.1, 4.1, and 5.1 is extended to David Weir, Graphic Artist, Audio-Visual Services, University of Regina, Regina, Saskatchewan, Canada.

Library of Congress Cataloging in Publication Data

Taschow, Horst G., 1921-
  The cultivation of reading.

  Bibliography: p.
  Includes index.
  1. Reading (Elementary) 2. Reading (Secondary education) I. Title.
LB1573.T347   1985   428.4'0712   84-29383

ISBN 0-8077-2775-X
ISBN 0-8077-2710-5 (pbk.)

Manufactured in the United States of America
90 89 88 87 86 85   1 2 3 4 5 6

Contents

Acknowledgments	viii
Introduction	ix

PART I: READING IN THE HUMAN CONTEXT

1. Reading: A Part of Human Communication — 3
- Communication — 3
- The Triad of Communication: Sender–Message–Receiver — 4
- Kinds of Communication — 6
- Language Development — 11
- Replying to Messages: Response and Feedback — 16

2. Reading: A Description of Human Communication — 20
- Basic Knowledge in Understanding Reading — 20
- Lifelines to Reading — 24
- Emotion — 24
- Cognition — 31
- Psychomotor Abilities — 34
- Active Reading through REIVA Processing — 37

PART II: READING IN THE TEACHING CONTEXT

3. Reading: A Synthesis of Developmental Processes — 43
- How Reading Begins — 43
- Processes That Contribute to Reading — 45
- Reading and Cognitive Development — 52
- Encouragement — 61

4. Becoming Ready — 63
- Sources of Reading Readiness — 63
- Preparing for Reading — 65

Ready to Teach Reading	71
Perceptual Awareness	77

5. Basic Information in Reading — 79
Transition from Home to School	79
Graphophonological Information	81
Graphic and Phonic Constituents	86
Patterns of Patterns	93
Phonics	94
Word Recognition	97

6. Advanced Information in Reading — 100
Syntactic Information	100
Semantic Information	102
Information Processing	106
Guiding Thinking in Reading	110

7. Reading in Different Content Areas — 119
Reading in Basal Readers	119
Content Reading	126
Organizing Instruction for Reading Comprehension	127
Acquisition of General and Subject-Area Vocabulary	131
Textbook Reading Comprehension	134

8. Teaching Reading — 138
Instructional Procedures	138
Reading in Basal Readers: The Directed Reading Activity Method	138
Reading in Linguistic Readers	149
Other Approaches to Teaching Reading	150
Eclectic Approaches to Teaching Reading	155

PART III: READING IN THE READER'S CONTEXT

9. Toward Independent Reading — 161
Grouping	161
Oral and Silent Reading	162
Toward Independent Study	167
Correlates of Using Knowledge	170

10. Different Readers — 178
What the Research Literature Says	178

Toward More Acceptable Forms of English	183
Pluralism in Monolingual Instruction	192

11. Evaluating the Reader's Reading — 196
Using Assessment for Evaluation — 196
Formal Testing — 200
Informal Testing — 203

References — 217
About the Author — 238
Index — 239

Acknowledgments

Although the content of this text is my responsibility alone, the making of the book is owed to many:

> To Dr. Ned D. Marksheffel, who will remain an unforgettable teacher, researcher, and writer; to Dr. G.E. Richert, the former Dean of the Faculty of Education at the University of Regina; and to my colleagues here and elsewhere for their critical comments, communications, writings, and readings, all of which made it increasingly difficult, if not impossible, to distinguish my own ideas from those who shared similar ones;

> To the President's Research Fund and the Graduate Studies Special Project Fund for financial assistance;

> To Susan Liddicoat of Teachers College Press and Susan Keniston for editorial assistance;

> To my daughter, Cornelia Daniela, for her patience and understanding in typing the final manuscript; and above all to my dear wife, Ursula Maria, whose constant encouragement and untiring love inspired my professional career and the writing of this book.

Introduction

The Cultivation of Reading is written from a psycholinguistic perspective to assist teachers-in-training to prepare for reading instruction in grades one through eight. This book can also be used by practicing teachers, teacher's aides, remedial reading teachers, consultants in reading and language arts, and teachers of adult education classes who know that what has been learned about reading and its teaching in the classrooms must be steadily refreshed, supplemented, and modified in the light of new knowledge. In addition, this text can assist parents to clarify for themselves basic issues in reading, which often become confused through overpowering but uninformed publicity.

The three major parts into which this book is divided examine reading in the *human context*, the *teaching context*, and the *reader's context*. Part I contains the first two chapters. In Chapter 1 reading is described as one of the four communication abilities practiced among teachers, students, chalkboards, and books. Chapter 2 describes basic knowledge in understanding reading, with its affective, cognitive, and psychomotor characteristics that lead to a strategy of active reading communication. Part II, which comprises chapters 3 through 8, examines reading in the *teaching context*. Chapter 3 presents reading as a synthesis of developmental processes and is based on various theoretical positions. Chapter 4 examines the development of reading readiness and its parent-teacher partnership, together with becoming ready to teach reading. Chapter 5 investigates the basic information that is essential to the teaching of beginning and advanced reading. Chapter 6 studies advanced information on reading, including processing models and reading-thinking strategies. Chapter 7 discusses teaching for reading comprehension in basal readers and different content-area textbooks. Chapter 8 describes instructional procedures that are used in basal reading programs, in linguistic readers, and in other approaches in teaching reading. Part III deals with reading in the *reader's context* and contains chapters 9 through 11. Chapter 9 describes how to become an independent, lifelong reader by examining the modes of reading, study techniques, and some correlates of using knowledge. Chapter 10 discusses different readers in terms of linguistic features of languages other than English. Chapter 11 examines the use of formal and informal instruments in the assessment of reading performance.

Each chapter has the special features of introductory purpose questions and summaries for each main section.

Throughout, this book reflects my position that reading is a synthesis of human processes, not a mere product of skills agglomeration. Teaching reading, as it should be pursued, means challenging students to think according to their own physical and sociopsycholinguistic development, so that they can reach the greatest possible proficiency in reading. In our literate society success in life is with all those children who learn to read effectively.

Part I

READING IN THE HUMAN CONTEXT

CHAPTER 1

Reading: A Part of Human Communication

Purpose questions for this chapter:
- What are the processes in communication?
- How is reading related to communication?
- What are the four basic language abilities?
- How are they used in communication?

COMMUNICATION

Mother said to Bobby, "Put the grocery bag on the table." "There are flowers on the table," replied Bobby. Just then, Father walked into the room, looking at Bobby. Blaring music from another room filled Father's and Bobby's ears. Through the open door they could see the TV pictures. From upstairs someone called, "Don't make so much noise. I have to read an assignment in my social studies book."

This is communication. One person speaks to another; flowers "speak" wordlessly; eyes seek eye contact; musical noises clamor for earful attention; TV flashes visual pictures; a calling voice expresses dissatisfaction; and information is extracted from print.

Communication is the sharing of ideas, thoughts, information, gestures, and feelings from person to person (Harris & Hodges, 1981, p. 57). Communication may take place between persons of a social unit and between persons and mechanical devices such as tape recorders, telephones, and computers. Communication may also occur between persons and plants, persons and animals, and persons and objects. Communication may happen in a dynamic relationship between daughter and mother, husband and wife, and others. Finally, communication is a means for transmitting written or printed messages in books, signs, telegrams, or any other such materials.

In every instance, a message is conveyed from one source to another. Messages are sent and received in three different modes: through oral language, written language, and sign-gesture language (see Figure 1.1). Oral language extends to speaking and listening, written language to writing and reading, and sign-gesture language to visualizing and observing. Of those, speaking, writing, and visualizing are produced and expressed; listening,

FIGURE 1.1. Functions and Modes of Language

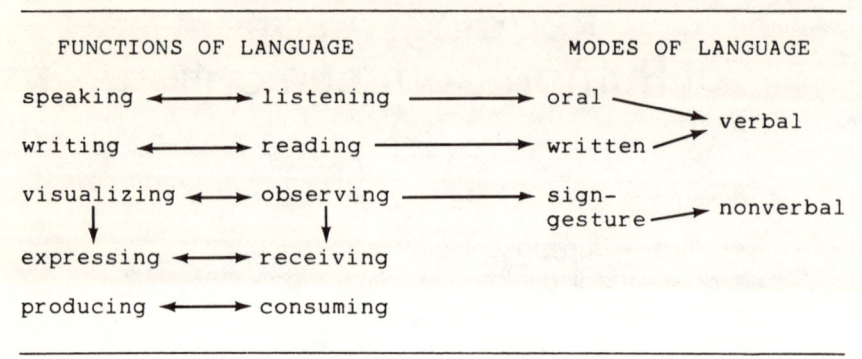

FUNCTIONS OF LANGUAGE	MODES OF LANGUAGE
speaking ⟷ listening ⟶	oral ⟶ verbal
writing ⟷ reading ⟶	written ⟶
visualizing ⟷ observing ⟶	sign-gesture ⟶ nonverbal
expressing ⟷ receiving	
producing ⟷ consuming	

reading, and observing are consumed or received. Oral and written language are verbal, and sign or gesture language are nonverbal.

Nonverbal language, or kinesic behavior (Scheflen, 1972), may accompany oral and written language but can also be used by itself to communicate, as in sending "smoke signals." Whatever mode or modes of communicating are used, thinking is an invariable ingredient in all the verbal and nonverbal abilities.

Most of the time, people communicate through oral language. Children, too, encounter oral language first, through listening and speaking. This first encounter is known as first-order processing (Emig, 1977), which usually develops without formal instruction. Reading and writing, or second-order processing, usually develop with formal instruction and are essential in handling written language (Hennings, 1982).

THE TRIAD OF COMMUNICATION: SENDER–MESSAGE–RECEIVER

Communication has three distinct coordinates: a sender, a message, and a receiver. A sender produces a message that, after it is encoded into a symbol system of sounds, graphics, and/or visuals (gestures), is transmitted to a receiver. This is the triad of communication, a closely related threesome.

In the sender's mind are thoughts, feelings, or information ready to be communicated. Because the sender cannot transmit mental images, the message must be encoded into a system of symbols that the sender knows. The symbolized message is called the psychological context. It is colored and permeated with the sender's human feelings, values, biases, interests, attitudes, and motivations, all developed from the sender's past experiences. The encoded psychological context is transmitted through speaking, writing, printing, gestures, signs, light flashes, smoke, or other procedures that transmit the symbols to the receiver, who must decode the message.

Reading: A Part of Human Communication

The receiver can decode the message into the language of the sender, provided that the sender's systems of symbols and experiences are familiar and common to those of the recipient. Should the receiver not share these systems, difficulties arise in understanding the message.

The prerequisites for interactive participation in successful communication (this word is derived from the Latin word *communicare*, meaning to participate) are embedded in and grow out of the sender's and receiver's sense of sharing in a common environment. Since the receivers only hear sounds or see symbols, they must be able to add meaning from their own background experiences that will match with the senders' intended meanings.

To experience what sharing in communication means, read and try to understand this message: *I saw a cyprinoid*. No doubt you can identify and pronounce the visual patterns. Now, try to add meaning to them from your background experiences. Are you experiencing difficulties with the meaning of the word *cyprinoid*? Little can be gained from contextual clues surrounding this word, so, unless the reader/receiver of this message shares background experiences in common with those of the writer/sender, no meaning can be gained from this message. It cannot be understood unless the receiver knows what a cyprinoid is. While the receiver is able to say and recode the words, their meaning is lost because of a lack of background experiences with this specific kind of vocabulary.

Suppose you receive these written messages: $\alpha\nu\theta\rho\omega\pi o\sigma$; *puella cantat*; *j'ai un chat*; *llueve*; *ich schreibe*. Unless you have background experiences in recognizing, pronouncing, and adding meaning to the words in Greek, Latin, French, Spanish, and German, in that order, they will remain meaningless and empty, and you will be unable to communicate intelligently.

This basic pattern, the triad of communication, can repeat itself indefinitely, thus becoming a communication chain. After the sender has sent the message, the sender waits for some kind of a response or feedback from the receiver. Whatever the response may be, the triad of communication begins again, only in reverse order. The receiver becomes the sender who sends a symbolized message, reflecting his or her social context, which will be received by the former sender, who is now the receiver. As long as the dynamics of sending symbolized messages, receiving them, and responding to them continue, communicative interactions continue as well.

Summary

Communicating is a daily human experience in which a sender transmits a message to a receiver. To understand the message, both sender and receiver must share a similar communicative system and common social and cultural experiences. Without these, there can be no appropriate feedback.

KINDS OF COMMUNICATION

Figure 1.1 showed that messages can be communicated from sender to receiver in oral, written, and sign-gesture language. These modes correspond to the sender's speaking, writing, and visualizing and to the receiver's listening, reading, and observing. Speaking, writing, reading, and listening are verbal language functions pertaining to words in any form, while visualizing and observing are nonverbal language functions that do not use words in either formulation or solution of a task.

Nonverbal Communication

In nonverbal communication, messages are transmitted by gestures, body movements, facial expressions, pictures, and many wordless procedures. The physical setting and social environment are very important to the effectiveness of nonverbal communication.

Metacommunication. Imagine being stranded in a faraway place where the people live in a different social context and listen to, speak, read, and write a language different from yours. You talk, but no one understands you; they talk, but you do not understand them.

You are hungry. You look around and you spot a place that looks like a shop where bakery goods are sold. (In this example, all nonverbal communicators are noted in parentheses.) You enter, and you note a particular odor (olfactory impression). You see baked goods in disarray on somewhat dilapidated shelves (physical setting). The vendor appears (eye contact) from behind a partially torn and not-so-clean curtain in equally not-so-clean clothes (physical and human environment). The vendor talks to you in a language you do not understand. You, in return, manage to smile (facial expression) and simultaneously shrug your shoulders and move your head to and fro (bodily action) to "tell" the vendor, "I cannot speak your language." The vendor smiles (facial expression) and nods (bodily action), thus responding to the received nonverbal communication. You point (hand gesture) at what looks to you (foreign, "other"—social context) like a loaf of bread, though different in color, shape, and size (your own social context). The vendor takes the loaf of bread, again responding to your message, holds it up for you to see (bodily action). You smile, easier than before, and nod vigorously to show acceptance by opening your purse to reach for the money. You collect several coins, stretch out the palm of your hand (bodily action) with the coins visible for the vendor (offering), communicating, "Here is the money to pay for the bread." The vendor takes some of the coins, you put the remainder back in your purse. You take the loaf of bread (bodily action), smile (facial expression), hug the bread, and wave your hand (bodily actions), communicating "thank you and good bye." Then you leave the shop. The nonverbal communication between you and the vendor, with a loaf of bread as the psychological context, is completed.

The way in which the two communicators conducted their nonverbal communication may be referred to as *metacommunication* or *paralinguistic communication*. This is a system alongside verbal language but without words, which Hittleman (1983) describes as "patterns of cues and signals meaningful to the members of a cultural group or social organization" (p. 19). Metacommunication also can refer to what goes along with nonverbal procedures in an effort to communicate messages without words.

Visuals and Movements. Nonverbal communication does not end with body language. It can include paintings, drawings, graphics, photographs, movies, filmstrips, and all other visual materials that are and can be intentionally or unintentionally displayed. Dance, ballet, and pantomime, performed intentionally, are other modes of nonverbal communication. All these modes are both expressive and receptive. They are expressive from the viewpoint of those who paint, photograph, and film and those who perform through bodily movements. They are receptive from the viewpoint of those who look at and observe what is displayed and what is performed. The former are the senders, the latter the receivers of the nonverbal communication messages.

These modes of nonverbal communication assist people of all ages from around the world, of differing ethnicities and languages to communicate among themselves. They are particularly helpful communicators for ideas generated among children and between social groups (Furth & Wachs, 1975).

Wordless Reading. Reading and comprehending visuals such as printed nonverbal business signs and those that direct traffic in public places and reading wordless picture books are said to be part of visual literacy. Read & Smith (1982) point out that, in wordless picture books, children learn to interpret actions through lines, shapes, and colors. Their thinking processes are stimulated by finding sequences, choosing main ideas, drawing conclusions, and arriving at judgments. In using wordless picture books as well as pictorial illustrations, teachers can not only focus on reading subskills but also catch readers' attention and guide them to extract information not readily given in the text (O'Donnell, 1983).

Verbal Communication

Verbal or linguistic communication conveys messages among individuals and groups by using spoken and written language. The basic ingredients of verbal language are words, numbers, and any other written notations. However, in this discussion, I am concerned mainly with transmitting meaning as encoded in the graphic symbols or letters that form words, which form sentences.

The basic symbolic language features are words. Words expressed orally are the generic agents in speaking-listening communication, and words expressed graphically are the generic agents in writing-reading communication.

Oral Communication. When the mode of communication consists of oral reading, the reader is the sender of the author's or writer's printed message, while the one who listens to the message is the receiver. This is an oral-aural relationship, in which the sender speaks (oral) and the receiver listens (aural). In order to understand the author's printed message, the oral reader first decodes (that is, goes from code language to meaning), then encodes the meaning into oral language to be heard by the listener, who, in order to understand it, decodes the encoded message. In cases where the oral reader is able to say a word but does not understand its meaning (as in the previous example of *cyprinoid*), the result is not oral reading but word calling and sounding out (Goodman, 1976, p. 481).

Silent Communication. When the mode of communication consists of silent reading, the writer's message on the printed page is the sender and the reader is the receiver. This is a graphic-interpretive relationship, in which the sender is the printed page (graphic) and the receiver reads silently (interpretive). The silent reader goes directly from print to meaning, while the oral reader moves from print through sound to meaning.

Meaning. Oral and written language both make up the expressive functions in communication that use words as language symbols. Words in themselves have no meaning; rather, the meaning comes from people and their responses. What one word, one group of language symbols means to one person does not necessarily mean the same to another person. Each individual must decide what that word is to mean in that situation, at that time, and for that purpose. For instance, the sound and orthographic patterns of the word *dog*, by itself, in an utterance or visual word sequence, may call forth such varied meanings as a quadrupedal, carniverous, domesticated animal; an idolized pet; a man's best friend or worst enemy; a watchdog; a seeing eye dog; a water dog; a sun dog; a worthless fellow; a mechanical device; or even ruin. Meaning depends on the experiences and memories of the person, as well as the surrounding words in a sentence, as in *The ship crossed the channel yesterday* and *Channel five will bring the movie*.

Without meaning, a word is either an empty sound or noise or just a visual squiggle. Meaning is the word's indispensible component. As in the example of *dog*, a word represents a category under which many different referents are possible; hence, a word is generic in that it denotes not one but a group of referents (Vygotzky, 1962, 1977).

The teacher in grade one talks of the dog as the friend of humans and shows a picture of a shepherd dog with the word *dog* printed underneath. The teacher tells of how the dog helped people, saved their lives, and prevented them from dangers and how, in turn, people cared for, liked, and loved the dog. Children add to the teacher's comments from their own experiences of having and caring for their own dogs or neighbors' dogs. Common experiences of sender and receiver make this communication possible. The person who is left out here is the child who was attacked by an animal that looked like the one in the picture, the child for whom the picture (nonverbal language) called forth a meaning different from what the teacher intended it to be.

Vocal Intonation. In oral communication, prosodic features of intonation and pitch used by the sender-speaker may evoke a variety of interpretive meanings in the listener-receiver. Utterances are shaded by pitch, the rise and fall of a voice. Sequences of pitches result in intonation patterns that give the tune of the sentence. Intonation patterns in utterances help the receiver-listener to understand the intended meaning of the sender-speaker. "*We* will go now" contrasts in intonation with "we will go *now?*" (Cazden, 1972).

In addition to intonation and pitch, accenting different syllables aids in the understanding of what is to be communicated. In the utterance, *he saw the object and could not object to it*, the word *object* is differentiated by stressing either the first or the second syllable. While stress appears to differentiate the homonym *ob*ject from o*b*ject, it is the meaning to be conveyed that directs the voice to place the spoken accent of either part of the word.

Try stressing each of the following words in turn, and you will see how different vocal behavior may affect the meaning of the utterances:

Bill is tall. (The speaker compares *Bill* to someone who is not as tall as *Bill*.)
Bill *is* tall. (The speaker knows Bill *is*.)
Bill is *tall*. (The speaker knows Bill is *not short*.)

Alternating stressed and unstressed syllables or words results in rhythm: *Bill* is a *tall* boy.

Vocal behavior is also marked by inflectional voice variation, depending upon the meaning to be communicated:

No. (It is not.)
No! (Don't do it.)
No? (Shall I or shall I not?)
Noooo! (How disgusting.)

Intonation, stress, and voice inflections are components of the speaker's vocal behavior, adding timbre or voice quality to the spoken sounds and amplifying the sender's intended meaning. These aids are not present in silent processing, however, but they may be suggested by punctuation marks, different typefaces (usually italics), indentations, and other visual markings.

Registers. What the sender-speaker wants to say orally and what the sender-writer wants to express in writing depend on the choice of words by which the message is communicated. The kind of words the sender thinks to be appropriate for the situation or event is known as the register of the language (F. Smith, 1982, p.87). The utterances *I ain't no understand* and *I have not understood* represent two different registers, different by the choice of words and the manner in which words are grouped together.

Registers of oral and written language are also influenced by sentence length, active and passive voice, and the usage of pronouns. Teachers usually form questions using more words than children will use in forming answers. The teacher asks, "Who went to the supermarket?" to which the child replies, "Mother." Similarly, and perhaps also to accommodate and simulate children's ways of speaking, sentences in basal readers are usually shorter than those found in other textbooks. Likewise, registers in a cookbook are markedly different from those in a novel. The cookbook gives directions in short sentences, phrases, or words; the novel abounds with long, complex sentences describing whatever happens.

Differences in register depend on subject, addressee, and context. There are two kinds of registers: the addressor-subject register and the addressor-addressee register. The addressor-subject register reflects the language and jargon of professions, trades, and sports in which technical, specialized knowledge is shared with the addressees, who are assumed to be knowledgeable in these subjects. In giving a complex mathematical formula, the addressor expects the addressees to know what this formula represents and when and how to apply it.

Take, for example, the formula $\bar{X} = \Sigma X/N$. Do you know what each member of the formula stands for? The character $\bar{X}$ represents the mean or the average of a number of scores, known as raw scores, which come from a standardized or teacher-made test the students have taken. The symbol $=$ means that what follows is equal to $\bar{X}$. This value is arrived at by finding the sum (Σ) of the scores (X) and using the division process (symbolized by the slanted line /) to divide by N, the number of students who have taken the test. When each character has been properly interpreted and the computations have been completed, the mean score, or $\bar{X}$, for this particular performance will have been found.

In another example, the addressor assumes that the addressee has specific knowledge when communicating that *the substrata factors are thought of* through listening and speaking. This can range from a modest word bank of about 3,500 to an immense accumulation of about 48,000 different words.

One researcher has estimated that normal, unimpaired children at the age of six have acquired a vocabulary of about 7,800 different words (Bartlett, 1981, p. 34), a figure that may differ somewhat between middle-and lower-class children. Those with smaller vocabularies, however, are just as skilled in learning as other children are. Because of the tremendous growth in listening and speaking vocabularies during the preschool years, most if not all words in the beginning basal readers are new only to the children's *eyes*.

When formal schooling begins, children in first grade face, without being aware of it, a lopsided learning proposition, because their listening and speaking vocabularies outshine their beginning reading vocabulary. Then when reading words and sentences is sufficiently mastered, the reading vocabulary outshines their writing vocabulary. Thus, within the four language abilities, listening and speaking vocabularies together with basic syntactic development have a head start during the preschool years, while reading and writing vocabularies await their acquisition and development at the time when formal schooling begins.

While it is commonly assumed that this gap narrows and closes gradually with formal and informal learning during the school years, Blass, Jurenka, and Zirzow (1981) have shown that an appropriate classroom environment can stimulate oral and written language communication by recording and giving messages. Children and sometimes teachers and principals write notes that are kept in the classroom to be read and answered. Likewise, poems, jokes, and experiences are written down, collected, and placed on the reading table to encourage further development of reading and writing vocabularies.

Language Teaming

Children, of course, use their vocabulary to make themselves heard, by orally reiterating the messages of signs, pictures and captions, and even their own scribbling. When analyzing this kind of language production, as was said already, listening does not always precede speaking, nor do reading and writing follow in that order. Students need combinations of language abilities when reading orally, copying from the chalkboard, or writing down spelling words. Listening, speaking, reading, and writing team up to make any of these complex activities possible.

The concept of language teaming can assist teachers in understanding the composite and often complementary nature of the learning processes of oral reading, spelling, copying, and dictating. What, for instance, must an individual do when reading orally? At lease two different basic language abilities receptor skills acquired through active participation in what is heard and seen and in how the messages are perceived, interpreted, and evaluated. Speaking and writing are processor skills that activate speech and hand muscles to produce oral and written language.

Although it is generally believed (Hall, Moretz, & Statom, 1976) that the four basic language abilities are acquired in sequence, there is no hierarchical order between and among them. Language abilities also interrelate. Speaking leads to listening, reading leads to speaking and listening, and writing—which may begin with listening—leads again to reading. Particularly, writing is not an outgrowth of reading in the sense that reading should be learned before writing should begin.

Integrating Reading and Writing

Montessori (1964) stated that "writing precedes reading," that experience has shown that writing and reading "are not absolutely contemporaneous" (p. 296). Harste, Burke, and Woodward (1979) suggest that growth in both reading and writing or the written/printed language is a sociopsycholinguistic process and should be studied in the social context. Research by Lehr (1981) supports further the view that reading and writing should be integrated to improve instruction in both areas. Seaver and Botel (1983) describe a first-grade teacher's typical day, during which instruction consists of integrating reading, writing, and oral communication. During instruction children respond to literature by retelling, enacting, debating, and composing; they respond to self-selected reading by pacing themselves in their own ways; they use oral, written, and graphic composing to discover, explore, and integrate personal interests; and they respond to investigating and mastering linguistic systems in all subjects by examining the forms of language and their relationships. Auten (1983b), in reviewing the research, asserts that the global, complex skills of reading, writing, speaking, and listening work together with thinking in a language system that assists in categorizing, abstracting, and storing experiences. Auten (1983a), in another research summary, maintains that reading and writing are a mutual support system. Boutwell (1983) reports that early in third grade reading becomes an integral part of writing and vice versa. Marta, a third-grade student became a "reader of her own writing . . . and a writer of her own reading" (p. 725).

Vocabularies

With the development of listening, speaking, reading, and writing, vocabularies develop as well. Smith and Johnson (1980) report estimates of how many words children possess in their vocabularies, acquired mainly

From Listening to Speaking

For a long time it was thought that listening began at birth. Recent literature from Europe, however, indicates that listening begins "in utero." Tomatis (1978) conjectured that the earliest human communication occurs between a pregnant woman as the sender and the fetus as the receiver, as "the child hears the voice [mother's] speaking and extracts the emotional sense from it." In return, the fetus sends information to the mother as "she feels him, senses him and sees him." Tomatis also thinks that it is "through the sound that he [the child] begins to integrate the basis of his mother tongue" (p. 65).

As the infant arrives and embarks on its earthly path, listening still is the major input. Soon the infant learns to distinguish the sounds of its mother's and father's footsteps approaching the crib. The infant listens to its own crying and learns that crying rushes a parent to the scene to tend to real or pretended needs. The infant listens to its own babbling sounds, responds to them by babbling more, and turns into a chatterer. This word comes from the Middle English word *chatteren*, meaning to imitate. The infant turns into an imitator who listens and produces speechlike sounds rapidly in staccato style. Linking sounds together, the infant doubles up syllables that sound like "mama, dada, doodoo," to which adults attach various meanings. From this vocalizing and sound imitating, further listening transforms playful speech into the beginning of purposefully produced and understandable speech sounds.

Refining Speech

Holophrases or one-word sentences like *cup* may have such various meanings as, *Where is my cup? I want my cup of milk*, or *Give me my cup of milk*. Holophrases develop into two-word phrases and then into more complete sentences. At the age of three, children speak in four- to five-word sentences; by the age of four and five, children have acquired all the common and basic sentence structures (Maxim, 1980). As children's interest in groups of words becomes more and more contagious, their listening and speaking vocabularies expand steadily (Durkin, 1978, p. 379), as do their abilities to make themselves heard more expressively.

In general, what children understand, how they speak, and the words they use in speaking are well developed by the time of school entry. At this point children have acquired, through the receptive mode of listening, large vocabularies, which they use through the expressive mode of speaking to communicate with anyone around them or with themselves.

The receptive mode, then, is not a passive intake of what is heard in listening and what is seen in reading. Instead, both listening and reading are *as neurological subsystems of brain assemblies which gain an interfacilitation* (J. Holmes, 1967, p. 20). As was the mathematical formula, this is an example of a subject-focused register in which the addressor is more concerned with the subject matter than the immediate understanding by the addressee.

In daily teacher-student communication the addressor-subject register can impede the reading-learning process by using an instructional language that is not understood readily by the students. DeStefano (1980) explains that the language instruction register (LIR) "can have important instructional consequences, especially if the teacher has formed the prior belief that a student's definition of terms in the LIR 'fits' the teacher's" (p. 812). What DeStefano is saying is that teachers should not assume and take for granted that students have in their heads the same or similar meanings—or any meanings at all—for new words, terms, and concepts that teachers use, whether or not they are necessary for instruction in a certain topic.

The register of addressor-addressee focuses on establishing and maintaining social relationships (Thorn & Braun, 1974). Social situations in which communication occurs determine the tone, lexis or words, and grammar of the language used in conveying a spoken message from sender to receiver. Various addressor-addressee registers are used in all social situations, including school situations or wherever and whenever people are together.

Children use different addressor-addressee registers when they talk among themselves in and out of school, when they ask the teacher, or when they address the school principal. In the same vein, addressor-addressee registers change when greeting friends and occasional acquaintances in the street; when exchanging pleasantries of "How are you?" and "The weather is nice today"; when inquiring about the stock market; and when expressing concerns about the diagnosis of the heart specialist.

Summary

In verbal communication, messages are sent and received among individuals and groups through the verbal signals of spoken and written language that correspond to sociocultural settings and customs. Verbal communication almost always is accompanied by nonverbal language, depending on the social environment, occasion, and purpose. At times, nonverbal language may be perceived as being an even more important part of communication than verbal language.

LANGUAGE DEVELOPMENT

The goal of language development is to acquire the abilities to listen, speak, read, and write with certainty, fluency, and speed. Listening, speaking, reading, and writing are referred to as the four basic language abilities.

are involved: reading and speaking. The former is a receptive activity, and the latter is an expressive one. If the reader is lacking any degree of proficiency in either one of them, certainty, fluency, and speed in oral reading are interfered with. Any slight speech impediment may make the oral reader uncertain in pronunciation and intonation, uneasy in the flow of words, and hesitant in proceeding to the end of a sentence. Thus, reading and speaking equal oral reading.

The spelling of words that are spoken by the teacher also involves language teamwork. Listening and writing, which are interrelated receptive and expressive language activities, result in spelling. Before students can write out the words orthographically, letter by letter, in proper sequence according to usage, they must be heard and perceived as spoken by the teacher. Listening, then, is the beginning of spelling. After the received sound patterns make sense to the recipients and are recognized as a word in their listening and speaking vocabularies, the recognized sound pattern must be unscrambled into acceptable usage of orthographic representation. Thus, listening and writing equal spelling.

Spelling, however, can include yet another equation of listening and speaking, in the case of oral spelling. When the teacher asks how a certain word is spelled, students listen first to receive and then to match the sound pattern with one of those in their listening and speaking vocabularies. Then the letter names that compose the word are recited in their correct sequence. Thus, listening and speaking equal oral spelling.

Copying, another instance of language teaming, consists of reading and writing. Students engage in receptive and expressive language activities in order to take written or printed material (preproduction) from the chalkboard or a book page and duplicate it in their notebooks (postproduction). Thus, in this sense of reproducing original text, reading and writing equal copying.

If learners learn better by repeating aloud to themselves what they are about to write, they interrelate speaking and writing, which at this time are both expressive activities. The same expressive activities are employed when students, after they have memorized a passage, recite it to themselves while simultaneously writing it down. Thus, in both instances, speaking and writing equal written recitation or repetition.

Summary

Communicating, it is thought, begins "in utero" with listening, which develops after birth into speaking. Listening and speaking form the basis from which reading and writing develop. These four basic language abilities facilitate human learning by interrelating receptive and expressive language activities.

REPLYING TO MESSAGES: RESPONSE AND FEEDBACK

Communication is not completed unless the receiver replies to the message received from the sender. A reply to a message can be either a response or feedback, which can be of interpersonal or intrapersonal nature or a mixture of both. In the expressions *interpersonal* and *intrapersonal*, *inter* means between and *intra*, within. Thus the former indicates that two or more persons communicate, while the latter indicates that a single person alone communicates internally. While interpersonal communication is easily observable, intrapersonal communication may not be.

As I said, a reply to a message can be a simple response, such as an answer to a question. This response ends the exchange. Feedback, on the other hand, is a reaction that may judge or change a process or a result. Feedback may extend to a feedback loop in which information is sent back and forth to either modify or control a process in progress (Harris & Hodges, 1981, pp. 116–117).

Interpersonal Communication

In interpersonal communication, the sender and the receiver communicate in a way that is seen and heard by both and, depending on the intensity of movements and volume of voices, also can be visible and audible to near and distant observers.

As so often happens, when a message has been received and a response has been given, the communication terminates unless the sender sends a new message. This is often typical of teacher-student communication, where the teacher poses the questions and the student responds. With the student answer, the communication ends, and a new question is produced. Thus the communication is sender centered, that is, kept alive by the sender alone, as shown in the example given in Figure 1.2.

```
FIGURE 1.2.    One-way, Sender-centered
               Interpersonal Communication
```

SENDER	RECEIVER
I'm going to the game. ⟶	I am, too.
When are you going? ⟶	Don't know.
Let's go together? ⟶	O.K.

FIGURE 1.3. Mutual Interpersonal Communication

SENDER		RECEIVER
Are you going to the game?	⟶	Yes, I'm going.
Sure, I'll come.	⟵	Are you coming?
When do we go?	⟶	Let's go now!

A different kind of interpersonal communication occurs when you talk with your friend, when the teacher talks with the principal, and when the mother converses with her daughter. The sender produces a message, encodes it, and transmits it to the receiver, who, after decoding and thinking about the symbolic message, answers with an encoded response or feedback. The receiver becomes the sender, who transmits a new message to the former sender, who is now the receiver. This mutual exchange and sharing of roles, as illustrated in Figure 1.3, can continue for as long as both parties wish.

Intrapersonal Communication

In intrapersonal communication, messages can be received either from without or from within. Messages from without are sent from an external source. When they are received, they may be dealt with immediately and then stored in long-term memory, or they may be stored away immediately to be dealt with at a later, more appropriate time. As shown in Figure 1.4, these messages are not replied to publicly.

As an example of intrapersonal communication stimulated by messages from within the person, see Figure 1.5. Here, the person is both sender and receiver. As sender, she recalls information about metamorphosis and begins to communicate within herself about it by sending and receiving her own thoughts.

These two examples of intrapersonal communication suggest that, after the messages have been received, the receivers take the time to think about them before actually producing either oral or written responses. Both kinds of intrapersonal communication, alone or in combination with interpersonal processes, together with response and feedback, are found in and can be observed during all phases of reading instruction.

FIGURE 1.4. Intrapersonal Communication
              Stimulated by an Outside Source

| SENDER | RECEIVER |

It appears that George
has withdrawn from par-
ticipating in the group. ⟶ Why would he do that?
                              ↓
                            What may have happened
                            between the last counsel-
                            ing session and now?
                              ↓
                            I must listen again to
                            the last taped session:
                            perhaps . . . ?

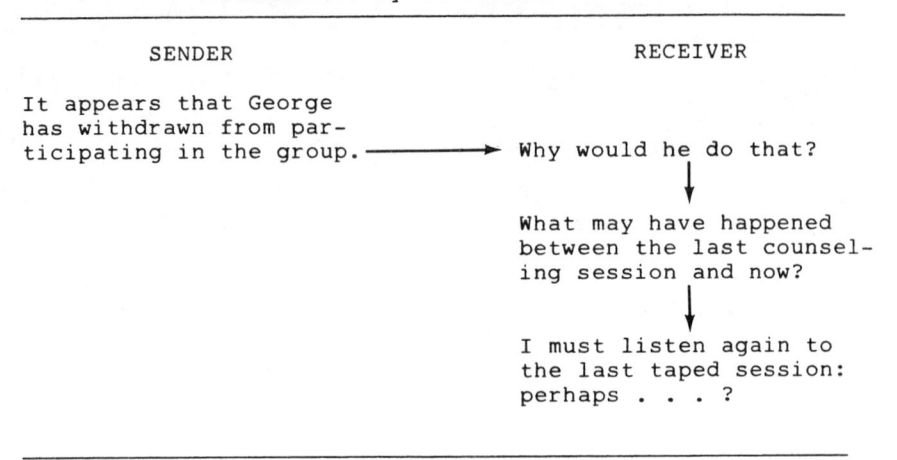

FIGURE 1.5. Intrapersonal Communication
              Stimulated by an Internal Source

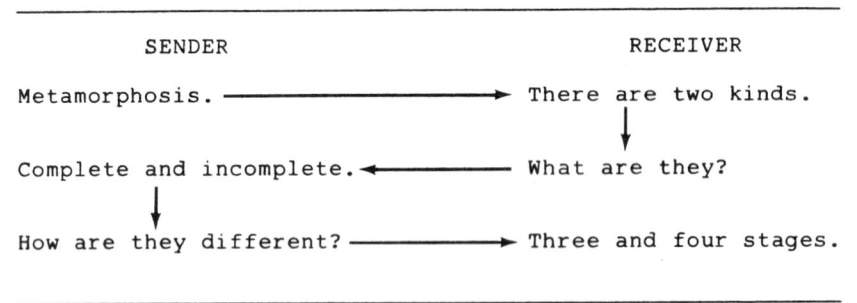

| SENDER | RECEIVER |

Metamorphosis. ⟶ There are two kinds.
                         ↓
Complete and incomplete. ⟵ What are they?
    ↓
How are they different? ⟶ Three and four stages.

Special Communication Awareness

In every classroom there are students who need more time than others to decode incoming messages and encode outgoing ones. Their interpersonal communication processing proceeds at a slower pace. Often, however, their need for more time clashes with the competitive spirit and the more aggressive pace of the faster-working students, who are always ready to comply with a teacher who is anxiously awaiting a response. In this sort of classroom atmosphere the slower-working students not only are penalized but too often are forgotten and ultimately pushed indirectly into withdrawal. There they remain, within themselves, at the expense of active participation in the reading-learning processes.

Summary

Interpersonal and intrapersonal verbal and nonverbal communications are constantly ongoing human experiences and practices that affect all people in all walks of life. In our schools, interpersonal and intrapersonal communications occur formally during reading and other classroom instructions and informally during recess times and after-school activities.

Interpersonal communicative relationships can involve simple responses or more complex feedback loops in which receiver and sender reciprocate their roles in sending and receiving messages.

Intrapersonal communication can be stimulated either from without or from within the individual. Once the message is received, it remains within the individual, who will think the message over and make appropriate private replies.

CHAPTER 2

Reading: A Description of Human Communication

Purpose questions for this chapter:
- What are the roles of words, syntax, and semantics in reading?
- How does emotion affect the reader's processing of print?
- How does cognition influence reading?
- What do psychomotor abilities contribute to reading?
- How does one guide students from product-oriented learning to process-oriented learning through reading?

BASIC KNOWLEDGE IN UNDERSTANDING READING

In *Hamlet* Polonius asked Hamlet, "What do you read, my lord?" Hamlet replied, "Words, words, words" (Act II, Scene 2).
    Words are the stuff sentences are made of, and meaning is what puts the words in a sentence. A word stands for a concept and not directly for a thing; it is a unit that is pronounceable and meaningful either by itself or together with another word.

The Function of Words

    All words share one basic function, which is to assist in expressing total meaning in a sentence. To fulfill this main function a word must associate with other words. In written language words can be seen because they are separated by white spaces from the preceding and the succeeding ones. In oral language, however, it appears doubtful that single words actually can be distinguished from one another without knowing the language (F. Smith, 1982, p. 72). Children are often unable to tell how many words are in a group of spoken words, as in *come here*, which they hear as one word /kumeer/.

While all words serve the function of meaning, Weaver (1980) suggests that we think of words being either content words or function (signal) words. Content words are nouns, verbs, adjectives, and adverbs, while function words are noun determiners, auxiliary verbs, conjunctions, and prepositions. The word *ball* is a content word that carries various meanings by itself. The word *the* is a function word that carries meaning only when in the company of another word, as in *the ball*, where *the* contributes the meaning that it is this ball and no other one.

Words and Morphemes

From the linguistic point of view, a word may also serve as a morpheme, which is the smallest meaning-bearing unit of the language. The word *cat* has one morpheme but the word *cats* has two morphemes. The adding of the ending *s*, which is another morpheme, alters the configuration or appearance of the word *cat* and its pronunciation, structure, and meaning.

There are two kinds of morphemes: free and bound. The word *cat* is known as a free morpheme, while the letter *s*, when attached to the free morpheme *cat*, is known as a bound or combining morpheme. Free morphemes, such as *cat, ball, girl, boy, foot*, and others are groups of sounds that carry meaning by themselves. Bound morphemes carry meaning only when combined or bound with other free morphemes, such as in *cats, balls, girls, boys*, and *footings*.

Nevertheless, the meanings of free morphemes depend upon whether they are used in isolation or in context. In isolation or outside the context, free morphemes carry lexical or denotative meanings represented by definitions that can be "looked up" in the dictionary. Within context, however, free morphemes carry full and precise contextual meanings that can be obtained from the surrounding words in the total sentence environment.

The morpheme *cat* has various lexical entries that range from a domestic to a wild species to a slang usage denoting an inanimate caterpillar tractor. The exact meaning a word is meant to convey in isolation is difficult, if not impossible, to know. Only when a word appears in an appropriate context, which usually is a sentence, can its full and precise meaning be determined. While *Bob saw a large cat* is a sentence, little is said about the cat. When, however, further words are added, as in *Bob saw a large cat, which was one of the mountain lions that endangered the construction site*, the usage of the word *cat* is no longer ambiguous.

In the following examples, note the various ways the lexical meanings and the precise contextual meanings of the common English word *see* can be used in oral and written expressions:

Can you *see* the tree on top of the hill?
Now *see* here young man!
Do you *see* what I mean?
The old woman will never *see* youth again.
Come and *see* me about your marks.
See that you finish all your work.
Let me *see*—where did I put it?
With extra money I will be able to *see* through the difficulty.
I cannot *see* Judy acting so childishly.
Did you *see* stars when you hit your head on the sidewalk?

It is only within the total sentence environment that the reader can decide on the full and precise contextual meaning of the free morpheme.

Syntax and Semantics

When morphemes are organized into patterns that show sequence and structure, as in phrases, clauses, and sentences, arrangements result that are known as syntax.

Syntax puts the elements of language together and determines the word usage as well as the way words are placed together (McNeil, Donant, & Alkin, 1980, p. 132). Syntax, like graphophonic and semantic information, is a part of the system of language. Kolker (1983, p. 16) suggests that syntactic rules for combining words into sentences develop along with sound and meaning. As we have seen earlier, meaning occurs in the company of other words. Conversely then, how words are put together determines meaning. Syntactic influence on meaning becomes clearer when we play with word orders, as in the following: *The hunter hunts the lion* and *The lion hunts the hunter*.

Chomsky (1965, p. 16) recognized syntax, semantics, and phonology as the three major components of generative grammar and explained that (1) syntax deals with the formation of sentences, (2) semantics deals with the study of meanings and how meanings are assigned to strings of words, and (3) phonology deals with how strings of words are pronounced and receive sounds. While growing up and learning a language, children develop, according to Chomsky, "an internal representation of a system of rules that determine how sentences are to be formed, used, and understood" (p. 25). Chomsky's statement is of special importance to all who teach reading to children who have developed a system of rules for a dialect or a language other than "standard" English.

Syntax, which puts words together into distinctive patterns, is a part of grammar. Grammar, as we have seen, encompasses syntax together with phonology and semantics. How a person orders words in a sentence; how one uses inflections, classes of words, natural gender, and verb-subject-pronoun agreements; and how one uses connectives to show grammatical relationships "characterize the knowledge a person has of his or her language" (Downing & Leong, 1982, p. 88).

The study of meaning and the meaning of meanings is known as semantics. It is the knowledge of what meaning is given to which words as they are used to express what one wants to communicate. In the following sentences, *The fish eats the fisherman* and *The fisherman eats the fish*, the meaning of the two sentences is not determined by the individual words, which are exactly the same, but rather by the reader's ability to reconstruct meaning as based on the reader's previous experiences, the reader's familiarity with the concepts, and the reader's knowledge of how language works and how meanings are assigned to strings of words (Harris & Smith, 1980, p. 39).

Understanding the total meaning of words in an idiomatic expression is different from understanding the meaning of strings of words in a sentence. An idiomatic expression such as *Bob flew off the handle* is either known or not known. If the receiver does not know this expression but tries to figure it out by adding the separate meaning of each word, the result may be a kaleidoscope of unrelated words and even more unrelated meanings, as in

> *Bob*—a boy, a man, a male, not a girl
> *flew*—took the airplane
> *off*—away from
> *the*—this, not any other one
> *handle*—object to hold onto, hang onto

Of course, this word-by-word meaning procedure will never convey the meaning of the idiomatic expression, which says that Bob is angry and just how angry he is.

Comprehension is defined by Harris and Hodges (1981) as "the process of getting the meaning of a communication" (p. 60). To comprehend what has been read orally and silently is, of course, the main purpose of reading, a common goal that is confirmed in the literature ranging back to Huey (1908), and up to present-day writings.

Summary

The basic constituents of a sentence are the words, and the free and bound morphemes are the smallest meaning-bearing units. Morphemes or words appear in syntactical order, thus forming sentences. The process of getting the meaning to and from the printed symbols rests with the individual reader, who decodes the words' meanings in isolation or in context. While lexical meanings can be given to isolated words, full, precise contextual meanings can only be determined from the total sentence environment.

LIFELINES TO READING

A lifeline is defined as a route over which supplies are brought to sustain life. Reading, too, has lifelines over which the reader sends messages of what and how to process print. As readers involve themselves in learning to read and reading to learn, they engage the whole organism, not only the mind, in complex, purposeful processes by coordinating emotional, cognitive, and psychomotor abilities.

Biglmaier (1979) called emotion, cognition, and psychomotor abilities the dimensions of reading and described each dimension in terms of its major criterion. Thus, emotion is connected with interest, cognition with understanding, and psychomotor abilities with certainty, fluency, and speed. In all, the three dimensions of reading have five criteria (p. 39). I prefer to denote emotion, cognition, and psychomotor abilities as the main characteristics and list interest, understanding, certainty, fluency, and speed as the subcharacteristics of reading, all of which bring life to reading.

Let us take each characteristic and describe it in some detail and examine it according to its quantitative and qualitative distinctions and its contributions to reading.

EMOTION

Emotion is characterized by reading interest, by which I mean the reader's interest in, attitude toward, motivation for, and spontaneity in grasping the psychological context communicated.

Reading Interest

Interest and reading combine with attitude and motivation to form reading interest, which is a household word in reading instruction. Having an interest in reading and finding reading to be interesting are different from saying this book is interesting and this book is boring. Being interesting or not being interesting is not a quality that rests with a book or an object. Interest is within the reader or the person. Interest is a state of mind. A book or an object is as interesting as the reader or viewer makes it. Readers who maintain that books are either interesting or boring "are unaware of their responsibility to generate interest" (Ortiz, 1983, p. 113).

Interest is one of the affective factors that develop and maintain a desire for reading. Children who are fascinated with the printed words, who ask questions about words, who in general seek books and look at them (Knight, 1983, p. 29), show the kind of interest that generates further reading. This desire should be recognized, nurtured, and cultivated by the teachers during everyday reading instruction. Interest is a powerful motivator and is used as a key component not only in elementary-school reading instruction but also in instruction for beginning adult readers (Heathington & Koskinen, 1982).

Interest is present when readers get engrossed in what they read and thus develop even keener interest to pursue special subject-matter areas. This results in specialized knowledge and additional achievement, which Guthrie (1981) describes as having "higher than average knowledge or superior acumen in the object of interest" (p. 984).

Quantitative Distinction. The quantitative characteristics of reading interest can be observed in the manner in which children handle, hold, and look at books; turn pages; inspect pictures; and display their willingness first to point at and name letters and then to pronounce words and sentences as found in the basal readers and other reading materials.

Likewise, during beginning reading instruction, children can be encouraged to record the number of lines and later the number of pages they read orally or silently. Also, children can count how many content and how many function words are on a page or in a given segment of print. In a more advanced practice, readers can count function words that belong to nouns, adjectives that describe nouns, or adverbs that modify verbs.

To get preschool children interested in reading wordless picture books, children can be asked to count how many times boys or girls or both appear in their red, blue, and yellow sweaters or how many times and in how many pictures children find a black squirrel or other animals.

All these performance examples can be measured by, for instance, coloring the number of correct findings in vertical columns. The important point is that each child has his or her own record, which we hope will spark further reading interest.

Qualitative Distinction. The qualitative characteristics of reading interest are established by noticing if and how the children are able to identify the content in basal readers and other subject books and reading materials. Children should notice how stories, their events, and the people in them are similar or different; whether they are liked or disliked; and how people acted and how children wished they had acted. Qualitative distinction rests in the interest children display in wanting to answer questions that vary in degree and level of difficulty, progressing from giving one-word, factual answers to giving factual main ideas and factual sequences, and perhaps even to asking questions themselves and answering them.

Another contributing distinction is the quality of basal readers and subject-matter books, including their appearance, layout, and organization. The quality of workbooks and teacher-made exercises is important, too. These aspects influence and partially determine (1) gradients of interest in, (2) favorable or unfavorable disposition toward, and (3) willing (active-constructive) or unwilling (passive-destructive) behavior regarding participation in the learning experiences.

It is important to know, when judging quality of reading interest, that children's attitudes, motivations, and background experiences come to bear on their reading behaviors. Children who have failed repeatedly in oral reading may first dislike and later hate oral reading and then all reading, in school as well as adult life. Extensive dislikes can be extended to disliking teachers, books, classmates, and then the entire school as an institution and a place of learning.

Attitude

An attitude is a predisposition to behave in certain ways toward certain targets, not necessarily as they really are but as they are perceived to be. For example, a poor reader may react negatively to the teacher who imposed the reading or to the book that was provided for reading, or to both.

Attitude determines strength and direction of actions undertaken. Attitude aids in forming and making up the child's lifestyle. Understanding this lifestyle is essential to understanding the child and his actions, which are approved or disapproved by himself and the society (Dinkmeyer & Dreikurs, 1963).

A favorable attitude, however, if it is without direction, does not necessarily compel one to read. An individual with good intentions may take a book in his hands, look at the cover, open it, turn pages, close it, and put the book away. While there was some kind of a favorable attitude in looking at and handling the book, no actions were directed toward actually reading it. The book was neither borrowed nor bought. Mathewson (1976) pointed out that favorable attitude must be combined with a strong action orientation. That is, an individual may not only look for a book and read it but may actually buy it and find a place to keep it at home, adding other books to it. It is generally agreed that, once successful reading has been experienced and enjoyed, such positive experiences will breed positive attitudes toward more reading (Dulin, 1978).

While attitudes often appear to favor specific types of reading, Ewing (1978) proposes a general attitude model toward all types of reading. This model is based on the proposition that too much specialization may omit "the importance of something more general, more fundamental than specific factors" (p. 157). In this vein, children who have developed a positive attitude toward general reading may produce and experience effective learning, whereas those who have developed a negative attitude toward general reading may produce and experience poor learning. The general attitude concept, however, appears also to be more in accord with present social psychology (Downing & Leong, 1982, p. 261).

Attitudes in the classroom during reading instruction can perhaps be best understood by learning how successful readers behave, how they perceive themselves when reading, how much or how little they enjoy reading, how willing they are to involve themselves in pursuing reading, and what reading means to them. Other important factors are what teachers think of the readers' reading and what the relationships are among the readers and the teachers.

Motivation

Motivation, another component of reading interest, is understood best in the sense of its being need and goal directed. In learning to read and reading to learn, students must have a need that they perceive to be significant. They must have a goal that they perceive to be important, not for the sake of the subject matter itself or for the sake of grades, but rather for meeting expected demands of personal worth and security, usefulness for future life, self-expression, and self-esteem (Zintz, 1980).

Motivation must be considered an integral part of not only school learning but also life learning. In all learning situations motivation can be extrinsic (from without), it can be intrinsic (from within), and it can come from the subject matter and the materials to be learned.

Extrinsic Motivation. When young children are "bribed" by parents to be "good little boys and girls," they look for immediate rewards and gratifications. Children are then "good" for as long as the rewards last. If the rewards abate and diminish, children want more and more, and, if they do not receive, they demand. Thus, extrinsic motivation in the home is often short lived. So it is in the classroom. As long as motivation to read, to pay attention, to concentrate, to learn, or even just to sit still and listen is imposed externally, it will be of limited duration.

Parents as well as teachers know of the exasperating experience of calling for silence, attention, and discipline. This is done first in a low-key voice, which, when unheeded, intensifies and then swells to an almost unprecedented loudness. Only then do we realize that this kind of external motivation is not successful. The immediate reward systems of silver and gold stars, tokens, points, and prizes also are of limited value. While motivation at first appears high and intense, long-term effects are seldom, if ever, realized. In another, often-practiced instructional approach, filmstrips are used to motivate. Students appear attentive as they are viewing picture frames showing jungle scenes and wild animals. What happens when the viewing is completed? Are the students still "motivated" to learn eagerly? Generally not. Though extrinsic motivation does not inhibit learning, good effects do not begin until extrinsic motivation changes gradually to intrinsic and subject-matter-oriented-motivation.

Intrinsic Motivation.   Although extrinsic motivation varies with the intensity of pressure, force, or reward from parents or teachers, intrinsic motivation furnishes its own rewards. Intrinsic motivation is stimulated when school is "learningful" to the learners; thus, intrinsic motivation is tied up with the materials to be learned. Kempf and Lehrke (1975) point out that intrinsic motivation results from the activity itself, which is experienced as pleasant and in which the learner is at least moderately successful. While it is difficult to isolate intrinsic motivation from subject matter, "it seems neither realistic nor desirable to want to motivate students only intrinsically, namely, through the learning activity independent of its consequences" (pp. 65, 66).

If students do not have an intrinsic desire to achieve, they will do poorly on comprehension tasks (Mangrum & Forgan, 1979, p. 278). Students, who have no purposes for reading, lack concentration and experience difficulties in maintaining it. If they perceive the printed page to be uninformative, unenjoyable, and unappealing, they have no desire for reading. Although motivation is an elusive concept, teachers must do their best to nurture the motivation, good will, and desire to learn that most students bring to the learning task. The will to learn in itself is an intrinsic motive and has its rewards in its own exercise (Bruner, 1966, p. 127). Should this be missing, however, teachers must find some way to motivate students to learn (Power, 1982, p. 295).

Subject-Matter-Directed Motivation.   Subject-matter-directed motivation is explained as a turning toward the subject matter, a readiness to occupy oneself voluntarily with that material, to acquire further information, and to digest it (Kempf & Lehrke, 1975, p. 65). From this interpretation it appears that subject-matter-directed motivation is different from extrinsic and instrinsic motivations. While extrinsic motivation most often is initiated by the teacher or another outside force and intrinsic motivation is initiated by the readers from within, subject-matter-directed motivation is initiated by the reading task to be done. The subject matter first sparks the reader's attention and curiosity, which then pushes the reader on to find new information. This, in turn, generates further interest to continue to read, and newly attained ideas keep alive the reader's concentration and desire to delve deeper into the subject matter till the reader's needs are satisfied. At some point, not necessarily identifiable, subject matter and intrinsic motivation merge to become an inherent and inseparable quality of reading, learning, and life itself.

Background Experiences

Background experiences that students have and bring to the reading-learning task direct interest, attitude, and motivation. What the children know through experience, either favorable, unfavorable, or somewhere in between, will influence the intensity of motivation, the strength and direction of attitude, and the likes and dislikes of subject matter. Background experiences determine the children's facility, scope, and range in adding meaning to what they listen to, speak, read, and write.

The importance of a reader's background experiences and how they affect the beginner's learning are discussed widely in the professional literature. From Huey (1908) to the most recent textbooks on reading, authors emphasize the need for appropriate background experiences for new learning. Background experiences are essential in order for a reader to connect information from the text to that already stored in the reader's head (Wilson, 1983).

In cases where students lack essential background experiences for learning through reading and studying text materials, teachers face the often-difficult task of filling the gap. Failing to do so may block any benefits of the present reading experiences. As Hayes and Tierney (1982) have shown, teachers attempt to meet this challenge by providing an "interpretive bridge between the unfamiliar material and the knowledge which students do have" (p. 258).

In reading, children apply prior knowledge all the time. Prior knowledge or nonvisual information (F. Smith, 1982) is information that readers already have "behind the eyeballs" (p. 10). This knowledge is not just that of subject matter, essential as it may be, but in addition it is knowledge of the relevant language and of how to read. These latter two are information readers have to supply or bring to the printed page, because they are not found on it. Reading materials that are too difficult to read, where readers have to pay attention to every word and thus become anxious, will result in inability to read. The lack of nonvisual information makes reading impossible; moreover, according to Smith, "there is a limit on how much visual information the brain can handle at any one time" (p. 11).

Overloading the reader's brain occurs when reading materials are or become too difficult, when visual information processing becomes too demanding, and when nonvisual information decreases or becomes insufficient. To avoid a breakdown in the processing of the text, demand for and supply of both visual and nonvisual information must be kept in balance so that the reader, although being challenged to stretch the mind, can still interact successfully with the print.

Direct Experiences. There are, of course, two kinds of experiences, direct and indirect or vicarious. When the teacher and children from a city school visit a farm in the country, these children experience first-hand what a farm looks like. In direct contact with the farm family and the farmhands, children see, touch, and perhaps ride on a farm tractor and other machinery; they see and touch farm animals; they witness the milking processes and may even drink truly fresh milk. These children experience directly what a farm looks like, what has happened on a farm, and who works on it and what kind of work is being done.

Vicarious Experiences. Other children, who are not able to visit a farm, are exposed to it through reading about it and, perhaps, through seeing pictures and filmstrips. These children may be less fortunate, but they can gather farm information through indirect or vicarious experiences. These experiences can be reasonably good substitutes for direct experiences. In fact, sometimes vicarious experiences are the only way to learn about a subject, as with reading about space travel, faraway lands, and past social and political events.

Summary

The processing of print cannot occur without readers' reactions to it. Interest, attitude, and motivation are the major movers from within and from without the reader. Interest rests within each individual reader, as books or other objects are neither interesting nor boring by themselves. Teachers of reading must explore and make use of their students' reading interest. Attitude determines the strength and direction with which a reader approaches reading, and attitude also plays a strong role in forming the reader's lifestyle. The latter, at least in part, provides the basis for understanding a reader's actions before, during, and after reading. Motivation, as another force within human emotion, is either extrinsic, intrinsic, subject-matter directed, or a combination thereof. Background experiences and nonvisual information also are important factors, which, together with emotion, are powerful movers and energetic shapers in determining active and constructive participation during reading.

COGNITION

The second main characteristic that brings reading alive within the reader is cognition. Its subcharacteristic is understanding, which combines with reading to produce reading understanding.

Reading Understanding

Understanding involves interpretation, assimilation, accommodation, adaptation, and equilibration. Cognition or the act of knowing depends on perceiving, recognizing, conceiving, judging, and reasoning, all of which lead to understanding. Reading understanding, then, means grasping the ideas represented in print and apprehending clearly the nature and subtleties of the reading content and becoming thoroughly familiar with them.

Quantitative Distinction. The quantitative characteristcs of reading understanding can be assessed by scoring the percentages of correct answers given by the students to the questions they receive pertaining to the content of a paragraph, story, or other printed materials. During instruction, teachers give a silent-reading assignment. After the assignment is completed, teachers want to assess what the students have read and how much they have learned; that is, how much they remember and are able to give back orally or in writing. Teachers ask various kinds of questions of the students, who respond by answering the questions or giving other feedback.

The number of correct answers and their respective percentages result in a quantitative measurement of performance for each student and for all students together. But it must be remembered that the obtained results are only for one particular reading performance, done at a particular time for a particular purpose and under certain circumstances.

Qualitative Distinction. The qualitative assessment of reading understanding distinguishes the mental processes and their difficulties. The meaning of the word *difficulty* must be understood in terms of the variability of the reader's skill, perseverance, and patience when experiencing mental hardships in acquiring information, solving problems, and evolving new ideas. Questions should vary in difficulty between as well as within cognitive levels. They should test (1) memory, which includes fact, definition, generalization, and value; (2) translation; (3) interpretation, which includes comparison, implication, inductive thinking, quantity, and cause and effect; (4) application; (5) analysis; (6) synthesis; and (7) evaluation (Spache & Spache, 1977). Each type of question demands varying intensities of thought processes from the reader, as well as reorganization of the thoughts and ideas received in the communication.

Assimilation and Accommodation. Cognitive processes are characterized by organization and adaptation, which are both continuous and ongoing processes. Assimilation and accommodation are complementary processes in adaptation.

The noun and verb *assimilation* and *assimilate* are terms that make one think of taking in or incorporating food into one's own body. According to Jean Piaget's concept, however, assimilation may be thought of as "taking in" the external environment in such a way that the organism or the individual does not change (Piaget & Inhelder, 1969). Paterson (1977) takes a somewhat different view that, in assimilation, the organism adapts the environment to itself (p. 73); however, the individual still does not change. The individual takes in or assimilates new experiences with already acquired schemata that have been stored in the mind.

In accommodation or in accommodating, on the other hand, the organism changes in order to meet the demands of the environment. Through reading, schemata change as the reader processes and assimilates new information and experiences (Modolfsky, 1983, p. 740). Think of an already existing framework in which there are "slots" waiting to be filled as the reader fits new ideas and thoughts into the framework (Tierney & Pearson, 1981). Thinking-through a story to fully understand its content or to solve a problem, the reader relies constantly on existing schemata. If these schemata or any combination of them do not exactly correspond to and fit the unfamiliar problem, the child has to activate, add to, and modify the schemata so as to arrive at a possible intelligent solution. Modifying mental structures, or schemata, to fit reality is called accommodation (Harris & Hodges, 1981, p. 4).

Equilibration. In modifying a new learning situation, the learner changes to meet new demands, that is, adapts to new learning environments.

Think of the new information you assimilate or process while studying. The new knowledge throws you into a state of unbalance, of disequilibrium. This unbalanced disposition forces you to restabilize your mental actions. You attempt to adapt the old knowledge to the new, to bridge the gap between them, to regain a state of equilibrium. According to Piaget and Inhelder (1969), you equilibrate to maintain a balance between assimilation and accommodation. What is important in reaching equilibration is that the learners activate within themselves the necessary forces to coordinate this development.

Cognitive Style

The different ways in which human beings act upon their environments by listening, speaking, reading, writing, learning, and thinking are referred to as the different cognitive styles. They represent the ways individuals approach situations and their related problems and eventually solve them.

Logan (1983), in reviewing research on cognitive style and reading, advises that students develop a cognitive style for reasoning, thinking, and solving problems in their daily reading instruction and in their independent reading. He cites Scott and Annesley (1976), who refer to cognitive style as the "modes an individual uses in perceiving, organizing, and labeling aspects of his/her environment, or, put another way, apprehending, transforming, and utilizing information" (p. 704).

Teachers recognize the fast- from the slow-moving, -working, and -thinking children, as well as the meticulous, scrupulous, and punctilious ones from the untroubled, unconcerned, and indifferent children. Teachers also know of those who learn without reading or studying very hard or for too long a time versus those who need to read and read again and again and study hard and harder over prolonged periods of time.

Let us now explore three cognitive styles: the impulsive, the reflective, and the passive/active.

Impulsive versus Reflective. Helfeldt (1981) contrasts the impulsive and the reflective thinkers as follows: The impulsive thinker is quick in responding to questions and suggestions without being overly concerned with whether or not answers and information are correct. Children with an impulsive cognitive style show high risk of response uncertainty; that is, they do not consider adequately, in accordance with the task on hand, the alternatives that may be possible to reach a more satisfactory, effective, and applicable solution to a given question and a presented situation.

Children and adults with a reflective cognitive style give careful consideration over time before acting on questions, requests, and suggestions. In subject-related performance, as in reading, answering questions, problem solving, and other reading-learning tasks, students who are reflective and thoughtful exercise greater control over behavior and the use of language than the impulsive child, in relationship to replying to instructional demands.

Passive/Active. Although at first glance the two conditions of being active and passive appear to be opposites, they are rather complementary to each other. To receive a message, the recipient must be willing to be, for the duration of the message at least, in a *passive* state of either listening to or reading what is to be communicated. The passive state of receiving indicates the reader's receptive discipline, without which the noise of the message may be heard and the visual symbols seen but its content will not be understood.

Once the message has been received, the recipient then must be willing to become *active* by reacting to the received message. Thus, in this communicative relationship the individual's passive receptiveness and active responsiveness are complementary to each other.

In day-to-day instruction of teacher-student or book-student relationships, Elkind (1976) postulates, effective reading comprehension requires receptive discipline of mind and body, together with the willingness to receive and to respond to messages.

Summary

Reading understanding takes effect with the act of knowing or cognition. How much and at what level knowledge is understood through reading can be assessed quantitatively and qualitatively. Cognitive processes, which are influenced by assimilation, accommodation, and equilibration, not only affect but also are being affected by the reader's cognitive styles. Impulsive and reflective styles assist teachers in understanding how students utilize received information. Receiving information and replying to it require states of passive receptiveness and active responsiveness.

PSYCHOMOTOR ABILITIES

Psychomotor abilities are characterized by reading certainty, reading fluency, and reading speed, which define the reader's state of being almost free of doubt in processing graphophonic, syntactic, and semantic information and being able to process them fluently and expeditiously.

Reading Certainty

Children's reading certainty can be observed through noting their accuracy when speaking and writing words and sentences and their sureness when approaching and executing oral and silent reading. In the day-to-day reading instruction these objectives can be broken down into smaller purposes.

In the beginning grades, for example, the reading certainty can be expressed through having no doubts in first recognizing and then naming small and capital letters and then groups of letters in alphabetic and non-alphabetic order. This would be followed by pronouncing the sounds of strings of letters and strings of words with proper intonation. In advanced school grades, reading certainty can be expressed through handling new, unknown, and difficult words in isolation and in context and through using them in oral and written responses and communications.

Quantitative Distinction. These observable actions can also be measured quantitatively by first counting all correct responses and then expressing them in percentages and, if so desired, in mean scores and other derived norms. In written performances such as teacher-made tests and quizzes, raw scores of the number correct can be obtained and converted to various quantitative measures. These can assist students in all school grades in assessing their mastery of the assigned tasks. Care must be taken, however, that quantitative results are not used to embarrass, to intimidate, or to punish students for not having performed as well as other classmates.

Qualitative Distinction. From the qualitative point of view, a good way of assessing reading certainty is to arrange systematically words according to initial, final, and medial letter positions. Exploring how letters and letter clusters are alike and not alike and how they sound, and then how they can be substituted for other possible ones to make new words with different sounds, helps in teaching visual and auditory discrimination. Similarly, reading students' miscues (in which students may distort meaning or call forth words that are not in the passage but otherwise do not alter its meaning) reflects the strengths and weaknesses of the reader's oral reading strategy (Richek, List, & Lerner, 1983, p. 128).

Reading Fluency

Reading fluency in oral communication can be described as being able to pronounce utterances cohesively, coherently, and smoothly, in thought units rather than a staccato word-by-word fashion. Reading fluency in writing can be described as being able to form letters without interrupting the stroke of the pen from the beginning to the end of a word.

Quantitative Distinction. This is made in oral reading by noting violations of word and sentence coherence, cohesiveness, and smoothness. In written language, we look for the ability to write with ease and readiness, especially in the formation of ascending and descending letters and the connections that string them together to form words, which are then strung together to form sentences. The number of correct or incorrect performances can be converted into percentages; repeated performances can be used in assessing reading fluency.

Also, a different assessment is possible when counting associative responses to a given word. For instance, in classroom application the teacher says the word "brick" and records within a predetermined time limit of three minutes all correct student responses that are associated with the given word.

Such quantitative exercises can be extended to larger utterances and be practiced throughout the school grades.

Qualitative Distinction. Quality in reading fluency is characterized by speaking easily and smoothly and by being facile in speech. Quality is further noticed in expression, pauses, and how effortlessly the prosodic elements of language are flowing. Quality in written-word fluency is expressed in agility or mental action and nimbleness of thought, comprehension, and resourcefulness in completing and composing stories, solving problems, and initiating and working out new ideas.

Reading Speed

The third and last psychomotor subcharacteristic is speed, which is noted in how quickly or slowly a reader reads, beginning (usually silently) at the top of the printed page and moving the eyes horizontally and then vertically from line to line down to the bottom of the printed page.

Quantitative Distinction. Reading speed can be described as the rate of reading, which is derived by finding the ratio between the total number of words read silently or orally and the amount of time it took in seconds or minutes. The obtained results express the average number of words the reader has read, or pretended to read, per minute. From the quantitative point of view, accomplishing high rates or unusually high rates of reading may and too often does mean that thousands of words have been *seen* but not *read*, at the expense of comprehension.

Qualitative Distinction. In assessing the quality of reading speed, we determine whether the reader's mind attaches meaning with the same speed as the eyes race along and down the printed lines. To achieve the highest possible reading speed while maintaining reading comprehension requires that the reader be able to change speed as the demands of processing print change. This means that readers must have reading flexibility. Readers are flexible when they are able to adapt their reading speed according to the reading task, including the difficulty of the vocabulary, the concepts, and the surface and deep structures. The surface structure of the printed passage refers to the visual input of the words and their letter sequences and how words are arranged into sentences. The deep structure, however, is the meaning to which a printed sentence refers. From the qualitative point of view, understanding determines the reading speed, not the number of words glanced at and counted.

Summary

Reading certainty, fluency, and speed, which constitute the psychomotor reading abilities, support and strengthen the student's progress from a dependent, outside-regulated reader to an independent, self-disciplined reader. Without these abilities, readers find it burdensome if not self-defeating to process print. But when reading certainty, reading fluency, and reading speed work together with the reader's emotion and cognition, the reader's whole organism engages in reading to extract meaning from text effectively, efficiently, and economically in pursuance of significant, meaningful, and experiential learning.

ACTIVE READING THROUGH REIVA PROCESSING

Students are on their way to active reading when they generate interest from within, when their attitudes direct them toward goals that are achievable, and when they move voluntarily and intentionally from teacher-imposed, extrinsic motivation to self-directed, subject-matter-oriented, intrinsic motivation. The reader's emotional, cognitive, and psychomotor assets will not only support effort and exertion in processing print but will also move product-oriented learning to process-oriented learning.

It is my conviction that only process-oriented learning can meet adequately the challenge of the ever-increasing knowledge explosion that is pushed on by an increasingly automated technology. REIVA processing, a program developed by me over a number of years, is designed to assist teachers and students in moving from product-oriented to process-oriented learning, in and through reading.

The first public forum at which REIVA was presented was the Twentieth International Reading Association meeting, held in New York City in May 1975. Following this, REIVA was tried out in regular classrooms, clinical settings, and Adult Basic Education instruction. After some changes, it was presented again in 1980 at the Eighth Plains Conference in Bismarck, North Dakota; and then again one month later at the First Rupertsland Reading Conference in Winnipeg, Manitoba. About a year later, it was taken to the Fifth Transmountain Conference, in Lethbridge, Alberta. It was presented in its present form in 1982 at the Tenth Plains Regional Reading Conference in Omaha, Nebraska.

REIVA processing induces readers to generate within themselves the following processes, which lead to extracting meaning from print: reflecting (R), exploring (E), investigating (I), verifying (V), and applying (A). The

FIGURE 2.1. Relationships Between and Among the Five REIVA Processes

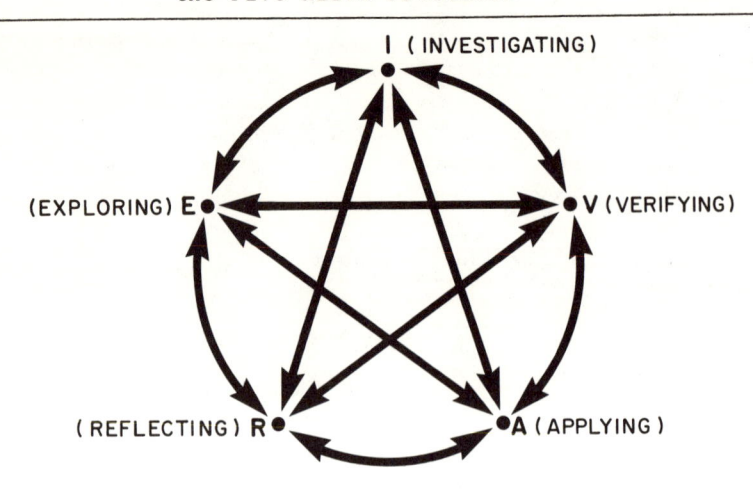

relationships between and among these processes are presented in Figure 2.1. They are defined as follows:

1. *Reflecting* requires the student to sit back; gather thoughts, ideas, and information; and think quietly and calmly through intrapersonal communication.
2. *Exploring* requires continued intrapersonal communication through constant searching for and calling up of acquired knowledge, with the intent of sifting through it to evaluate what does or does not apply to the new task at hand.
3. *Investigating* requires the student to move from intra- to interpersonal communication, to hypothesize judiciously, to examine closely, to study systematically, and to work diligently on the principal issues of the new learning.
4. *Verifying* requires the student to substantiate the "is" reality from the multitude of "might-be" possibilities and then to either accept or reject the hypothesized findings.
5. *Applying* requires the student to employ what has been learned by applying it critically to new but similar learning situations. These may require support and clarification through any of the previously described processes.

To make these five processes more accessible for use, examples are given in Table 2.1, which lists the names of the processes and describes them through questions that illuminate their importance to lifelong learning.

TABLE 2.1. Moving into Active Reading

Process	Content as Question	Relation to Life-long Learning
Reflecting	What background experiences need to be recalled? What knowledge is or is not relevant?	Reviving what is known by recollecting willingly and thinking calmly for oneself
Exploring	What and/or how much is known? What and/or how much is not known? What purpose(s) need to be set? How will purpose(s) facilitate new learning?	Searching storehouse of knowledge to determine what is there and what is needed to reach understanding
Investigating	What materials need to be studied? What new concepts need to be developed? What details need to be learned? What assumptions or hypotheses must be posed?	Purposeful, systematic inquiry into newness by using multi-sensory approaches and multiple material resources
Verifying	How can I prove what was hypothesized? What support is or is not available? What can be accepted? What must be rejected?	Confirming and substantiating by establishing evidence through screening "is" reality from "might-be" possibilities
Applying	How significant was new learning? How experiential was newness to the learner? How meaningful is it for new learning? What transfers can be made?	Employing results diligently to acquiring further knowledge, solving new but similar problems, evolving new ideas, and reading for enjoyment.

REIVA's uses are independent, utilitarian, and universal, and indefinite, encompassing the reader as a whole person. REIVA is independent because its processes are not bound to one another and can be independently activated by and performed from within the reader. REIVA is utilitarian because its processes are applicable to a wide range of personal actions and reactions. REIVA is universal because its processes are broad and versatile. Finally, REIVA is indefinite because its processes have no distinct limits in relationship to one another.

Experience has shown that these mental processes are commonly applied by all people, knowingly or unknowingly, around the globe, regardless of color, creed, and tongue. In fact, you, the reader, are using these mental processes at this very moment. There is a growing awareness of the need to bring these human mental processes back into human consciousness so that they will become more fully recognized and used as a focus in all daily instruction and in particular in the teaching of reading.

Part II

READING IN THE TEACHING CONTEXT

CHAPTER 3

Reading: A Synthesis of Developmental Processes

Purpose questions for this chapter:
- How do the eyes behave during reading?
- Which are the processes that contribute to reading?
- How can reading be described?
- How do different stage theories of cognitive development relate to reading?
- How does encouragement or discouragement affect learning to read?

HOW READING BEGINS

Reading is learned by reading, just as swimming is learned by swimming and skiing by skiing. There are many physical and mental processes that must function together to permit the swimmer to glide partially submerged through the water and the skier to coast over the snow. Likewise, many physical and mental processes must function together to permit the reader to process print and extract meaning from it. This is reading. With what does it begin?

A reader who decides to read. After this decision, the reader must undertake some preliminary actions, such as selecting and getting the reading materials and finding a well-lit place that is free from distractions and otherwise suitable for pursuing reading.

Thus, the reading act consists of important physical actions that get one ready to read, yet these physical actions are nothing more than reactions to the mind that generated the interest and gave the directions to prepare for this activity. Once these are complete, the reader is ready to engage in the actual act of reading, by letting the eyes make contact with the printed symbols.

Actual reading begins when the eyes contact the print. Print is usually composed of strings of black squiggles known as letters that are printed or written, usually on white paper. Letters form words, groups of words, or word patterns that make sentences, and sentences make paragraphs. When the eyes gaze or look constantly at a word or group of words, the eyes stop or make a fixation pause. During a fixation or eye stop, complex psychoneurological processes transfer to the mind the visual input of strings of letters or word patterns. Then the eyes move on to the next fixation. The direction of moving on is usually from left to right and is executed in a swift and jerky progression, called saccadic movement. The term *saccadic* is derived from the French, *saccade*, meaning to jerk or jump. The eyes jump from fixation to fixation. During a saccade or a jerky movement from one fixation to another, no clear vision is possible. Only during a fixation when the eyes are motionless do the eyes see and have a clear vision of the printed symbols (Crowder, 1982, p. 7). Should the eyes move too quickly to the next fixation without having fully "registered" to the satisfaction of the mind what the text said, the mind will direct the eyes to regress or fixate. In regressing or moving back, the eyes move in the opposite direction, from right to left, then go onward again, toward the right and the end of the line. When one line is read, the eyes make a return sweep from right to left and then downward one line, skipping from the near end of the finishing line down to the near beginning of the following line.

When the eyes "intend" to see too much in a single fixation, then the mind cannot assimilate and accommodate all the input, resulting in inadequate perception and poor comprehension. This will make the eyes regress. Regressions also take place when readers encounter difficult words, phrases, numbers, formulas, and concepts that interfere with comprehension. For example, read the following terms related to the eye and see what happens: *aniseikonia*, *heterophoria*, and *ophthalmology*. You may have experienced difficulty in oculomotor adjustment and in adjusting the eye movements to the unfamiliar printed materials, on the one hand, and in processing essential nonvisual information on the other hand.

Often it is said that readers should expand the input or the number of words taken in during one fixation, thus reducing the number of fixations that the eyes must make in a line. As you will recall from the discussion of reading speed in Chapter 2, however, the importance of reading lies not in the quantity of words seen, but in the quality of meaning extracted from print. While single words may be recognized quickly during a fixation pause, the mind may need more time to process their meaning, which, together, have more importance than the individual words alone.

For example, the words in the sentence *The small child runs to the mother* may be seen and recognized in perhaps two fixation pauses and quickly pronounced with ease and intonation. Yet the mind may have many different ways of attaching meaning to and interpreting this sentence. Thus, the reading act extends beyond seeing, recognizing, and even pronouncing words and sentence patterns to getting meaning that must be interpreted and integrated.

Summary

Reading begins with getting physically ready to do the act in an appropriate environmental setting. Then the eyes take over by contacting the printed material, which they scan in saccadic movements, jumping from fixation to fixation in a left-to-right direction. Occasionally the eyes regress, only to jump forward again to the end of a line where they make a return sweep to the beginning of the next line. Comprehension and interpretation of nonvisual information or meaning gives substance to the visual cues, thus advancing reading toward its utilitarian purpose of extracting information for learning and enjoyment.

PROCESSES THAT CONTRIBUTE TO READING

Just as a river does not become a river without its many contributory rivulets, so does reading not become reading without its many contributory processes. As the rivulets supply a steady flow of water to the river, so do the reading processes give a steady flow of impulses of incoming information to reading. As the water flows through the riverbed, so do the impulses flow through the reader. Should the flow of water in the rivulets be slow, decrease, or even stop, the current of the river will become irregular and deficient. Should the flow of information be slow, decrease, or even stop, the processing of print in reading becomes irregular and deficient.

Contributories to reading are the processes of sensing, perceiving, thinking, learning, and becoming. Processes, of course, grow and expand as rivulets develop into streams. As shown in Figure 3.1, they flow together into reading.

Sensing

Sensory processing, or sensing, involves the visual/seeing, auditory/hearing, kinesthetic/moving, tactile/touching, olfactory/smelling, and gustatory/tasting senses. These are activated by input stimuli, which the individual perceives from either outside or inside the self. Of particular interest to reading are the visual, auditory, kinesthetic, and tactile senses.

Seeing. Visual processing employs acuity and discrimination. Visual acuity or the sharpness of seeing clearly assists in distinguishing one word from the other by the white spaces on either side. Visual acuity also aids in perceiving distinct lines that pertain to one letter but not to the others. Straight, horizontal, vertical, slanted, and curved lines give the conventional

FIGURE 3.1.   Synthesis of Processes
                Contributory to Reading

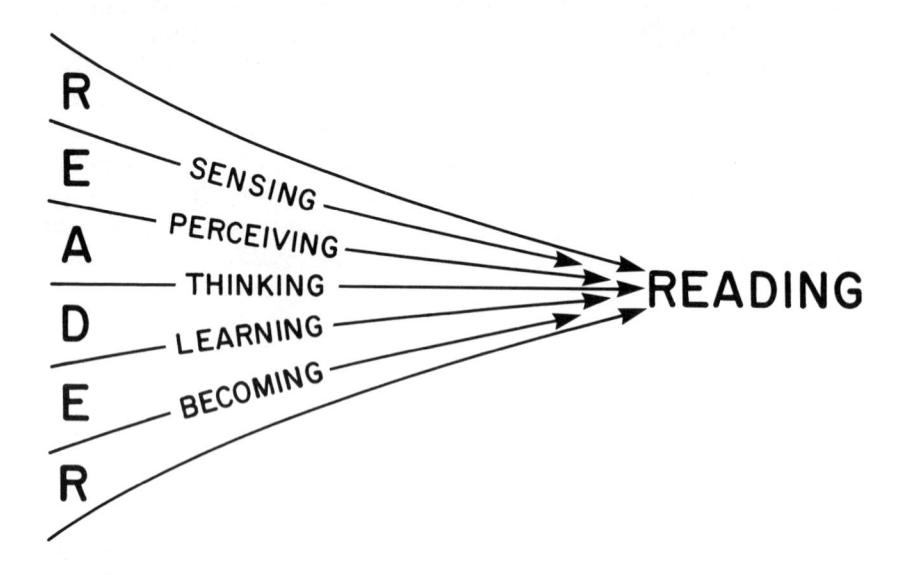

```
R
 E    SENSING
  A    PERCEIVING
         THINKING ─────────►READING
  D    LEARNING
 E     BECOMING
R
```

form to each letter by which it is recognized as a character or symbol of the English alphabet.

Visual discrimination is the reader's ability to perceive similarities and differences by sight when letters and words are presented in text or in isolation. The beginning letters in *b*all and *b*ill look alike and are the same. But the beginning letters in *b*all and *h*ill look almost alike but are not the same. When *b*all and *b*ill, and *b*all and *h*ill are in context, meaning together with visual discrimination will determine if the beginning letters are the same or different; when in isolation, where meaning depends entirely on the reader, visual discrimination alone must determine whether the beginning letters are the same or not. When visually processing the word *ball* as compared to the word *bell*, Yaden (1982) reports that readers use both horizontal and vertical letter dimensions and also contrast the separate letters (p. 237).

To accomplish visual discrimination, the eyes proceed in a left-to-right direction, inspecting and distinguishing letters and words. When letters in mixed order are rearranged into their proper sequence, visual sequencing occurs, as in arranging the letters *a, t, u, b, o,* to make the word *about*. Similarly, visual sequencing is at work when letter clusters in their set order are found in different words, as with *ight* in l*ight* and fr*ight*, and *ough* in th*ough* and c*ough*.

Hearing. While vision processes the letters seen by the eyes, hearing processes the sounds heard by the ears. Like vision, auditory processing also involves acuity and discrimination. A letter is seen, a sound is heard. Auditory acuity is the keenness of hearing that both blends speech sounds together and discriminates initial, medial, and final speech sounds in words. Auditory discrimination abilities are necessary to distinguish the utterances *pin* from *pen*, *pin* from *bin*, and *sun* from *sum*.

Speech sounds that correspond on a one-to-one relationship to the letter sequence of a word form a sound-letter correspondence as in the words *pan* and *ton*. In these and other similar words, each letter according to its position in the word receives its sound, and when the sounds are blended together, each letter can be recognized by its own sound. Not so, however with many words of the English language, which contain letters that are written but not pronounced as in the words fin*e*, pan*e*, li*gh*t, and *psy*ch*o*logy. This noncorrespondence from letter to sound also indicates that words have their own visual appearance or visual "gestalt," which can be in agreement with or be different from their sound "gestalt," or how words are pronounced in the English Language. These differences between oral and written language also suggest that the letter name can be different from its sound when this letter is part of a word's total sound gestalt as in the words p*e*n and b*i*n. The letters *e* and *i* are not the same as their sounds heard. Finally, in oral reading, visual and auditory processing must work together not to recode letters to sounds but to produce sound patterns according to the meanings to be communicated.

Moving. Going from reading print to writing, the reader-writer employs the kinesthetic senses through movement perceptors in muscles, tendons, and joints. Fine motor movements direct the pencil to draw the lines that form the letters and connect them in proper spatial sequence, forming strings of letters and strings or words.

Imagine yourself studying for an exam. As you read, you rephrase what you learn, recite it in your own words, and write it down on paper. You do this because, through repeated experience, you know that this process helps you to recall more effectively than just reading alone. The motor movements you use in writing are kinesthetic pathways that become one of the major input modalities in acquiring information. Simultaneously, your writing is supported by movements of the muscles of your speech apparatus as you recite what your eyes have seen. This whole process—seeing what is to be learned by reading it or by using the *visual* input modality, saying it and thus employing the *auditory* modality, and writing it down and thus using the *kinesthetic* modality—is known as the VAK procedure (Richek, List, & Lerner, 1983, p. 186).

Touching. Blind persons or those who are severely visually impaired use the tactile senses or the sense of touch when they read. They use Braille, a tactile reading-writing system that was devised in the beginning of the nineteenth century by Louis Braille, a French teacher of the blind. This tactile writing system uses the alphabet letters expressed in a combination of raised dots that are read by touching them. In Brailling, a blind person uses the tactile modality as the primary input channel for acquiring information.

The tactile modality may also be employed in the beginning of learning to read. Children in this learning situation touch letters made of sandpaper, felt, or any high-contrast material. In particular, children who have difficulties in learning to read are taught systematically to use their *tactile* senses in structured combination with VAK, their visual, auditory and kinesthetic senses. This results in VAKT or the visual-auditory-kinesthetic-tactile technique, which was first used in the 1920s by Fernald and Keller (Fernald, 1943). The VAKT technique reinforces learning by using a combination of movement and touch together with visual and auditory processing, and it is still utilized today in remediating various reading difficulties (Brown, 1982, p. 202).

Perceiving

Once the reader has visually identified and recognized clusters of printed symbols, blended them together in accordance with their relative speech sounds, and given meaning to them, perceiving is in progress. How one perceives depends upon the readers's interest in, attitude toward, and prior experience with the subject matter.

How is perceiving explained? Harris and Hodges (1981) say that perceiving is "the crucial link between incoming stimuli and a response that is meaningful" (p. 323). Downing and Leong (1982) suggest that perception is not a passive taking in of external stimuli, but a skill that, as it develops, enables the reader to cope "with larger and larger chunks of the text" (p. 24). Larger chunks consist of long words or more than one word, and processing them requires a larger or more extended perceptual span from which the reader picks up information during a single fixation (Buurman, Roersema, & Gerrisson, 1981). Results from this study yielded a maximum perceptual span of 25 to 31 character positions (p. 234). For instance, the word *antidisestablishmentarianism* contains twenty-eight character positions, and the sentence *The house stands on the hill* consists of twenty-nine character positions, including letters and white spaces. At least in silent reading, a reader who can process larger chunks may require only one perceptual span to collect the information from these two examples.

To extract meaningful information from print also requires readers to perceive sequences of letters in words and words in sentences, as in *hate* and *heat*, and in *The ball hit Bob* and *Bob hit the ball*. Perceptual training, both visual and auditory, is widely used in the elementary schools to remediate reading problems (Wepman, 1958; Frostig & Horne, 1964). However, recent investigations by Mann and Goodman (1976) not only warn against "fractionating" educational practices but also emphasize that there is little evidence that perceptual training improves reading. Instead, they suggest the use of criterion-referenced instruments (see Chapter 11) as an alternative to perceptual training.

Thinking

Perceiving may be thought of as the covert junction, unobservable to the eye, where graphic-phonic information or lower-order processes join to interact with cognitive or higher-order processes. Thinking appears to depend on the kind and amount of perceptual data received from past experiences and from relative knowledge received from the text.

Dewey (1933/1960) referred to thinking as the act of turning over thoughts in the mind and giving serious consideration to possible doubt, resulting in the hesitation one may experience while pursuing a certain task. Doubt and hesitation, however, may lead directly to a search for the facts that will resolve these uncertainties.

REIVA, as discussed in Chapter 2, can be used to guide the reader to thinking. REIVA begins with reflective thinking, which Dewey called "the better way of thinking" (1933, p. 3), and leads the reader through investigating and verifying alternative choices, information, or positions, thus reducing uncertainty (F. Smith, 1982, p. 127) and gaining greater certainty.

Thinking itself should challenge the reader to progress to higher-level thinking by engaging the mind in questioning and finding answers through interpretation, application, analysis, synthesis, and evaluation. If assessments of reading comprehension during elementary and secondary school remain mainly on the level of having students answer literal questions and do not extend to inferential questions, students are not challenged to develop their thinking abilities toward the greatest possible intellectual growth. Furth characterizes this rather unfortunate instructional situation "the thinking-reading gap" (1978, p. 43).

As meaning lies in the interpretation given to words in context by the readers, higher thought processes need to develop to encompass more complex possibilities. Thinking abilities must be refined if comprehension is to go beyond the literal level of mostly recalling from memory or finding facts in printed materials (Dallmann, Rouch, Char & DeBoer, 1982, p. 17). Thinking is involved in attempting to solve problems and remove uncertainties. Thinking is also applied when meeting a new situation, when matching it against already-stored information to identify it, and when determining what has been or can be learned from it.

Learning

The overworked slogan "learning to read and reading to learn" still carries an important message to teachers of all grades and subject-matter areas. Whatever the slogan's interpretation may be, the fact remains that reading is learned and a skilled reader has learned to read by reading. Johann Wolfgang von Goethe (1749–1832), a renowned European poet, dramatist, and philosopher, wrote toward the end of his life, "The dear peole do not know how long it takes to read. I have been at it all my life and I cannot say I have reached the goal."

Formal school instruction in reading in all grades and subject-matter areas can assist individual learners to move from beginning and relatively unskilled reading to more advanced and skilled reading. Reading as a learned processing ability fosters change from a teacher-dependent reader into a teacher-independent one. Because learning is a covert process, it can only be observed through the responses the reader gives after having read, that is, by noting how learning has changed the behavior of the learner. For instance, through reading the research about the damage that smoking does to our health, many smokers change their behavior by giving up smoking.

Learning is also influenced by the ability to pay attention over a longer duration of time. Children who exhibit short attention spans or whose attention is decreasing as the demands of learning increase during the school day, may lack appropriate nutrition, as suggested by Pertz and Putnam (1982). In reviewing pertinent research, they observed malnutrition's damaging influence on learning and concluded that deprivation through improper diet "in affluent countries is less frequently recognized but no less damaging to children" (p. 705).

Learning is usually what is done in school, with a prescribed program, but there is also learning through reading in the workplace. A recent study by Mikulecky (1982) confirmed that students read less often in school than most workers do on the job. Workers "read for a number of purposes including reading to learn, reading to do, and reading to assess," while students in school "read primarily to learn" (p. 413). Failing to comprehend the reading materials encountered in the workplace means failing to learn what is essential to the actual work operation. Thus, the somewhat illiterate person with inadequate reading skills "will have disappointed himself and failed to meet the expectations of the employer" (Guthrie, 1983a, p. 668).

Becoming

As in learning, *becoming* implies a process of change by which earlier stages of development are incorporated into later ones (Allport, 1963, p. 28). Becoming involves development, which, according to Lawton (1982), is the universal sequence of "physical, intellectual, emotional, and social changes occurring as a person passes from birth to adulthood, evolving the possibilities provided by maturation, experiment, the environment, and individuality" (p. 6).

Bibliotherapy has a place in becoming. Jalongo (1983) advocates teachers' use of bibliotherapy with their students. Books can help to promote the students' socioemotional growth and can provide enjoyment, new insights, and discoveries.

Schools can foster becoming through growth in different directions for different students, by way of instruction that spans a broad spectrum from academic engagement and task participation to group initiative (p. 863). Furthermore, schools can assist students in becoming well-informed, participating adults by encouraging secondary students to read to primary students as well as to children in day-care centers and their own younger brothers and sisters (Smale, 1982, p. 209).

Reading as a Synthesis

Based on the preceding discussions of the contributory processes that make reading possible, I now offer a description of reading as a synthesis of contributory processes that interrelate, interact, and integrate with other life processes so that readers are able to communicate with themselves and with others through reading.

It is hoped that this succinct description may challenge the readers of this book to compose their own explanation, perhaps definition, of reading. For, having none, how does one teach reading? Of course this description may be criticized for what it lacks. It says nothing about recoding from letters to sounds and sounds to letters, or about decoding words and attaching meaning, or about directly processing print into meaning, or about the reader bringing meaning to segments of print. Undoubtedly, these subactivities, and many others not yet discussed, are important. Yet I believe they are subsidiary to the contributory processes described in this section. Likewise, this description has said nothing of reading skills, an expression we have heard so many times.

Downing (1982) asks whether we should speak of *reading skill* or *reading skills*. He refers to psychologists who explain that a "skill" is a complex set of processes that are cognitive, attitudinal, and manipulative (p. 535). "The key feature of every skill," Downing advises, "is the integration of the complex set of behaviors that make the total pattern. Integration is learned through practice" (pp. 536–537). A skill has subskills, some of which, as research tells (McNeil, 1974, p. 426), are learned concurrently while learning to read.

To foster yet more reflection on reading, readers of this book may want to think about E.B. Huey's statement (1908), which clearly recognizes the difficult task of describing and defining reading. He wrote: "And so to completely analyze what we do when we read would almost be the acme of a psycholinguist's achievement, for it would be to describe very many of the most intricate workings of the human mind as well as unravel the tangled story of the most remarkable specific performance that civilization has learned in all its history" (p. 6).

Summary

The sensory processes of seeing, hearing, moving, and touching, together with perceiving, thinking, learning, and becoming, are the processes that contribute to reading. All these processes interact and integrate through the reader's ability and willingness to activate their dynamic potentials so that they flow together and synthesize to extract meaning from the text. Reading was described as a synthesis, based on the contributory processes that make it possible. This description and Huey's statement on reading should challenge the readers of this book to compose their own descriptions or definitions of reading, without which one cannot teach reading.

READING AND COGNITIVE DEVELOPMENT

The integration of the contributory processes makes reading possible to the degree that teachers and students are concerned with processing print to extract meaning. This concern ranges from trying to decode letters and words to using prior knowledge to gain meaning. Some readers can do this and some cannot. The range of differences between can and cannot is anchored in the individual differences in the ways in which knowledge develops.

Cognition

Cognition is the act or the process of knowing. Knowing results in knowledge, which is organized and structured in our heads. Knowing leads to understanding, and what is understood clearly leads to *cognitive clarity*. As Downing and Leong (1982) explain, cognitive clarity probably develops out of cognitive confusion or not yet being able to understand and to think clearly.

But students who have reached cognitive clarity do understand clearly and are able to think clearly (p. 109). However, it should not be assumed that "cognitive confusion will automatically give way to cognitive clarity which is essential to reading" (p. 111). Vernon (1971, p. 79), for instance, found that cognitive confusion results when children fail to understand that the limited number of twenty-six letters in the English alphabet can make an unlimited number of words. Cognitive clarity is achieved when the same children learn to understand that, in fact, a limited number of letters can make an unlimited number of words.

Using the following example, experience how cognitive confusion, even though only momentary, may give way to cognitive clarity. The following twelve letters of the English alphabet—a,a,a,c,e,h,k,n,s,s,t,w—can make over 100 well-known English words!

Knowing how cognition develops and how to use its development, teachers can recognize and understand clearly why some students are more able to do what others cannot do, at least not yet. At the same time, such knowledge will also aid teachers in thinking clearly about the preparation and organization of reading materials and reading approaches.

Stages of Cognitive Development

What makes even a limited study of the stage theories of intellectual development rewarding for students in reading is to know that brain-growth stages are now a scientific fact, not a theoretical notion (Epstein, 1978). Human brain growth occurs "primarily during the age intervals of three to ten months, and from two to four, six to eight, ten to twelve or thirteen, and fourteen to sixteen or seventeen years and that these stages correlate well in timing with stages found in mental growth" (p. 344), although "their universality is not yet proven" (p. 356).

Unfortunately, school curricula in general and reading curricula in particular seem to have paid little attention to stages of intellectual development, although Piaget's theories appear in many books on reading and the notion of stages of intellectual development can be traced back about sixty years. It would appear that, ideally, intellectual input would be most effective during the brain-growth spurts.

Our discussion on stage theory and development will focus on their possible implications for reading. The theories to be discussed are those by Alfred North Whitehead (1861–1947) of England, Maria Montessori (1870–1952) of Italy, Leo Semenovitch Vygotzky (1896–1934) of the Soviet Union, Jean Piaget (1896–1980) of Switzerland, and Jerome Seymour Bruner (1915–) of the United States. The thinking of these educators has had lasting influence on educational thinking, theorizing, and practicing throughout the world, and is the basis for continuing research.

Whitehead: The Rhythm of Education. Whitehead made it clear that the contents of different subject areas should be taught only when students had reached the proper level of mental development. He called the development from level to level the *rhythm of education* (Whitehead, 1958) and said that "lack of attention to the rhythm and the character of mental growth is a main source of wooden futility in education" (p. 29). Within each rhythm there are cyclic processes that repeat themselves in relation to intellectual progress.

Whitehead, however, did not apply the cyclic processes specifically to reading. Nevertheless, in teaching reading, cyclic processes probably occur when, for example, the single letter *s* is introduced in its initial position, as in the word *sing*. Then, in later instruction, the same initial letter develops with another consonant to become *st*, as in the word *sting*; *st* later develops into the beginning letter cluster *str*, as in *string*.

In Whitehead's stage periodization, children between the ages of two and four develop from perceiving objects through bodily activities to the acquisition of oral language. Language, however, is not yet governed by systematic procedures or rules of syntax, which develop within the next cyclic spurt that ends about the age of seven or during the second year in school.

Between the ages of eight to twelve spoken language is mastered, which leads to classifying objects and to keener perception and greater stabilization of emotions. Striving toward greater precision ushers in more systematic order and progress, together with greater powers of observation, manipulation, and utilization of the child's mother tongue. The years between twelve and fifteen are dominated by a "mass attack upon language" (Whitehead, 1958, p. 34), which develops into abilities to generalize verbally and to achieve greater precision in science.

When Whitehead talked about the mastery of language, he also talked about reading. At about eleven years of age, children gradually increase their concentration on precise knowledge of language. While children are developing a "command of English," they also should be able to read fluently fairly simple French and should have precise knowledge of parts of Latin grammar.

In summary, Whitehead suggested that education should be perceived in terms of a rhythm within which there are repetitive cycles, thus indicating that education in general and learning in particular are not achieved in uniform and steady advancement and development. Accordingly, the human mind must not be packed with information that is useless or alien to the child. Instead, the mind must acquire knowledge in orderly and systematic sequences that are the "natural food for developing intelligence" (Whitehead, 1958, p. 41).

Montessori: From Absorbent Mind to *Erdkinder*. Montessori emphasized that, during the child's first period of transformation, that of the Absorbent

Mind, from birth to about age six, language acquisition develops mainly through absorbing words the children hear spoken around them (Montessori, 1964). Infants listen to the speech sounds adults and siblings produce. This induces the infants to absorb unconsciously vague and less distinguishable sounds, which leads them to exercise the muscles of the speech apparatus in general and those of the mouth and lips in particular. When the conscious mind takes over, closer to six years of age, articulate language emerges, leading to writing and reading. With the development of consciousness, the child moves from being controlled by the environment to controlling it (Patterson, 1977, p. 29). Montessori saw this accomplishment reflected in the abilities of children to conquer language in both spoken and written forms.

Writing begins a few weeks before reading. Both writing and reading are preceded by touching and looking at letters; this cooperation of the senses fixes the images of letters more quickly (Montessori, 1964, Chapter 16). In Montessori's Casa dei Bambini, or the Home of Children, the young learners experimented with didactic, graded materials that provided for sensory and motor training. This kind of instruction, Montessori suggested, lays the foundation for acquiring the basic symbolic skills that are important for the learning of writing, reading, and counting.

The end of this period of transformation not only coincides with the beginning of formal schooling but also signals the transition into the period of uniform growth, or childhood, from about six to twelve years of age. This is when children learn how to read, how to read more skillfully, and how to develop from the "sensorial, material level to the abstract" (Montessori, 1973, p. 11). As children are making commitments to extracting meaning from written words, they engage freely in abstract lessons and in these "years of plenty" accomplish a great deal of mental work. They gather undetermined quantities of knowledge, which makes it possible to reconstruct the whole when knowing only a detail or part (Montessori, 1976, Chapters 4 and 5). These cognitive developments relate directly to learning to read, as children move from initial recoding of letters into sounds, to decoding written or spoken language into meaning.

This period of relative stability is followed by the second period of transformation, adolescence, about 12 to 18 years of age. This period is mainly characterized by "doubts, hesitations, violent emotions, discouragement, and unexpected decrease in intellectual capacity" (Montessori, 1973, p. 101). These rather negative psychological characteristics yield to more positive ones when teachers strengthen adolescents' expectations, creative work, and self-confidence through using doubt and hesitation as challenges to seek and establish proof through hypothesizing and verifying. Adolescents reason and distinguish the real from the unreal, the correct from the incorrect, and what can be done from what cannot be done. They become what Montessori called *erdkinder*, or land-children, having "knowledge of one's own capacity" (1976, p. 102).

In summary, beginning with the Absorbent Mind, children experience developmental spurts that move them through stages of learning. With the growing interaction of language and further mental development, children not only learn to write, read, and count, but, more important, to grow from the sensorial to the abstract levels and from there to fully mature thinking *erdkinder*.

Vygotzky: From Primitive to Genuine. Vygotzky, like Whitehead, asserted that there are critical periods of sudden, forceful change that relate directly to the transition from one level of cognitive development to the next (Vygotzky, 1974). Vygotzky called the developmental period between birth and about two years the Primitive stage; from two to about four years, the stage of Syncretic "Heaps" or of Conglomeration; from four to about seven years, the stage of Associative Collection and Chain Complexes; from seven to about eleven years, the stage of Pseudo-concepts; and the age beyond eleven years, the stage of Genuine Concepts (Vygotzky, 1962/1977, Chapters 5 and 6).

In the Primitive phase, children explore their immediate environment of objects. Infants show signs of hearing adults speak and develop understanding of language long before they themselves actually begin to speak. Increased active exploration and investigation of almost everything moves children into the stage of Syncretic "Heaps" or Conglomeration at about two years of age. Children begin to form concepts by gathering together a number of objects in unorganized congeries or "heaps" (Vygotzky, 1962, p. 59). This is the start of real language development, when words begin to stand for images and when language imitations accompany playing. These "syncretic heaps" or primitive word groupings are arrived at by trial and error. Children experience, for example, that milk and drink, dressed and out, and doll and play go together and, through this togetherness, develop preconcepts (Smith, Goodman, & Meredith, 1976, p. 142). Toward the end of this second stage, children's thinking advances to include complexes, or groups of objects, united by bonds that are concrete and factual and are discovered through direct experience.

During the following stage, Associative Collection and Chain Complexes, children advance to the purest form of thinking in complexes (Vygotzky, 1977, p. 64), which ushers in concrete thinking. Thinking in complexes is limitless and gives the child the power to include more and more individual members within any original group. Complex thinking develops into the stage of Pseudo-concepts and Potential Concepts.

Thinking now looks like conceptualizing at adult level, and it could just as well be mistaken for abstract thinking. In reality, however, children have formed only an associative complex that is still embedded in the concrete and visible relatedness of objects and limited to a kind of perceptual bond. Nevertheless, pseudo-concepts are the link between thinking in complexes and in concepts.

To reach true conceptual thinking, verbal communication with adults is essential. At about eleven years of age and thereafter, children move into the stage of Genuine Concepts. Thinking advances to analyzing and synthesizing, to coping with scientific concepts and testing them, as well as to using deductive and inductive reasoning. "Only the mastery of abstraction, combined with advanced complex thinking, enables the child to progress to the formation of genuine concepts" (Vygotzky, 1962, p. 78).

In summary, beginning with the Primitive stage and progressing to the stage of Genuine Concepts, language and thinking develop in spurts to maturity. A difference, however, is noted between the development of oral and written language, because "written speech is different in both structure and mode of functioning" (Vygotzky, 1962, p. 98). Vygotzky agrees with Montessori in the sense that reading and writing as well as arithmetic, grammar and science will develop better with adult assistance. Through appropriate adult guidance in and out of school, children can develop a more profound base of knowledge than when left to themselves without appropriate formal and informal instruction in school and at home.

Piaget: From Sensorimotor to Formal Operational. In the child's Sensorimotor period, from birth to about age two, Piaget suggested that spontaneous movements and reflexlike activities show the beginning of assimilation, accommodation, and organization. Manipulating materials lays the foundations for experiences, while engaging in magical beliefs indicates the threshold of intelligence. Toward the end of this period, thought development leads to some problem solving not only by external or physical grouping but also by sudden internalized comprehension or insight (Piaget & Inhelder, 1969, Chapter 1). For example, a child discovers that having a string attached to an object provides a new means to pull it to oneself.

The child's transition to the Preoperational period, from about two to age seven, is crucial in preparing and learning to read (Waller, 1977, p. 3). The child's mental growth during the early Preoperational/Preconceptual period from about age two to four, is particularly important in developing the ability to represent an object or event by means of language. To distinguish a signifier from that which is signified is absolutely essential for reading. The word *dog* has a symbolic function as the signifier but is not, the real dog. When children can say the word *dog*, they also know what it represents and what it means, without the dog being present. This exemplifies nascent (young, developing) language, which permits verbal evocation of events that are not happening at the moment (Piaget & Inhelder, 1969, p. 54).

Soon the child is ready to advance into the later Preoperational/Intuitive period, from about four to seven years of age. Symbolic functioning is leading the child from print to meaning. The child begins to differentiate symbols from signs. Symbols are the child's own creation as, for instance, simulating sleep or dressing up to visit grandmother. Symbols are private and idiosyncratic. In contrast, signs are representations of words from the environment. Signs that the child must learn are arbitrary and are shared by all living in that environment.

It is, of course, toward the end of the Preoperational period that children are introduced to formal schooling and with it to formal instruction in reading. If at this time children have not advanced from representational thought to symbolic functioning, they will not be able to learn to read or, at best, will have great difficulties and may experience failure in reading.

At about age seven to eleven, mental development spurts into the Concrete Operational period. The transition to this period requires that children have mentally developed from centration to decentration, from static to dynamic functioning, and from irreversibility to reversibility. Decentration means accepting that twenty-six letters in the alphabet represent forty-four sounds and that each letter has two graphic structures as a capital and a small letter. It means accepting that letters can be either a consonant or a vowel—or both, as *y* in *y*ou and b*y*—and that a word can be both a noun and a verb, as in *They run the run together*. Dynamic functioning means bringing to the task selective attention in order to inspect a word from beginning to ending and produce the sounds blended together according to the conventional total sound pattern of the word, as in *pin* and *pine*. Reversibility means being able to exchange letters and sounds to make different words and restore them mentally to their original state, as *leak* to *lake* and *heat* to *hate*.

Conservation of letters versus the changeability of sounds is another essential prerequisite in learning to read. While the letter *a* conserves its graphic representation, beginning sounds change, as in *at, ate*, and *all*, as do the medial sounds in *cat, call*, and *calm*. Seriating the letter and sound orders in words, as in *girl* and *grill*, and sequencing words in a sentence, as in *The fisherman ate the fish* and *The fish ate the fisherman*, are mental operations essential to extracting meaning from the text. Reading the basals and subject-area textbooks requires seriating, sequencing, classifying, numbering, and grouping of objects, events, actions, ideas, and thoughts, all of which are mental operations that must be developed during the Concrete Operational period.

At about eleven years of age and older, children enter the Formal Operational period. Mental operations move from concrete and present observations to hypothetical-deductive, combinatorial, and propositional thinking (Patterson, 1977, p. 98; Piaget & Inhelder, 1969, p. 131). Hypothetical-deductive operations make it possible to reason out hypotheses by examining many or all of the "might-be" possibilities in a search for the "is" reality. Combinatorial thought operations reflect the adolescent's ability to bring together factors in groups of two, three, or more, as well as to solve complex problems in which several elements are simultaneously contributing to a particular result or situation (Elkind, 1977, p. 100). Propositional thought operations are expressed in setting up if-then, either-or, neither-neither, or-both, or neither-or situations (Piaget & Inhelder, 1969, p. 136), which are all difficult in word and thought order. Nevertheless, these higher mental operations are needed if adolescents are to progress through reading from dependent to independent thinkers and readers and if they are to use textual information proficiently as the basis for analytic-synthetic reasoning.

In summary, Piaget's stages of cognitive development prescribe the mental operations that, though variable in chronological onset, must proceed in an invariable order. Although Piaget did not apply his cognitive stages directly to reading and reading instruction, each thought period suggests explicitly and implicitly what children can do and can be asked to accomplish in and through reading.

Bruner: From Enactive to Symbolic. Bruner postulated that human intellect develops discontinuously rather than smoothly. It grows through the modes of Enactive, Iconic, and Symbolic representation of the world (1973, p. 316).

During Enactive Representation, or the action mode, knowledge is gathered through doing, which provides "the necessary condition for the infant's achievement" (Bruner, 1966, p. 16). Visual, auditory, and tactile manipulation focus on sensory perception, through which children get acquainted with their external world. Words are signs, not symbols; they represent objects that are present. What can be done to objects and events defines what they are to the child, who has difficulty in separating the mental product from the act of perceiving (Bruner, 1978, p. 12).

Advancing to Iconic Representation, or the mode of imagery, the object to be perceived (the percept) becomes "relatively autonomous from action" (Bruner, 1973, p. 317). That is, the child uses "a set of summary images or graphics that stand for a concept without defining it fully" (Bruner, 1964, p. 310). Images are of simple organization, are limited and unstable, and lack flexibility. Nevertheless, this imagery or iconic representation appears to be useful in the first years of schooling, when children attach "arbitrary labels to things and objects which are visualized" (Patterson, 1977, p. 143). Learning that symbols refer to things but are not the things themselves is less dependent on imagery than on the mental growth of the ability to conceptualize. Graphic representation of language at this stage is arbitrary and is dependent on knowing its symbolic code.

When children are able to use language as an instrument of thinking, mental growth has arrived at Symbolic Representation. This is the mode in which "the transformational apparatus of grammar [aids] in the solution of mental problems" (Bruner, 1978, p. 14). Children are now equipped to use spoken and written language to organize, categorize, set up possibilities and conditions, integrate, interrelate, and draw conclusions. Applied more specifically to reading, these qualities mean that readers are no longer restricted to reading the lines but are becoming free to read between and beyond the lines and "go beyond the information given" (Bruner, 1973).

In summary, the Enactive, Iconic, and Symbolic modes are the means by which the individual represents or constructs the world and by which the world is represented to the individual. None of the modes is separated from the others. Instead, Enactive Representation continues when Iconic Representation develops, which continues into Symbolic Representation, and one interacts with the other. Thought processes that begin with the dialogue of speech and gestures between children and parents lead to the process of trying, by which "we recast the difficulty into a form that we know how to work with—then we work it" (Bruner, 1979, p. 93).

Queries on Cognitive Development

Thinking about age periodization of cognitive development in terms of stages during which cognition develops invites questions for which answers are not yet readily available and must be left for future research to answer.

Age periodization is said to move cognitive development from one level to the next. Why and how does it happen in stages? When moving through the stages, are there changes taking place in the structure of the mind prior that must occur before proceeding to the next stage of cognitive development? Prior to a new stage of development, does the brian expand? If so, why and how?

Other questions that pertain to the various theories as well as to the manifestations of the various stages in the development of intelligence beg further answers. Of the five theories of cognitive stage development presented here, is any one theory more suitable than the other for the teaching of reading from the teacher's point of view and for learning to read from the student's point of view? How do teachers know when students are at or about at the stage of formal operational development? How do they know when and why students are not at this or any other particular stage? How do these mental spurts develop in those children whose level of intelligence is lower than normal? Do they manifest lower-than-average achievement during any of the stages, do they move slower from stage to stage, or does the mental development stop at a certain stage? If so, why and how?

Of course, we recall that, according to Piaget, the progression of the stages is constant but the ages at which the stages manifest themselves can and do vary. That is, a developmental stage does not need, and perhaps should not be expected, to coincide with a person's age.

While questions still remain on stages of cognitive development, perhaps Alfred North Whitehead's statement can be used as a challenge to teachers in general and teachers of reading in particular, as we search for answers. In 1922, Whitehead stated in *The Aims of Education* that "different subjects and modes of study should be undertaken by pupils at fitting times when they have reached the proper stage of mental development" (1958, p. 27).

Summary

The five different theories on stages of cognitive development presented here can be used by teachers in planning effective instruction. Knowledge of the stages of development may contribute in many ways to teaching reading. It is proposed that new learning should be encouraged during brain-growth spurts, when students will be better able to absorb new knowledge, think through what ought to be learned, participate in the new learning experience, and stay alert in solving problems and in evolving new ideas. When cognitive development moves through slow-growth periods, teachers should consider reinforcing and enlarging upon what has been learned, including helping those students who need additional practice in any phase of reading instruction.

ENCOURAGEMENT

Although it is important that teachers understand the stages of cognitive development, they must also be sensitive to the dynamic emotional forces operating from within and from without each person. These affect all of us, but in particular they influence those who learn to read, read to learn, and learn to learn. These forces are called encouragement and discouragement. Remember the last time you felt discouraged or encouraged by what you had done or what someone had done to you. You know from experience that encouragement or discouragement comes from parents, teachers, the work one does, and from the environmental circumstances one lives in (Dinkmeyer & Dreikurs, 1963, p. 87 ff).

Encouragement is not a tangible reward, such as gold stars and other materialistic give-aways. Encouragement is not just empty words glibly spoken. Encouragement is acceptance of the person as a person, a sincere smile, a hand that helps without doing the work for the child, a displayed positive behavior that is noted as such by the recipient.

Children in the beginning stages of learning to read need to be encouraged without being compared to more skilled readers, without being told again and again that they cannot read, are lazy, or don't want to do it. Children at home and in school must be given opportunity as well as time to prove to themselves and to their parents and teachers that they actually can read and accomplish some work. The opportunity to contribute will establish self-confidence, which in turn will foster willingness, which will spark eagerness to live up to expectations and, with success, will prompt achieving even more than was originally expected.

Encouragement invites success and forestalls discouragement and unnecessary failure. Both encouragement and discouragement shape children's mental representations and perceptions of the world around them.

Encouragement in reading will result in positive, constructive, productive behaviors, while discouragement will result in negative, destructive, unproductive behaviors. Children who can read are encouraged by their accomplishment, while children who cannot read are discouraged by their failure. For too many readers at too many times, failure to learn to read has become an accepted way of life in school.

Summary

Children's cognitive development is accompanied by the dynamic forces of encouragement and discouragement. The former spells success and self-confidence, the latter failure and self-defeat—either temporarily or for the long term.

CHAPTER 4

Becoming Ready

Purpose questions for this chapter:

- How did the concept of reading readiness develop?
- What are some factors indicated by research to be essential in reading readiness?
- What do parents and teachers contribute to readiness?
- How can readiness be advanced for early reading instruction?
- How is perceptual awareness involved in beginning reading?

SOURCES OF READING READINESS

It was not until the year 1925 that the term "reading readiness" appeared in the reading literature. In the *Report of the National Committee on Reading* (Gray, 1925), the concept of reading readiness as a preparatory period in the child's total reading development was initially recognized. The report indicated that lack of readiness could be compensated for through appropriate reading instruction and that readiness to read could be cultivated through appropriate prereading instruction. The important message, however, was that whether or not a child learns to read depends on the child and the initial reading instruction the child receives in school.

This position emphasized instruction, so it was soon questioned if not opposed by those who espoused the maturational position. The latter put the onus on nature and what the child has received at the time of conception; the former put the onus on nurture and what the child has received during home and preschool training and how appropriate the child's prereading instruction has been as a basis for learning to read.

Nature's Endowments

The early literature assumed that readiness was best left in the hands of nature, which, through heredity, predetermined the unfolding of the child.

Gesell proposed a concept of neural ripening through developmental stages as the essence of children's growth and life (Ilg & Ames, 1955). With this fairly lawful development of intrinsic neural ripening or maturation, stages follow one another in an almost inevitable order. At some point during these patterned stages, children acquire the ability to learn to read (Durkin, 1983, p. 44).

However, with the advance of testing, particularly intelligence testing, the mental-age concept was looked to for more definite answers regarding when or when not to begin the formal teaching of reading. In fact, the much-acclaimed study by Morphett and Washburne (1931) advised teachers to postpone the teaching of reading until children had reached the mental age of 6.5 years, before which they should "avoid any effort to get a child to read" (Washburne, 1936, p. 127).

At this point, it becomes essential to understand the concepts of mental age (MA), chronological age (CA), and intelligence quotient (IQ). Mental age indicates the level of development in intelligence or mental growth that has been achieved in relationship to the chronological age, or life age. For instance, an average six- or seven-year-old child will have a mental age of six or seven, respectively. Thus, MA is the distance that the child has traveled mentally. This should not be confused with the intelligence quotient, which is a measure of the rate of mental growth. That is, IQ indicates the rate at which the child has traveled to reach that level.

Nurture's Influence

In more recent years, the notion of postponing reading until children reach that magic number 6.5, has been overshadowed by the concept of nurture, which takes into account the impact of the environment on the development of intelligence. From this point of view, the emphasis on explaining reading readiness shifts from heredity to the home and school environment. Emphasis is on the child and his or her physical and mental performances as supported by ancestral endowments. What the child can do physically and mentally constitute the child's ability, which is influenced by informal and formal educational experiences in and out of school.

The kinds of training, instruction, and experiences preschool children encounter and are exposed to at home and in kindergarten assist in determining their attitudes, interests, and motivations toward beginning reading instruction. The importance of how children are brought up at home and later in school was clearly recognized and attested to in the second *Report of the National Committee on Reading* (Gray, 1937), which was released only twelve years after the first. To those responsible for teaching reading in schools, its message was unequivocal in pointing out that "process and direction of growth are determined by all the experiences that children encounter, both in school and out of school. Accordingly, good teaching utilizes . . . the latter as well as the former and helps the child to associate them appropriately and to see their significance" (pp. 13–14).

Asbell's report (1967) on a 30-year child development study recognizes the impact on intelligence not only of environment but also of parental inadequacy of affection and attention as well as of inadequacy of school instruction. The latter points to what kinds of reading programs or materials are used, how effectively they are implemented, and, perhaps most important, what the teacher's knowledge is about the teaching of reading.

Rupley and Blair (1978) also pointed to teacher effectiveness in reading instruction and concluded by asserting that "the teacher accounts for a major portion of [the] pupil's reading achievement and is a primary factor in determining whether children will be successful in learning to read" (p. 970). Mason (1980) rallied behind the parents and affirmed that parental influence together with educational television "has apparently increased children's knowledge about reading" (p. 205).

Summary

Since its first appearance in the literature in 1925, the concept of "reading readiness" has sparked controversial dialogues concerning the role of nature and nurture in readiness to read, as well as their implications in teaching reading and learning to read. The assumption that a child's mental age is the sole determiner in learning to read has been counterbalanced by the recognition that a child's preschool experiences and the kind of instruction given interact with the mental factor to furnish the basis for learning and reading.

PREPARING FOR READING

There is much agreement in the reading literature that many factors influence and are essential to a child's reading readiness; however, disagreement prevails as to what these factors and their functions are, how important they are, whether one is more significant than the others in becoming ready to read.

Reflecting briefly on the accounts in the literature, some basic factors found to be important as precursors to reading instruction will be described.

Basic Factors in Child Readiness

Gray (1937) listed the following factors as being essential to beginning reading instruction: (1) reasonable facility in the use of ideas and in having command of simple English sentences, (2) a relatively broad speaking vocabulary and range of background experiences, (3) accuracy in enunciation and pronunciation as well as in visual and auditory discrimination, and (4) a keen interest in learning to read (pp. 81–85). Harrison (1939), in his effort to identify essential factors in reading readiness, suggested the mental factor and the abilities to see likenesses and differences, to remember word forms, to do abstract thinking, and to have a memory span for ideas (pp. 8–9).

Betts (1946) called for recognizing the needs of the learners and their experiences, social adjustments, interests and attitudes, chronological ages, mental maturity, perception of relationships, memory span, background information, language facility, motor control, and sex differences. They also should have good auditory, visual, and color discrimination, good visual efficiency, and general good health. They should be free from neurological disturbances (pp. 116–137).

Harris (1961) cited as major factors to reading readiness those of age, sex, general intelligence, visual and auditory perception, physical health and maturity, freedom from directional confusion, background experiences, comprehension and use of oral English, emotional and social adjustment, and interest in reading (p. 26).

Downing and Thackray (1971) recalled earlier attempts to categorize the many factors under broad headings and suggested four general groups: physical factors; environmental factors; emotional, motivational, and personality factors; and intellectual factors (p. 15).

Ransom (1978) suggested six major areas that she thought require maximal functioning before reading readiness is indicated: psychomotor skills, sensory factors, perception, the cognitive and affective domain, linguistic patterns, and personal experiences (p. 4).

King (1978) reviewed ten research studies on the effectiveness of direct versus incidental teaching in prereading instruction. She identified twenty-eight basic skills, which she grouped into five areas: listening to stories read, picture reading, auditory discrimination, visual discrimination, and forming associations (pp. 508–509).

More recently, Dallmann et al. (1982) repeated much of the same factors already cited, while Rubin (1982) added speech improvement, left–right orientation, and developing comprehension skills (pp. 46–49). May (1982) considered among other factors, those of decoding and comprehension of print, phonic analysis, letter recognition, visual and auditory memory, letter-sound association and auditory blending, following oral directions, oral vocabulary, and being able to think about what is read (pp. 188–214).

While many factors and their groupings appear to be arbitrary, research has nevertheless recognized some of them as being important to reading readiness. Research by Richek (1977–1978), Hillerich (1978), and Hiebert

(1981) identified visual and auditory discrimination, oral language, following oral directions, using oral context, print awareness, letter recognition, blending, sequencing, and listening comprehension.

Partnerships in Readiness

The target of becoming and of being ready is the child. The movers are the parents and later the teachers; however, they are movers only from without and must work together with the child, who, from within, is his or her own mover in becoming ready. The child, the parents, and the teachers may be perceived as the prime movers, while the wider family circle, neighborhood environment, nursery, and kindergarten may be perceived as secondary movers. Prime movers deal constantly with the child over prolonged periods of time, while secondary movers deal intermittently with the child over shorter periods of time. In varying degrees, at different times, and for diverse purposes movers communicate messages directly and indirectly, consciously and unconsciously. Messages and how they are delivered touch and influence children's physical and mental development and growth and ultimately shape and determine readiness or unreadiness for successful or unsuccessful schooling.

What this means is that the readiness of any child arriving at and being in school must never ever be posited on the child alone. Children prior to school age have not lived—existed—in isolation to suddenly appear from nowhere at the time of school entrance, to be massed together in a classroom where readiness tests of questionable content and child relatedness lay claim, and often sole claim, to determine readiness to read. Quite the contrary, the child, parents, and schools form an alliance or a partnership in which efforts and interests toward reading readiness are shared by all concerned, with responsibilities and with respect for the roles each partner has to act and to fulfill.

Figure 4.1 attempts to capture this three-way partnership of child with parents and teachers, while two-way arrows signify their reciprocal influences on reading readiness. Let us now examine some of the contributions that these partners make to a child's reading readiness.

Contributions of Parents and the Home. Parental influence on readiness occurs in the immediate home environment, among the family, whose members relate first to the pregnancy and later directly to the newborn. It may appear that because of an infant's helplessness in regard to life sustenance, the infant is acted *upon*. Yet, the infant is not the passive receiver but actually the active demander around whom family life centers. Just as the expectant parents got ready for the infant's arrival, the infant, supported by the parents, gets ready for life. What happens during the years from birth to school

FIGURE 4.1. Relationships in Reading Readiness Among Child, Parents, and Teachers

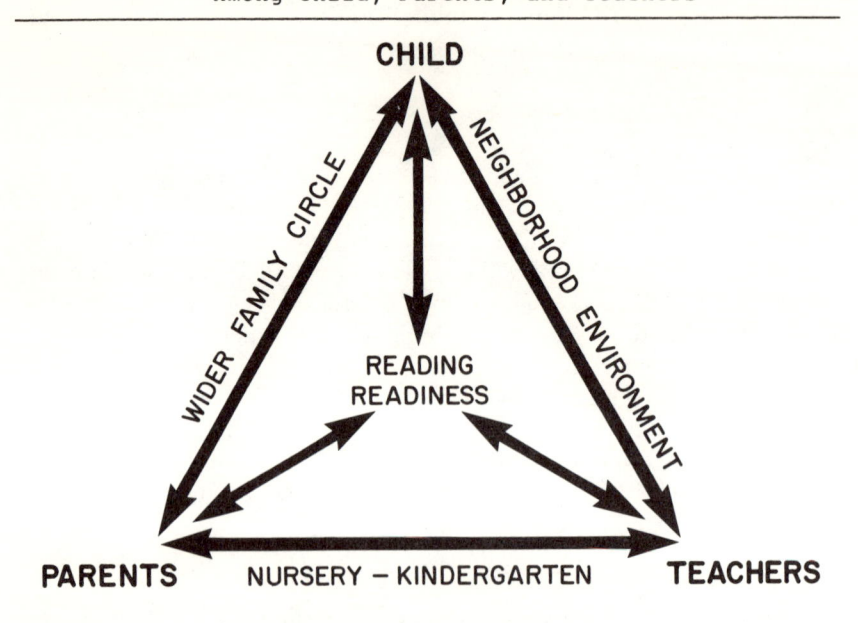

```
                        CHILD
                         ↕
              ╱                    ╲
          ╱  ↑                    ↑  ╲
   WIDER FAMILY CIRCLE    NEIGHBORHOOD ENVIRONMENT
      ╱                              ╲
    ╱       READING                    ╲
   ╱        READINESS                   ╲
  ╱     ←            →                   ╲
 PARENTS  NURSERY – KINDERGARTEN  TEACHERS
```

entrance will influence the infant's subsequent development. The growing child is both the recipient and the sender of messages as well as the recipient and the mover of actions.

These formative years at home are marked by the complexity of interrelationships and interactions among the child and his family members. These reciprocal relationships provide the foundation for physical development and environmental experiences, as well as for cognitive growth and intelligence (Richek et al., 1983, p. 28). Parents' social and emotional well-being structure a favorable or unfavorable home environment, which, according to studies by Abrams and Kaslow (1977), contributes to making good and poor readers.

Children's readiness may be said to relate to parents' readiness for their children. Parents are their children's first and most important teachers. Parents and their homes are the primary shapers of children's readiness by providing the immediate social environment in which the use of language develops and is practiced, as well as by cultivating attitudes and interests toward life in general and learning in particular. Parents or parent substitutes are responsible for moving their children toward literacy before formal schooling begins (Mass, 1982, p. 670). Literacy in this sense means oral language ability, which, as Fox (1976) reports, "may be considered a basis for developing reading skills" (p. 670).

This emphasis on the parent-home interrelationship and interaction with the child should not be interpreted to exclude other experiences that enrich the child's background for reading. Traveling, experiencing country and city life, visiting museums, attending concerts, watching symbolic plays, and participating in many other educational encounters expand and diversify experiences and thus add to the quantity and quality of the child's listening and speaking vocabularies, facilitate mental functioning, and assist in schema formation (Vukelich, 1978).

Environmental exploration and investigation lead to reading and understanding symbols and signs and never fail to whet children's curiosity for what the black squiggles really say on commercial establishments, television shows, and advertisements. Words on cereal boxes, storefronts, and signs become children's first experiences in visual word recognition, as whole-word patterns in meaningful setting and context (Mason, 1980). Mason reports that parent-child communication and the child's cognitive development and linguistic awareness of print influence progress in reading. Based on his studies, Mason suggests a natural hierarchy of knowledge development in learning to read words by realizing that letters are discriminable patterns, that letters provide clues for reading, and that sounds in words are determined by letters (p. 203).

Durrell and Murphy (1978) note that, of the twenty-six letters in the English alphabet, the names of twenty-two letters contain their phonemes. The exceptions are the consonant letters h, q, w, and y. The authors claim that "a child who knows letters well enough to identify them by name will be more aware of differences between words than a child to whom letters are nameless shapes" (p. 387).

The role of parents as teachers of their children does not and should not stop when the preschool years at home come to an end. Rather, parent involvement as part of the teaching team is an important educational concept. Research has confirmed that comprehensive, sustained parent involvement in which parents serve many roles has a positive effect on the school's ability to do its job (Strickland, 1982). Parent involvement can provide and perhaps assure continuity in the lives of children between home and school and can relate positively to their attitudes and academic achievements.

Contributions of Teachers. The day of reckoning for parent-child readiness comes when the child arrives at the classroom and begins learning to read. At the same time, this calls for teacher readiness.

How prepared is the teacher to teach reading? Is the teacher able to organize the classroom successfully to create a social environment that is most effective for learning? How does the teacher utilize the time that the student is engaged in learning? Are opportunities to learn given through occupying students with reading a text and then discussing and reacting to it? How are the students involved in oral reading, writing, and other language-performance activities (Aulls, 1982, p. 450)?

Through these introductory questions, we can see that it is undeniably the teacher who bears the responsibility for making instruction in reading efficient and effective. Good teaching means good classroom management, including setting attainable goals, selecting appropriate reading materials, and providing time and opportunity for student feedback. While organization of teacher effort, time, and knowledge is essential, effective teaching does not stop with managerial talents but reaches out and actively engages teachers and students in "inspiring moments of mutual discovery" (Guthrie, 1982, p. 638).

What, then, makes teacher effectiveness possible? Effectiveness does not reside within the teacher who is always sure and certain of being right because of having a teaching certificate and some years' teaching experience. Rather, effectiveness resides within the teacher who lacks that certainty, who has doubts, and who knows that much learning needs to be done and that learning never stops. "That enables a teacher to be effective. For *only* an uncertain person can learn; *only* an uncertain person can show how learning is done" (MacGinitie, 1983, p. 679).

A good teacher is uncertain and skeptical about the basal reader series, with all its tempting ready-made accessories, and about the hardwares and softwares of microcomputers. A good teacher does not assume that these will be superior over other instructional methods, will "fit" students and their learning styles, and will solve students' difficulties. A good teacher is aware that student failure to achieve will certainly pigeonhole readers into various categories, such as remedial readers or disabled readers.

Teacher readiness is a dynamic that comes with the *seeking* teachers, who are always inquiring by reading professional literature and trying different approaches based on and kindled by research. Seeking teachers know their own limits in knowing and teaching abilities and seek out additional information. Seeking teachers guide students in engaging in their own seeking, and they share and accept uncertainty in favor of sterile yes and no answers.

Teacher readiness goes beyond administering a certain reading program, which may be appropriate for some students but not for others. Teacher readiness is the matching of academic knowing with the professional ability to reach the students and to communicate with and inspire them. Teacher readiness goes beyond mastery learning, where "the learners who master the task get to sit and wait for the others" (Davis, 1982, p. 610).

The concept of readiness must not be confined exclusively to instruction in the primary grades, rather, it should be extended throughout the entire school curriculum in elementary and secondary classrooms. Bruner (1978) plainly states that "one *teaches* readiness . . . [which] consists of mastery of those simpler skills that permit one to reach higher skills" (p. 29). Dupuis and

Askov (1982) urge content teachers to recognize "motivation and readiness are ongoing, a constant concern for teachers" (p. 113).

While reading readiness within the often-narrow scope of schooling is directed by tunnel vision toward comprehension of some sort, reading readiness in preparing students for the labor force cannot be dismissed lightly. To identify facts; to remember, synthesize, and convey information; and to prepare overviews of operations and agreements (Guthrie, 1983c, p. 383) are the goals of reading on the job, which adds another dimension to teacher readiness in upper-elementary and high-school instruction.

Summary

Child-parent-teacher readiness sets the stage for reading instruction to begin and to continue successfully. While it should be remembered that children develop and mature within the child-parent-teacher partnership, it must also be recognized that they mature in different kinds of partnerships that often are not synonymous with current societal demands, expectations, and practices. What happens to children during the formative years before school entrance will influence and determine their subsequent development. These beginnings will be more formally enriched or impoverished, advanced or retarded by the quality of teacher readiness. Teachers must be aware that readiness goes beyond the teacher's technical talents, it must extend beyond the primary grades, and it must prepare the student for entering the labor force.

READY TO TEACH READING

Child-parent-teacher readiness provides the basis on which to start reading. The teacher must build on whatever readiness the parents have given to their children.

Prospective teachers know that reading is a synthesis of processes involving purposeful communication, language, and thinking, to which children bring their attitudes, interests, experiences, language dialects, concepts and schemata. Teachers know that reading is not a set of skills that, once learned, constitute reading. Teachers know that the various processes that interrelate, interact, and integrate make reading possible.

The teaching of reading can begin when instruction is matched with what children have learned; this becomes the readiness base for new learning. The following discussion on beginning and advancing reading reflects the dynamics of reading readiness that is encouraged by matching children and instruction, rather than by committing them to books with which many of them get disgusted.

Beginning Reading Instruction

Reading is thinking, and thinking occurs in some context. When the sound patterns representing the names of Bill, Linda, and Sandy are heard, the receivers of the sounds, the listeners, perceive and think of them in some experiential context; that is, children do not perceive the names as indistinguishable and nonunderstandable noises. Equally, reading as thinking must be pursued in children-related context, not in isolation of it. It cannot be for the sake of reading as a means in itself.

Children's names, can quite easily become the starting point of beginning reading instruction. Children talk about what they do; soon, from this children's talk, the teacher can write a simple sentence on the chalkboard: *Bill, Linda, and Sandy play ball*. Through talking or intercommunication, children also learn that there is more than one Bill and one Linda in the class and that the different activities they do lead to the construction of new sentences.

Since reading begins with visually contacting print, each word name, that is, each Bill and Linda, can be compared with the names of the other boy and girl who have the same names, Bill and Linda. These names are placed together, one below the other rather than side by side, so that the children can see whether they are similar or different. Once they are found to be alike, the two names of Linda and Sandy can be compared. They are found to be different. The three steps that should appear on the chalkboard or a large piece of paper are

| Bill | Linda | Linda |
| Bill | Linda | Sandy |

What should be compared is the whole word, then its parts, and then the whole word again.

While children pronounce, they not only see but also print what they say. Guided by selective attention, the four basic language abilities of speaking, listening, reading, and writing are integrated with auditory and visual discrimination as well as left-to-right sequencing. Depending, of course, on planning and purpose, words like *ball*, *bell*, *bill*, and *bull* may be looked at in various contextual settings, or the word *play* may be used to generate such new words as *playing*, *player*, and *playpen*. While these are new words in terms of how they look in print, they are old ones because they are already in children's listening and speaking vocabulary and hence are meaningful to them.

What is particulary important in beginning reading instruction is to uphold children's knowing that print carries meaning and that, in order to get that meaning, they must be able to read. What matters most is the continual opportunity for children to experience the process of extracting meaningful information from print. That is what reading is all about.

Whichever words children are able to identify and recognize, whichever words children know, are the ones that should be "read" in a variety of printed and written materials. Children should be looking for these words in books of different sizes, makes, and appearance; in newspapers, magazines, and comic strips; on printed and written notes produced in different handwritings. These activities make the beginning readers aware of and drive home the point that the purpose of reading is to get through the printed representation to extract the meaning, which comes from the reader by way of print. There probably is no more effective way of teaching than beginning with what children know and using their knowledge in cracking the code.

At least in early reading instructions, cracking the code should start with the students, thus bringing their experiences to the foreground. They verbally exchange their experiences with other students by talking about what they have seen on the way to school, what they are doing after school, and so on. At any time, through skillful guidance, teachers can move children's intercommunications toward the purposes and goals of further instruction in reading. Most important, however, is that children remain actively involved, even then when instruction is more teacher directed.

When children's responses—their thoughts—are written down, their interest, motivation, selective attention, and concentration will engulf them in what they do. They know that it is their production—their language and their words—that they see emerging in print. Even though there is some teacher direction and purposeful teacher guidance needed, it is the children's work that is meaningful to them, in accordance with their background experiences.

What must be thoroughly understood is that what is happening here represents the children's total universe, the psychological context of which is related to their real world. They have seen how their thoughts were put together in print, how the content was synthesized, and how the very same content can be separated or analyzed into sentences, words, and letters that also can be synthesized. This is the process of synthesis-analysis-synthesis.

Reading begins by reading the children's whole story, which represents *synthesis*. Reading the whole story together orally lets the children hear the total sound universe. This accomplishment builds self-confidence and extends encouragement to those who need it most. While reading aloud, children follow the teacher, who becomes the model for reading fluency, voice intonation as the means for expressing feelings, and voice pauses as indicators of punctuation.

Analysis is represented in instruction that begins with the whole story and breaks it down into sentences, phrases, words, and, when necessary, letter clusters and single letters. Sentences and parts thereof are enunciated without distorting the sounds, which are naturally blended together. Analysis may lead finally to single sounds that are enunciated according to their phonemic values in relation to letter names (Durrell, 1980). Letter-sound relationship can be demonstrated by using words whose beginning sounds actually say the name of the letter when it is in the initial position of the word. For example, the letter *b* says its name in the beginning sound of the word *bee*tle, as do *c* in *ce*dar, *d* in *dea*ler, *g* in *gee*, *j* in *jay*bird, *p* in *pea*ch, *t* in *tea*spoon, *v* in *ve*hicle, and *z* in *ze*ro.

Durrell (1980) reports that the ability to identify the first letter or sound in a word when the first syllable is the name of the initial letter comes more easily than identification when the initial phoneme is not followed by vowels of the letter name (p. 160). When words like *bull, cat, dot, gain, joy, push, tame, vase,* and *zoo* are used, the letter name cannot be heard. Likewise, this difference may be observed for beginning sounds that say the names of the vowel letters *a, e, i, o,* and *u* in the initial position, as in *a*corn, *ea*sy, *i*ceberg, *o*ld, and *u*sing. When words like *about, elephant, it, on,* and *up* are used, the beginning sounds do not say the names of the beginning vowels.

In this and other approaches, analysis from word to letter and sound can be completed according to students' different learning needs. Then, words are placed back into phrases and sentences, and sentences are put back into the whole story, which again represents *synthesis*. The whole story then is read once more to enable the student to recapture its full and uninterrupted meaning. This leads to further explanatory discussions, which enlarge reading vocabulary as well as build new concepts or correct and revise already-existing ones in the storehouse of knowing.

Advanced Reading Instruction

The greater portion—and sometimes all—of the time of instruction in beginning reading is devoted to transposing print into speech. Print uses *grapheme* representation, which consists of consonant-letters and vowel-letters in single or cluster sequences. Speech, as in reading aloud, uses *phoneme* representation, which consists of consonant-sounds and vowel-sounds in single or cluster sequences. Letter-to-sound translation is said to be a grapheme–phoneme correspondence and is used to pronounce words seen in print. Sound-to-letter translation is said to be a phoneme–grapheme correspondence and is used in spelling words. Words like *can, pin, set, dot,* and *fan* are said to have a consistent consonant-vowel-consonant (CVC) letter and sound correspondence. They are known as CVC trigrams and have the highest

Becoming Ready 75

rate of usefulness among the few phonics generalizations in the English language (Emans, Harms, & McClain, 1973).

CVC Trigrams. In a controlled research study, Walmsley (1978–1979) reaffirmed the importance of categorizing CVC's by pronunciation pattern, meaningfulness, and frequency of occurrence. Walmsley regards the pronunciation of CVC's as an important decoding skill that assists in assigning correct sound value to a vowel between two consonants. No matter whether the CVC is a word by itself or a syllable within a polysyllabic word, there are about 2,646 possible CVC combinations. Some examples are

CVC (word)	*CVC (polysyllabic)*
fat	*cat*alog
bed	im*pene*trability
sit	un*fit*
pot	*pop*corn
cut	*nut*let

Of course, CVC combinations are present in many English words that, while being one-syllable words with a short vowel, have more than one consonant positioned at the beginning or ending, or at the beginning and ending. Consonants accumulated around a short vowel letter can form either real or unreal words such as *flush* and *flish*. When all possible CVC combinations of real and unreal words are constructed, Walmsley (1978–1979) reports that this will result in a universe of over one million items (p. 587). Some CVC combinations with their corresponding examples are

CVC	cat	CVC	cat
CCVC	spin	CCVCC	flash
CCCVC	split	CCVCCC	branch
CVCC	fish	CCCVCC	splash
CVCCC	match	CCCVCCC	stretch

When examining the CVC combinations, there is always visible a basic CVC combination, but the same CVC sound combination can not always be heard. In the CCCVC or *split* combination, the basic CVC or *lit* letter combination is clearly recognizable in print and so is its sound combination. But, in the CCCVCC or *splash* combination, the CVC or *las* letter combination is visually recognizable but not auditorily because the letter *s* combines with the letter *h* to form one final sound.

Additional Vowel Considerations. Since there are only twenty-six letters in the English alphabet, some letters or combinations of them have more than one sound. Listen attentively when pronouncing the following words and hear how the sound of the same letter changes. While the vowel letter *a* is conserved, its sound is not.

words	*sounds*
any	/e/
at	/a/
ate	/ā/
fare	/â/
father	/ä/
tall	/ô/

While in the above words it is possible actually to hear the changes in and to discriminate between the various /a/ sound pronunciations, this is almost impossible in the following words, which, in addition, appear to defy common phonics rules and generalizations:

words	*sounds*
lawyer	/oi/
mauve	/ō/
plaid	/a/
prayer	/â(r)/
rain	/ā/

It further complicates translating print to speech when we meet combinations such as *aw* in *law*yer and *law*n, and *au* in *mau*ve, *mau*dlin, and *Mau*ser. The varying sounds of the vowel-letter *a* appear to depend on the position and the number of vowel-letters in the word, as in *beau, beautiful, beater,* and *beatify*. Further attention must also be given to the contextual setting in which vowel-letter combinations occur, as in the sentences *Bill reads now* and *Bill read yesterday*.

Learning to read in the beginning stages can be further complicated when short vowel sounds become long vowel sounds and when additional vowel letters change the orthographic appearance of already known words as in *hat* to *hate*. Long vowel sounds depend on sound prolongation, tongue position, tongue elevation, and lip position. A long vowel sound is represented either by its corresponding vowel letter or by clusters of two or more appropriately sequenced vowel letters as in *chase, cheap,* and *cheese*.

Undoubtedly, the visual appearance of more than one vowel letter in different positions of a word invites confusion in pronouncing correctly the letter patterns. Regarding the effectiveness of sounding words out when not being certain of them, Durrell (1980) noted, "If a child does not know a word by sight, spelling is usually more effective than an attempt to 'sound it out'" (p. 160). It appears that spelling forces children to examine closely the word and the sequence in which one letter follows the other. It is questionable whether or not words can be spelled and pronounced before being known in speech and print. It may be next to impossible to either spell or pronounce correctly the words *phthisic, thought, light,* and even *cake* without having "learned" them before actually producing them in writing and sometimes in speaking.

Summary

In beginning and advanced reading instruction, a teacher cannot simply adopt a set of basal readers with their multiple accessories and assume that it should be used with all beginning readers. On the contrary, reading instruction starts with the children and remains child centered, even though teacher guidance must be there at all times. The approach is not to adopt, but rather to adapt various reading materials and instructional approaches to match the children who learn to read. In this light, CVC trigrams and their many combinations assist children in learning an important decoding skill, in attributing appropriate sounds to a vowel in the CVC patterns, and in pronouncing words they encounter most often in the reading of basal readers.

PERCEPTUAL AWARENESS

Perceiving as one of the contributory reading processes was already discussed in Chapter 3. In this section, perceptual awareness and how it affects learning to read will be explained. While perceiving in a general sense is the becoming aware of objects, events, and persons by means of the senses, perceptual awareness is an active and selective process that is influenced by the person's attitude and prior experience (Harris & Hodges, 1981, p. 232). Awareness emphasizes that a person is conscious and cognizant about what is perceived.

Both perceiving and perceptual awareness are important to reading. Reading requires not only the ability to distinguish between different words, as in *heat* and *hate*, but also the ability to make a perfect fit between cue and category specification (Bruner, 1973). The latter is the ability to class objects as being equivalent or nonequivalent. The word *heat*, with its cue *-eat*, fits into a category and can be classed together with the words *beat, meat,* and *seat*; while the word *hate*, with its cue *-ate*, fits a category and can be classed together with the words *date, fate,* and *late*. The ability to categorize with ease and fluency depends on how accessible any given category is to the reader and how frequently it is used. Correct or incorrect recognition of words may well be attributed to the degrees to which a reader has or has not used cue and category specifications.

The perceptual awareness of fit between cue and category specification is influenced and supported primarily by generic perception. In Bruner's words (1973) "whatever is perceived is placed in and achieves its meaning from a class of percepts with which it is grouped" (p. 8). In the sentence *The damage that the _____ wave has caused was extensive*, the blank space could be filled with either *heat* or *hate*. The choice will depend on the meaning with which the reader can identify; that is, it depends on the subjectivity of past experiences. This will be brought to bear in making a decision based upon perceptual veridicality.

Veridicality refers to the reality or truth of what is perceived; however, no two persons perceive exactly the same message in print or in speech. When the thermometer measures 104° Fahrenheit or 40° Celsius, there is likely to be a heat wave, which, when read as hate wave, does not concur with what could be expected. It is an error and shows nonveridical perception (Bruner, 1973, p. 11), because it does not even come near to what should have been perceived objectively. As in the case of 104° Fahrenheit, however, the ways in which individuals perceive themselves to be affected by such a temperature is each person's perceptual veridicality as it corresponds to the fact of extraordinary warmth. One person may feel quite comfortable, while another will not.

When students in any given grade read the same assignment, with the same printed words and sentences, different perceptions will emerge. Readers interpret print according to their own experiences, but influenced by the writer's thoughts. Since no two readers have exactly the same experiences, somewhat different interpretations must occur. If readers' experiences are inadequate, communication by means of reading or speaking is difficult, if not impossible, to achieve.

Summary

Perceptual awareness, which is the ability to make a more-or-less perfect fit between cue and category specifications, is influenced by generic perception and perceptual veridicality. Regarding the former, the reader perceives meaning from a class of percepts with which words are grouped. The latter refers to the nearness or closeness of meaning between what the sender intends to express in speech or print and what the receiver perceives the message to be.

CHAPTER 5

Basic Information in Reading

Purpose questions for this chapter:

- How is graphophonological information used in teaching reading?
- What are grapheme-phoneme correspondences?
- How and when are words identified and recognized?
- How are word lists to be used in teaching reading?
- How reliable are phonics rules?

TRANSITION FROM HOME TO SCHOOL

Children transit from home to school, from preschool to school, and from informal to formal education. To better understand who the children are, teachers of course look to the children's homes, to their parents or parent substitutes, who are the first to interact with the children while they are growing up and learning to talk. Teachers also want to look at children's nursery-school and kindergarten experiences (Anselmo, 1978, p. 130), where parent-child registers of day-to-day home living become influenced by different sets of experiences that no longer are determined solely by the parents.

At least during the first years of life, children, parents, and home constitute the first ecological system. In this environment, children's and parents' emotions, cognition, and psychomotor activities constantly, but not necessarily consistently, interact in a mutual relationship. Children are exposed to sound; they hear, listen to, and respond to what parents talk about and how they talk about it. Utterances, sometimes loving and caring, sometimes scolding and reprimanding, bombard children. Through these they develop listening and speaking vocabularies, speech patterns, attitudes, and behaviors pleasing or unpleasing to parents. During this time of development, children learn the function of communication by forming understandable sounds, then words, phrases, and sentences to express what they want or reject. In addition to developing speech, some children learn in their own ways to "read" by using whole-word memorization, sound-symbol relationships, letter-sound correspondence, and word-by-word reading (Lass, 1982, 1983).

This first ecological system of the child-parent relationship continues relatively undisturbed provided children remain at home instead of going to nursery and then to kindergarten.

Unless treated like Rousseau's Emile by being carried away from civilization, some disturbances will occur when children on their own begin to take excursions into the neighborhood, where they meet other children and their parents. Obviously, experiences different from the home ecology will be heard, felt, and known; through parental approval or disapproval these can either be encouraged or discouraged. When, however, neighbors' visits and outside playtimes become more frequent and of longer duration, the home ecology experiences differential influences. These extend over time and intensify when children, at least intermittently, leave the first ecological system to enter into a second ecological system in going to nursery school and kindergarten.

Goals, objectives, and purposes and how to achieve them are not only different from the home system but are also determined by people different from the children's parents. Different ideas and thoughts, different motives and incentives, and even different language dialects surround the children and imprint in their minds, leaving them with the feelings of a whole new universe of different learning experiences to explore. These, of course, increase when actual schooling begins.

Just as children earlier became aware that speaking makes parents and other people listen to them and that through speaking they can communicate their ideas, so they must learn that print and writing have similar functions and can do the same for them. Just as children learned to activate and use the complex functions of their speech apparatus, which made it possible for them to form understandable speech sounds and utterances, so they must learn to process print to read and write. As speaking has its own technical features to master, so has print. To understand the technical features of printed/written English, children must be taught to develop code consciousness (Agnew, 1982, p. 450).

When entering school, most if not all children know that signs stand for something that adults call words, from which they get meaning. While children are able to pronounce words, they are not sure about what they are and how letters make words. But children can reconstruct the messages from signs they see in newspapers, supermarkets, advertisements, and other locations. Children know when they see the signs that spell *Coca-Cola* that this is something to drink. When they see the *Safeway* sign, they know that this is the place where Mother goes to buy groceries. *Fraggle Rock* signifies their favorite television show. Reconstructing messages from signs is a psychological process, and recognizing graphic information is a linguistic process. Together, they result in psycholinguistic processing.

Children know that certain meanings are attributed to certain signs but not to others. Somehow they expect that print signals meaning, that meaning must be hidden in print, and that this must be the secret of reading that they come to school to learn.

GRAPHOPHONOLOGICAL INFORMATION

In learning to read, graphophonological information is essential. Graphophonological information refers to both letter and sound relationships. Graphic language, or the alphabetic writing system, is a representation of the oral language. At times, readers may turn a visual form into a sound form to test by trial and error whether or not certain words are recognized when heard. Aural recognition, however, is based on the assumption that these words, though unrecognizable in graphic form, are in the reader's listening and speaking vocabularies (Hittleman, 1983, p. 253). If not, no amount of decoding will make the word comprehensible to the reader. According to Goodman (1976), graphophonological information consists of graphic, phonological, and phonic information (p. 479).

Graphic Information

Graphic information may be retrieved from (1) written or printed orthographic representations of letters or graphemes; (2) letter clusters, words, and word patterns; (3) phrases, sentences, and their patterns; and (4) a whole script. Letters can be used to compose words, and words can be decomposed into letters. The former is a synthetic procedure; the latter, an analytic procedure. How much of each procedure is necessary to learn to read and to become a skilled reader has been debated repeatedly during the past century. Results of research show the importance of both.

Whole-Word Identification. Almost 100 years ago Cattell (1885) concluded from his experiments that words and sometimes phrases and sentences are read in word-wholes, phrase-wholes and sentence-wholes. Skilled readers could recognize and identify in a single, short tachistoscopic exposure four to five unconnected letters or, during the same short exposure, four to five words, provided these words formed a meaningful phrase or sentence sequence. Cattell's findings were confirmed by Erdman and Dodge in 1898. They restated that the length of a word and its general form, not its constituent parts, are what render it recognizable. That is, the total familiar arrangement of a word, phrase, and short sentence, not single letters, may be recognized during tachistoscopic exposures measured in milliseconds. These findings were supported by Huey in 1908, who stated categorically that "we, therefore, perceive the word as a whole" (p. 73). Present research contends that reading appears to develop from whole words to single letters (Forester & Mickelson, 1979).

Whole words, through their letter compositions, have shapes that one would guess might be a source of visual information for the reader. Rayner (1976) concluded from his studies that word shape is indeed a useful cue in teaching reading in grade one and beyond. Haber and Haber (1981) confirmed that, for both beginning and mature readers, word shapes are a useful source of visual information when given in the context of syntactic and semantic information. In a follow-up study, Haber, Haber, and Furlin (1983) provided additional evidence for the use of word length and word shape in teaching reading. Shimron and Navon (1982) report that written words may be identified by their visual features in a fashion similar to the way readers identify other familiar visual patterns. As these patterns are seen, Goodman (1973) suggests that perhaps readers see to a large extent what they expect to see. Thus readers' expectations may determine to what extent graphic information is actually used. This may be less than expected, especially since we know that the brain tells the eyes what to see and how to see it and also augments what is received with what has been stored. Readers know what they have seen only when the brain edits and interprets the incoming information (Hart, 1983, p. 43).

One can only speculate as to what Comenius would have replied to what is still unresolved today. It was he who, in about 1657, introduced in *Orbis Pictus* the whole-word method. When, however, Samuel Worcester, about 1828, introduced the word method in America, he made his belief clear that children "may learn first to read words by seeing them, hearing them pronounced, and having their meanings illustrated, and afterwards it [the child] may learn to analyze them or name the letters of which they are composed" (N.B. Smith, 1965, p. 86).

Letter Identification. Another aspect of print awareness is letter identification, where letters are identified before words and their meanings can be understood. This assumption is not a recent one; it dates back at least to the Egyptians, who developed a symbol system to represent speech sounds. From this beginning, the Phoenician and then the Greek and Roman alphabets developed, from which, in time, the present English alphabet of twenty-six letter representations emerged.

The first evidence of the alphabet method was found in the Hornbook, in about 1450, which based instruction in reading on the alphabet, list of syllables, words, and some religious selections (N.B. Smith, 1965, p. 7). The ABC books were followed by the *New England Primer*, about 1730, which attempted to teach letters of the alphabet in verse form. For instance, the letter M was learned by reciting "The Moon gives light/In time of night" (p. 23). Later editions offered the alphabet, consonants, vowels, double letters, and c ipital letters. These were followed by two-letter syllables, such as *ab, eb, ib, ob, ub, ad, ed, id,* and so on, which increased in length to six-syllable words.

Examining more recent positions on letter-by-letter identification to aid in word recognition, Marchbanks and Levin (1965) conclude that children who know letter names and are able to recognize them in words are better equipped to spot differences between words than children to whom letters have no distinctive forms. Broadbent and Gregory (1968) explain that digraphs and letter pairs, as in *ch*in and pa*th*, are favorable to letter identification in words. Durrell and Murphy (1978) claim that knowledge of letter names is an early indicator of reading ability and provides "the major support for words as visual semantic units" (Durrell, 1980, p. 159).

At the time of this writing, it can only be said that inconclusiveness still prevails in the research reports on letter-by-letter identification. Collins and Demos (1983) report on a study in which they surveyed instructional reading practices in grade one in sixteen countries. The study included eight European countries, Taiwan, Korea, South Africa, Guatemala, Canada and Newfoundland, the United States, and the Virgin Islands. From the survey they found that the greater percentage of total reading instructional time during the second half of first grade was spent in teaching letter-sound correspondences, while whole-word reading and sight-word instruction ranged second and third, respectively.

Phonological Information

Phonology involves the speech sounds as they relate to the surface structure of printed sentences composed of visual symbols. In the English alphabet, names of consonant letters, when vowels are added, stand for certain syllables and sounds, as with the consonant letters *b, c, d, g,* and *p,* which stand for the sounds of /bē/, /sē/, /dē/, /jē/, /pē/, respectively. Holmes (1973) observed that reading the written alphabetic languages, including English, seems inadvertently to involve transforming visual into spoken language.

In fact, I have been told by many classroom teachers on innumerable occasions that, unless children read out loud they have not read at all and therefore have not understood what they read. Reading appears to be reading only when it involves a grapheme-phoneme translation. Does this express the assumption, perhaps the belief, that sounding out carries meaning and to understand print it must be transformed into speech sounds? Yet, oral as well as written language use an arbitrary code (F. Smith, 1973) that "has [no] direct relationship to meaning and the real world other than that which its users assign it" (p. 24).

By insisting that oral reading is inseparable from and a prerequisite for understanding print, we compel readers first to recode or pronounce graphic representations and then to decode them for meaning. Recoding graphemes to phonemes and symbols to sounds is word-calling, not reading. Oral output or what is said, and aural input, or what is heard, are not meaning in or by themselves. Learning to read, particularly in its beginning stages, is often accompanied by recoding or attaching speech sounds to graphic symbols, which results in oral output or oral reading. Oral output is speech and can be said out loud or internally. When heard, it becomes aural input that must be decoded or given meaning, as in listening. However, a more direct route that avoids recoding word for word is moving directly from print to meaning, as skilled readers do in silent reading when processing syntactic and semantic information (Goodman, 1976, p. 482; F. Smith, 1982, p. 151).

Figure 5.1 shows the direct and indirect routes by which readers can extract meaning from print when reading either silently or orally. The direct route moves from print to meaning. However, during silent reading, readers

FIGURE 5.1. The Processing of Print into Meaning via Silent Reading (Direct Route) and Oral Reading (Indirect Route)

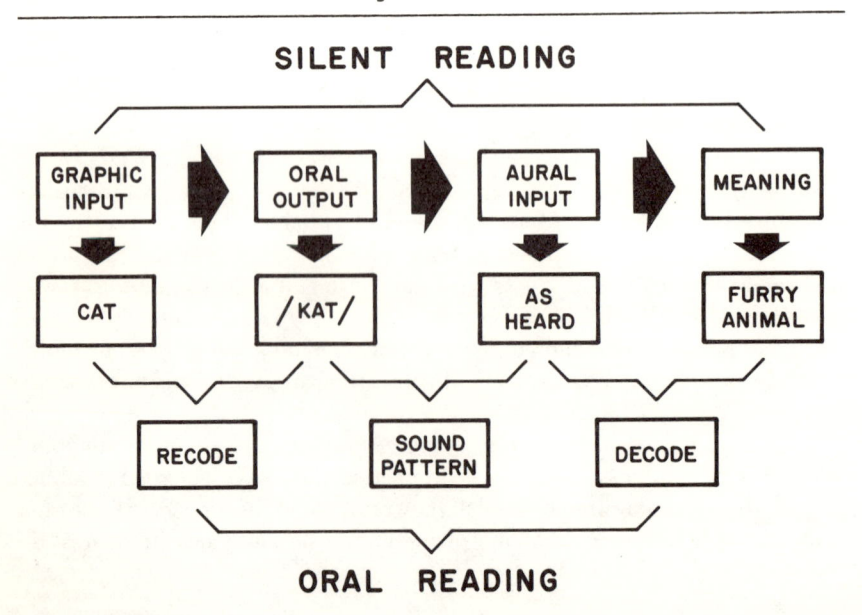

may whisper or vocalize as well as reproduce words inaudibly or subvocalize. Such behaviors may interfere with proficient reading, yet are regarded as "a natural part of the developmental reading process" (Richek et al., 1983, p. 292). The indirect route, on the other hand, moves the reader from print to meaning via oral reading. Studies have shown that unskilled, beginning readers depend more on such phonemic processing as an intermediate step between visual input and meaning output than skilled, silent readers (Smith & Kleiman, 1979).

Hardyck and Petrinovich (1970) report that readers appear to engage more in recoding when trying to extract meaning from difficult materials than from familiar and easy materials. To this, Baron and Baron (1977) add the suggestion that readers may choose the direct path more often when they feel competent with the words they meet. Shimron and Navon (1982) found that children and adults could not resist grapheme-phoneme translation when they were presented with Hebrew words. When both children and adults named Hebrew words, their graphemes were phonemically recoded. Since words in the Hebrew language have vowel signs to indicate their phonemic identity, the study showed, at least for the children, that correct vowel signs speeded up and facilitated the naming of the words. When, however, words were distorted by nonvowelizing or misvowelizing, children, again, were more sensitive than the adults to changes of the vowel signs. This clearly shows recoding appears to be more pronounced in children than in adults (p. 227).

Though research findings and other professional literature are not always in agreement, phonological information appears to be, at various times and on various occasions, useful to readers, both children and adults. Beginning and unskilled readers may use phonological information to support what they think the graphical information represents to them. These readers seem to say to themselves that they must make sure that this is what the printed words want them to say. Therefore, they choose the indirect path as a means to arrive at meaning. If they do understand, they think they arrived at meaning because they read orally, which of course is the same as saying that sound carries meaning.

Skilled readers, on the other hand, who identify words more rapidly, appear to extract meaning mainly by visual recognition plus occasional phonological recoding. It appears that these two processes occur almost simultaneously, which calls into question the practicality of constructing a spoken version (Holmes, 1973, p. 62).

Summary

Graphophonological information furnishes basic information that makes both silent and oral reading possible. Graphological information consists of letters that form words, word patterns, phrases, and sentences. Phonological information consists of speech sounds that form sound patterns that, when recoded, result in oral output that is used as a means to achieve meaning. Research acknowledges that unskilled readers usually recode print as speech and then decode, while skilled readers take the direct route from print to meaning and may refer to the indirect route only when reading becomes difficult.

GRAPHIC AND PHONIC CONSTITUENTS

In order to understand letter identification and the transformation of graphic symbols into speech sounds, a closer inspection of the graphic and phonic constituents of print is necessary. This appears warranted because of the frequency with which these constituents are used during beginning reading and in corrective and remedial reading instruction.

Graphic Constituents

Letters. A letter is an alphabetic symbol and, in English, is one of twenty-six characters that permit graphic representation and processing of the English language. Letters have forms that are seen, occupy space, and have specific names. They can be either capital, upper-case letters or small, lower-case letters. Letters in a word can be a mixture of both. Letters have geometric forms that are composed of rectilinear, curvilinear, and oblique segments. Each letter in the English alphabet, upper case and lower case, has a distinctive composite geometric form. Capital letters all have the same height, while lower-case letters are smaller and sometimes have ascending and descending vertical lines.

To assist the brain in visually distinguishing letter features, letter comparisons can be made to discover which features are redundant and which are specific. When comparing lower-case letters, the redundant features, for instance, may be the vertical lines, as in the letters b, h, and k. The distinguishing features are the geometric forms to the right of each vertical line. Different, however, are the distinguishing features of the capital letters, as in the letters A, B, and so on.

When letters have many features in common, they are more frequently confused than those that have fewer features in common. The letters b and d, often confused in what is called a reversal, have all features in common except the directionality of the attached circle to the right or left of the vertical line. It is the same with the letters p and q, except with vertically descending lines. Somewhat different are the letters n and h, the latter of which adds a vertically ascending line. F. Smith (1982, p. 117) cites groups of letters that are susceptible to letter confusion. These groups are *a, e, n, o, u; h, m, n;* and *f, i, t.* In contrast, the lower-case letters *r, s,* and *x,* have fewer features in common and therefore are less often confused.

Words. Letters are the stuff with which to make words. Words must be either identified or recognized. Words to be identified are those that have an unusual appearance for the reader, such as *tEaCHEr, ReAdINg,* or *hypopituitarism.* Words to be recognized are those that the readers have met before and are familiar with, such as *teacher, reading,* and *book.* Words that are recognized are actually re-known. Thus, word identification and word recognition really are not synonymous and therefore should not be used interchangeably. With the research on word versus letter effects still being inconclusive, but the teaching of reading still being a day-to-day reality, it makes sense to strike a tentative compromise for the benefit of both teachers and students. Thus, unskilled and beginning readers may be allowed to depend somewhat more on recognizing letters within words, as they may not have automatized word identification and recognition to the degree that more skilled readers have.

By easily identifying target letters embedded in words, skilled readers can concentrate on extracting meaning rather than on deciphering words. When skilled readers meet unfamiliar words, they do pause to look at the letters and try to sort them out and pronounce them to test the sound pattern against their speaking and listening vocabularies. They are flexible in applying efficiently phonic and structural analysis as well as configuration and context clues to identify unknown words.

Crowder (1982, p. 85) points out that word superiority depends on the strategies readers bring to the reading task, and Stanovich (1980, p. 47) reports that even young readers use context to facilitate word recognition. It appears also that high-frequency words are easier to identify and recognize than low-frequency words, and that, at least for some words, word shapes are important to speedy identification.

Phrases and Sentences. When reading phrases and sentences, skilled readers pick up chunks consisting of letter sequences. Chunking not only aids the visual system in processing more information but also aids memory. Cattell's research (1886) was echoed by Huey (1908), who wrote that "when sentences or phrases were exposed, they were either grasped as wholes or else scarcely any of the words or letters read . . . [and that] the reading was in larger wholes than letters" (pp. 72–73). Furthermore, help in word identification comes from semantic and syntactic constraints of phrase and sentence context, as well as from the position a word has within a sentence. Readers then use the "potent role grammar plays in reading" (Kolers, 1973, p. 45), by relating parts of speech rather than single words to each other.

The eyes make another contribution in picking up print. Numerous research studies on eye movement have shown that average grade-one readers require about 183 fixations to read 100 words. Adults require 75 fixations to read 100 words in common reading materials. When converted into the amount of visual information received from the print, grade-one readers have a ratio of 100:183, which means that they see about .55 words per fixation. Adult readers, by contrast, have a ratio of 100:75 and thus see about 1.33 words in a single fixation. This may depend on the typographical layout of the printed material, including length of words; for example, shorter words may be processed one at a time or in parts during one fixation. Processing, however, will be facilitated when readers are familiar with the subject matter, its vocabulary load, and the syntactic structure of the text.

Visual Discrimination. Another feature of the visual processing of print is visual discrimination, or the ability to perceive the distinctive properties of letters, words, and phrases, together with the ability to see likeness and differences. There are word patterns that can be readily discriminated because of their gross or maximal visual differences, as in the visual word patterns *horse* and *bake*. There are word patterns that cannot be so readily discriminated because of their minimal differences, as in *horse* and *house*. Finally, there are visual patterns that are very nearly alike, as in *pen* and *pen*, *bow* and *bow*. These are homographs (Harris & Hodges, 1981, p. 141), that is, words that are spelled alike but have different meanings, as a *pen* with which to write and a *pen* with which to enclose, or as a *bow* with an arrow and the *bow* of a ship.

Words may have the same initial letters, as in the words *b*oy and *b*ite; the same medial letters, as in m*a*ke and sh*a*ke; and the same final letters, as in fu*n* and te*n*. From the letters words receive their shapes. A total shape or configuration of a word in isolation may fit several words as in the word cat . This shape also fits the words *rat, sat, and, end, cut, nut, sit, set, sad, ink*, and many others. Learning to recognize words by their shapes alone and in isolation, as in sight-word learning, should be a matter of concern to all teachers (Groff, 1974, 1975). To avoid unnecessary hardship and failure, words should always be learned in and through context.

Conclusion. Contrasting research results leave little, if any, middle ground in the polarization between those who espouse letter-by-letter word identification and those who advocate whole-word recognition. However, from oral reports and my own observations in working with people of all ages in learning to read and to improve reading, readers appear to use both strategies interactively, guided by "what makes sense." The word *pneumonoconiosis* may be a fitting example with which any reader may try out the strategies and decide which would best serve in identifying this word.

Phonic Constituents

The phonic constituent of print is sound; it is used when print is pronounced out loud or read orally. Oral reading should not be confused with internal speech or subvocalization. Oral reading as used in school terminology and actual practice is neither a prerequisite to knowing words nor to extracting meaning from print to show understanding. Oral reading as so often done during reading lessons amounts to little more than recoding or word-calling, perhaps without realizing that "written symbols do not decode to sound in any reasonable fashion" (Holmes, 1973, p. 62). Reading instruction is dominated by oral reading, the greater portion of which is used too often as an end in itself. The already complex task of attending to visual input is made more complex by having readers attend almost simultaneously to matching visual word patterns to sound patterns.

Sounds. Sounds are all around us. The human brain receives, perceives, and interprets sounds either as meaningless noise or as meaningful communication. Sounds are produced conspicuously in oral reading and also can be meaningless noises or meaningful messages.

Individual sounds are phonemes. There are about forty-four English sounds for the twenty-six letters that make up the constitutents of the spoken and written English language. A phoneme is regarded as the smallest linguistic unit in spoken language. More precisely, a phoneme is not exactly a single sound, rather a class of closely related sounds constituting the smallest unit of speech that will distinguish one utterance from another (F. Smith, 1982, Chapter 10).

Pronounce aloud the words *bat, bet, bit, but*, and become aware of how the initial letter *b* is closely related to the vowel sounds that follow it and how the vowel sounds closely relate to the initial consonant. The closely related sounds make it impossible to pronounce the initial consonant letter as /buh/ or /bē/. In fact, the word *bet* does not begin with the sound of /buh/, for there is no such sound but noise; nor does this word begin with the sound of /bē/, for it is not a sound but the name of the second letter in the English alphabet.

Considering the same word *bet* in relationship to other words, the beginning /b/ as well as the following /e/ and /t/ are also distinguishing the word /bet/ from the words /set/, /bit/, and /bed/. That is, each sound element—beginning, middle, and ending—acts to distinguish a word from all other words.

Vowels. Vowel letters, singly or together, represent vowel sounds. The vowel letter in the word *bet* represents the vowel sound /e/ that makes the pronunciation of this particular word possible. The word *bet* cannot be pronounced as *but*, for the vowel sound /e/ makes this impossible. The vowel sound /e/ gives this word this particular sound pattern. In the word *team*, two vowel letters represent and form one vowel sound, which gives this word its particular sound pattern /tēm/ and not another sound pattern.

A vowel is "a voiced speech sound made without friction or stoppage of the air flow as it passes through the vocal tract" (Harris & Hodges, 1981, p. 351). Vowel sounds also depend on the shape of the mouth, the position of the lips, and the position and elevation of the tongue in the mouth. With the help of a mirror, movements of mouth, lips, and tongue can be observed in pronouncing the words *bat, bit, beat, ball, bull,* and *boat*.

Vowel Letter-Sound Combinations. In words such as *freight, sleigh, eight, bread, breath,* and *break*, two or more adjoining vowel letters represent a single vowel sound. This is called a vowel digraph. When two or more adjoining vowel letters makes a sequence of two or more vowel sounds, the result is called a vowel cluster, as in the words *aorta, piano, beatify,* and *beautiful*.

There are also words in which certain consonant letters—*l, r,* and sometimes *w*—control the preceding vowel sounds. In words like *far, sir, ball,* and *saw*, the consonant letters immediately following the vowel letters control the vowel sounds and are known as vowel controllers (Harris & Hodges, 1981, pp. 351-352).

Diphthongs also are vowel speech sounds. In the word *boil*, the diphthong begins with the vowel speech sound /o/. While pronouncing the *o*, the tongue position in the mouth changes toward the vowel sound /i/, to pronounce /oi/. The speech sound change occurs in the same syllable or the same phonological segment of the speech sounds (Harris & Hodges, 1981, p. 319). Additional examples of diphthongs are: *bee, bough, boy, buy,* and *oil*.

Consonants. Vowel sounds make the pronunciation of consonants possible. Without adding vowel sounds, consonants cannot be pronounced. Vowel sounds are added to consonants either as preceding or succeeding sounds. In the English language, the alphabet consonant letters *f, l, m, n, s,* and *x* cannot be named without the preceding vowel sound /e/ which makes /ef/, /el/, /em/, /en/, /es/, and /eks/ pronounceable. The consonant letter *h* takes on the vowel sound /ā/ to make /āch/, and the consonant letter *r* takes on the vowel sound /ä/ to make /är/. All other consonant letters are succeeded by the sounds of /ā/, /e/, /ē/, /ī/, and /yōō/, making pronounceable the names of the alphabet letters /bē/, /dē/, /jē/, /pē/, /tē/, /zē/ or /zed/, /jā/, /kā/, /wī/, /kyōō/, and /dubel yōō/ (pronunciation key based on the *Random House Dictionary*, 1968).

Basic Information in Reading

In the dictionary, a consonant is defined as "a speech sound produced by occluding, diverting, or obstructing the flow of air from the lungs" (*Random House Dictionary*, 1968, p. 287). When the flow of air is occluded, the consonant speech sounds *p, b, t, d, k*, and *g* result, which are known as plosives; when the flow of air is diverted, *m, n*, and *ng* results, which are known as nasals; and when the flow of air is obstructed, the speech sounds *f, v, s, z, sh, zh, j, ch*, and *th* result, which are known as fricatives.

Consonant Letter-Sound Combinations. Consonant sounds are either voiced or unvoiced. Three of the occluded consonant speech sounds, the plosives *b, d*, and *g*, are voiced, while the other three, *p, t*, and *k*, are unvoiced, as in *bill, do*, and *gem*, and *pull, ten*, and *key*, respectively.

Five of the obstructed speech consonant sounds, or the fricatives *j, th, v, z*, and *zh*, are voiced, while the remaining five, *ch, f, s, sh*, and *th*, are unvoiced, as in *jam, these, vein, zeal*, and *azure*, and *chin, fell, sun, sharp*, and *death*, respectively.

The three nasals, *m, n*, and *ng* are voiced consonant speech sounds, as in *ham, fin*, and *sing*.

Glides or semivowels serve as both consonants and vowels. The *Random House Dictionary* defines a semivowel as "a speech sound of vowel quality used as a consonant" and as "a speech sound of consonantal quality used as a vowel" (1968, p. 1197). Voiced semivowels or glides are *l, r, w*, and *y*; and the unvoiced semivowels or glides are *h, hw*. The voiced semivowel speech sounds are in words like *land, row, wet*, and *yes*; and the unvoiced ones are in *hill* and *what*.

Sound patterns reveal a three-position pattern of vowel and consonant speech sounds in initial, medial, and final places within words. This pattern can be built up systematically to serve any teaching situation, including both corrective and remedial teaching. Some examples of vowel positioning are

Initial	*Medial*	*Final*
arm, at, end, in, on, up	cat, warm, set, fin, cot, bun	abaca, Alabama, alpha eery, piano, zoo

Similar systematic arrangements can be tabulated for consonant speech sounds in the three positions (examples here are given only for two consonant speech sounds—/b/ and /d/).

Initial	*Medial*	*Final*
base, bin, bun den, dim, duck	label, liberal, squabble grader, riding, fiddle	dib, mob, tub lid, nod, wind

Consonant clusters are two or more consonant speech sounds that are succeeded or preceded by vowel sounds, as in *stretch*, *itch*, *screams*, *blends*, and *trains*.

A consonant digraph consists of a combination of consonant letters that represents one single consonant speech sound, as in *ph*oneme, gra*ph*eme, rou*gh*, *kn*it, and *gn*at (Harris & Hodges, 1981, p. 65).

Auditory Discrimination. Another phonic constituent of processing print is auditory discrimination. Printed word patterns have equivalent sound patterns that can be readily discriminated because of their gross or maximal sound differences, as in *pan* and *fur*. There are sound patterns that cannot be discriminated so readily because of their closeness in sound, as in *pan*, *pen*, *pin*, and *bin*. Finally, there are sound patterns that sound exactly alike, as in *to*, *too*, and *two*, and in *hare* and *hair*. These are also known as homonyms, which are words that sound alike but are spelled differently (Richek et al., 1983, p. 283). Homonyms, because they sound alike, must always be presented in meaningful sentences, such as: The airplane pilot *sighted* the ship. The building will be located on this *site*. The judge *cited* a passage from the lawbook.

Maximal and minimal differences among similar speech sounds can be observed by comparing initial, medial, and final sounds and their positions in sound patterns. For maximal auditory differences, listen to the initial sounds in *pan* and *fan*; for minimal differences, note the initial sounds in *den* and *ten*. For maximal auditory differences, listen to the medial consonant sounds in *reading* and *speaking*; for minimal differences, note the medial consonant sounds in *ringing* and *sinking*. For maximal auditory differences, listen to the final sounds in *rip* and *rig*; and for minimal differences, note the final sounds in *bet* and *bed*.

Summary

Letters are not only visually distinguished by their geometric forms but also by their redundant and specific features. Letters make words, which are either recognized or identified. Words already known are recognized, those to become known are identified. Proficient word recognition and identification lead to reading phrases and sentences. Efficient eye movement picks up letter clusters and letter patterns supported by visual discrimination that aids in distinguishing maximal and minimal differences in words.

Phonic constituents of print pertain to the production of speech sounds, sound patterns, and utterances. Speech sounds are combinations of vowel and consonant sounds that are blended together. Single and multiple consonant and vowel sounds can be identified in the initial, medial, and final positions of sound patterns. Because sounds are heard, auditory acuity and discrimination are necessary in order to perceive subtle sound likenesses and differences and to distinguish one sound pattern from another and attach meaning to it.

PATTERNS OF PATTERNS

Patterns of patterns occur when speakers and writers produce strings of sounds and strings of words. In both instances, oral and graphic patterns of patterns are not determined by their sounds and words but rather by the brain producing the message. In both instances, thought precedes language, which may or may not coincide with the ideas in the brain of the sender. In speaking, thoughts and oral language may be apart, for example, when speakers interrupt the flow of sounds to rethink quickly the choice of utterances through which to express more clearly their thoughts. In writing, thoughts and language may be apart when writers interrupt graphically the flow of words, or revise what is already written, to find "better" words and sentence structures to express more clearly their intended message.

In both instances, the brain's thoughts provide the deep structure that must be encoded into either oral or written language that is of corresponding surface structure. What listeners hear and readers see is the surface structure, which, when decoded, allows access to the sender's message.

In both instances, oral patterns of patterns are different from written ones. Speech enjoys temporary permanence only; print enjoys continued existence. Written discourse enjoys the luxury of visual markings separating paragraphs, sentences, and words through indentations, punctuations, and white spaces. Oral discourse relies on the voice to produce sound patterns of patterns through intonation, pitch, stress, and pauses.

Intonation is the melodic expression of the spoken language, characterized by the pitch or rise and fall of the voice. Intonation in the English language, which is nontonal, is produced by changing the voice pitch across sound patterns in order to express what the brain dictates, as in *Go* versus *Go!* and *Go?*; *Please, close the door* versus *Please, close the door!* and *Please, close the door?* Pitch and intonation assist in understanding and interpreting meaning.

Stresses and pauses are speech markers that help listeners to extract meaning more accurately from surface sound patterns. Voice stresses (here capitalized to differentiate) placed on sound patterns communicate different meanings, as in *OBject* versus *obJECT*, and in *JOHN was not here* versus *John was not HERE*. Pauses are slight vocal interruptions in sound patterns that are used to emphasize meaning and relationships of meaning.

Pauses of various durations are known as junctures, of which there are three kinds: cloze juncture, open juncture, and terminal speech juncture.

When sound patterns and utterances are produced by the brain through the voice without undue interruptions or repetitions, this speech pattern is known as cloze juncture. In cloze juncture, not only are the speaker's thoughts and language closely joined together, but also, and perhaps more important, the speaker's articulated speech sounds are seamlessly connected. When, however, thoughts and language become disjointed, slight and longer pauses will interrupt the seamless flow of speech patterns. This is known as open juncture. Undue interruptions of speech sounds, of course, also may interrupt the flow of meaning for both speakers and listeners. Finally, there is the terminal speech juncture, which is heard when the voice comes to rest at the end of segments of utterances or a sentence, or at the end of a question or after a demand.

Summary

Patterns of patterns consist of strings of sounds that make strings of utterances. These are produced by the brain in an effort to produce meaningful oral communication that is supported by appropriate voice intonation, pitch, stress, pauses, and junctures. These speech features assist listeners in extracting meaning from the deep structure of the speaker's encoded thoughts through decoding sound patterns of the aurally perceived surface structure.

PHONICS

Attaching speech sounds to letters and letter combinations results in a process called phonics. According to Harris and Hodges (1981), phonics is "an approach to the teaching of reading and spelling that stresses symbol-sound relationships, especially in beginning reading instruction" (p. 238).

Phonics and phonetics are often used interchangeably, but they are different. Phonetics is the study of speech sounds for all languages, and it is used by phoneticians to transcribe language according to the International Phonetic Alphabet, or IPA. Phonics, then, is a system of speech sounds that is applicable only to the English language and can be used successfully only in teaching the decoding of English words.

Synthetic and Analytic Phonics

Synthetic phonics is the blending together of single sounds and sound combinations that correspond to single letters and letter combinations. To pronounce the word *cat* with the help of synthetic phonics, the following three strategies are possible:

1. c /kuh/ + a/a/ + t/tuh/
2. ca /ka/ + t/tuh/
3. c /kuh/ + at/at/

Through the magic of blending, each synthetic phonics approach or strategy should result in a close approximation of the conventional sound pattern of the well-known domestic animal called *cat*.

Anyone who has had the opportunity to observe the painful working-out of a word using this method will wonder if this, indeed, is reading. Guthrie and Cunningham (1982) indicate that synthetic phonics just may not be the strategy to show how fluent reading occurs or to give the right notion of what reading is. Further, although it may help readers to learn individual sounds, they may find it difficult if not impossible to blend those sounds into words (p. 555).

A different approach is analytic phonics, which begins with a whole word, known as sight word. A word such as *cat*, already in the children's listening and speaking vocabularies, is taught as a sight word by writing it on the chalkboard. (Readers may recall that *cat* is also a CVC trigram.) When its graphic representation is learned, it is used to teach other words with the same sound patterns, such as *fat*, *sat*, and *rat*. Then, by comparing and contrasting known words with unknown words, children can use known words as matching indicators to decode unknown ones.

Comparing and contrasting words in the narrowest sense is known as rhyming, which uses regular linguistic phonic patterns (Richek et al., 1983, p. 184). This tends to limit the sight words used in writing stores (*A fat cat sat on a mat*), and it limits fluent reading to such words and requires waiting to learn other common linguistic patterns (*bet, met, set; all, ball, fall*). Limiting words to linguistic rhyming forestalls the teaching of regular common sound patterns by which "children use all the words they know to decode any word they don't know" (Guthrie & Cunningham, 1982, p. 559).

Perhaps an interactive approach using both analytic and synthetic phonics may be more realistic and practical for children and any classroom situation in teaching reading. One could begin with an analytic approach, using a whole word. The whole word *cat* retains its whole gestalt as a live animal as well as its whole sound pattern and its whole graphic representation. When, however, the need arises to compare and contrast *cat* with, say, *cut*, one could call upon the synthetic strategy. Children could then examine medial vowel sounds and vowel letters and be made aware how substituting medial vowels changes meanings, sounds, and graphic patterns and why these changes make new whole words. Following this, analytic phonics would take over again.

Articulation

Further consideration should be given to the chronological ages at which children can or cannot articulate certain sounds. While *sh*, *th*, *ch*, and *l* sounds can be articulated at age six and one-half, the sounds *s*, *z*, *r*, and *wh* do not come until the chronological age of seven and one-half (Robinson, 1955). Articulation is complicated further by dialectism and bilingualism. Non-English speakers, who have to learn sounds that are not in their first language, experience difficulties in pronouncing English sounds. Spanish speakers have no voiced *th*, *z*, *sh*, and *j*, as in *then*, *zoo*, *shoe*, and *jump*; while Chinese speakers have no voiced *j*, *l*, *r*, and *v*, as in *jump*, *low*, *row*, and *vow* (Carillo, 1976). These things must be taken into account in deciding when the logic of phonics may be efficiently applied to the synthesis of processes in learning to read. There may be a hierarchical order regarding when and how to present phoneme-grapheme correspondences and their irregularities and exceptions.

Phonics Rules

The irregularities and exceptions to usual common graphic representations defy most phonics rules. Consider the words *bough*, *cough*, *slough*, *dough*, *ghost*, *pighead*, *hiccough*, *taught*, *laugh*, *does*, *doe*, *shoe*, *telephone*, *shepherd*, *father*, *fathead*, *colonel*, and *salmon*. The purpose of phonics rules is to foretell, control, and direct with precision how words should sound; however, the rules forfeit their predictability in words like *come*, *done*, *some*, *axe*, *how*, *sow*, and *been*.

For a moment, examine the rule of the letter *e* when it is in the final position, as in the words *lake*, *bake*, and *cake*. While the *e* is not pronounced, it influences the preceding vowel letter *a* to become a "long" vowel sound. The question, of course, is how the rule stands up in the light of reading, which is done in the left-to-right progression.

To apply this rule so as to pronounce the word *lake* correctly, several steps must be successfully negotiated. The pronouncer's eyes must travel from left to right to "see" what is at the end of this word. When it is recognized that there is the letter *e*, the eyes must travel back in the opposite direction, from right to left, to await the brain's decision of how the position of the letter *e* may or may not affect the word's sound pattern. Of course, this decision may be made in relationship to meaning, which may or may not be available to the pronouncer. Or, the decision may be made on the precarious knowledge that the letter *e* in final position prolongs the sound of the letter /a/ in that word. Still if this "rule" is applied without meaningful interpretation, sounding-out errors will result. F. Smith (1973) notes that "sound dependencies in words run from right to left" (p. 87). Obviously, sound dependency can only mean unnecessary difficulties for a beginning reader, who, wasting a lot of precious energy, makes sharp explosive noises that represent one sound at a time in order to sound words out from left to right. Phonics rules appear to be neither predictable indicators of nor reliable rulers over the regularities of letter-sound correspondences. Even if phonics rules are learned, known, and applied, readers must still learn and know when these rules are not applicable and what the exceptions to the rules are.

This leaves the question of how many rules would be needed to establish the credibility of letter-sound correspondences within a given universe of English words. Researchers investigated the reading vocabulary in schoolbooks of six- to nine-year-old children. Of 6,092 one- and two-syllable words, the researchers found that the phonemes were represented by 211 different spellings. Of this total of symbol-sound correspondences, 166 rules accounted for the pronunciation of consonant and vowel correspondences with no fewer than 45 consonant and vowel exceptions. Of the 166 rules, 60 applied to consonant and 106 to vowel pronunciations. Of the 106 vowel rules, 73 governed the six single-letter vowels *a*, *e*, *i*, *o*, *u*, and *y*, and the remaining 33 rules governed combination-letter vowels (research by Berdiansky, Cronnell, & Koehler, 1969; reported by F. Smith, 1982, p. 140).

Regarding the use of phonics, the message for teachers is that there are no rules that reliably predict letter-sound and sound-letter correspondences.

Summary

Teaching reading via the use of phonics is anything but simple. Synthetic phonics is equal to putting single sounds and sound combinations together to make complex sound patterns. Analytic phonics begins with whole words, known as sight words. When comparing and contrasting is not applied to decoding new words, the learning of new sound patterns may be limited. Phonics instruction depends also on articulation, which may be influenced by chronological age, bilingualism, and dialectism. When using phonics to decode words, it was seen that the unreliability of phonics rules appears to hinder more than to facilitate the teaching of reading, particularly beginning reading.

WORD RECOGNITION

Word recognition occurs when a word is seen and perceived with little or no delay. Recognizing a whole word without delay is called immediate word recognition. Recognizing it with some delay is called mediated word recognition (Hittleman, 1983, pp. 256–257).

Immediate word recognition requires that the word to be recognized has been stored in the long-term memory before seeing it again. Words that are immediately and correctly recognized are in the reader's visual or reading vocabulary as well as in the speaking and listening vocabularies. When, however, the word is not immediately recognized, it is not in the reader's reading vocabulary but may be in the speaking and listening vocabularies.

Immediate word recognition is essential to reading fluently, effectively, and economically, both orally, and silently. This is perhaps more so in oral reading, because any slight delay in the flow of words is heard by the listeners. Oral reading is used to assess the reader's ability to recognize words either in isolation or in context. In isolation, words are read aloud when arranged in columns or when exposed on flashcards. In context, words are read aloud when arranged in sentences and short paragraphs.

Mediated word recognition can be applied to learning new words through intermediated processing of known spelling patterns that correspond to meaning. In this sense, mediated word recognition forestalls memorizing words by sight or learning words by their surface structure only.

Intermediated processing means applying what is already known. In this case, letter clusters, which are already known and can be decoded, are used in identifying new words. The student who knows the word *say* can apply *ay* in *play*, *playing*, and *player*, and in *delay*, *delaying*, and *delayer*. When the word *tab* is known, intermediated processing leads to words like *drab* and *establish*, just as *sang* leads to *bang* and *strangle*, and *nature* leads to *departure* and *agriculture*. Glass (1973) and his associates have assembled a list of 117 vowel and two-consonant clusters that can be used by teachers in teaching word recognition more effectively.

Using Word Lists in Teaching Reading

Word lists are collections of words that are selected according to their frequency rating in sets of basal readers as well as in common reading materials. In addition, words are sorted out according to grade levels. The following are some word lists that are often used in teaching reading:

1. Dolch Basic Sight Vocabulary (1953). This is a list of 220 words collected according to their frequency in basal readers and categorized into groups of words that appear most frequently in preprimer, primer, grade one, grade two, and grade three.
2. Fry's List of Instant Words (1957). This is another well-known list. It contains 600 words, 100 each for grades one, two, and three, and 300 words that belong to grade four.
3. Kucera-Francis Corpus (1967). This collection contains 220 words compiled by frequency of occurrence from over one million words from different sources of reading materials.

Basic Information in Reading

From a study of the use of five different word lists in teaching reading, I have concluded that their effectiveness depends on the purposes for which they are used (Taschow, 1977). There is perhaps, one basic principle in the use of word lists: Words should never be used in isolation but always in their contextual settings of phrases, sentences, and paragraphs. Without context or in isolation, words like *the*, *a*, *then*, *that*, *what*, and others remain nothing else but graphic patterns. When in context, however, they assist in shaping meaningful messages, as in *A dog is in the house*.

To work with words effectively, children may use 5"×8" (or 12½×20½ cm) cards. On one side of the card children print or write the word, and on the other side give examples of using the word in phrases and sentences, to show various meaningful interpretations. These cards can be used for learning to spell and to write, for learning dictionary skills such as alphabetization, for marking stress, and for making sentences and new stories. The words can be sorted into categories of graphic and speech sound patterns. In addition, the words can be used to generate new ones; for example, beginning with *sing*, the user could compose such sentences and phrases as *We are singing*, *Ann sings*, *Mother is a singer*, *We sang yesterday*, *The unsung hero*, *Singing out the praise*, and *We sing a song*.

Summary

Immediate and mediated word recognition are essential tools for advancing from beginning to skilled and fluent reading. Word lists, which present words in isolation, are useful when these words are learned in context and then practiced in a variety of applicable exercises. These exercises should always be derived from and based on meaning, rather than on meaningless drilling and memorizing.

CHAPTER 6

Advanced Information in Reading

Purpose questions for this chapter:

- What role does syntactic and semantic information play in beginning and advanced reading?
- How is printed/written information processed?
- What are some different kinds of thinking?
- How can a reading teacher help students to think?
- What is active comprehension?

SYNTACTIC INFORMATION

What is printed is visually and vocally accessible. What is accessible are the sentence and sound patterns. These patterns are constrained according to syntactic information about how words and sounds are put together. These patterns—what readers see in print and what listeners hear as speech sounds—are the surface structure, as are the writer's ideas and thoughts as encoded into written/printed symbols and the speaker's ideas and thoughts as encoded into speech sounds.

The psycholinguistic term *syntactic information* is derived from the linguistic term *syntactic component*, as discussed by Chomsky (1957) and Chomsky and Halle (1968). They postulated (1968, p. 6) that a syntactic component of grammar assigns to each sentence a *surface structure*, which also determines its phonetic form or total sound pattern. In addition, the surface structure gives access to the abstractness of thought, the meaning of the message, or the *deep structure*. The deep structure underlies and partially determines the surface structure. What kinds of words are selected and how they are put together conveys the message, as in *Bill hit Paul* and *Paul hit Bill*. Otherwise, the deep structure is irrelevant to the phonetic interpretation or how word patterns are vocally recoded. The syntactic component then consists of the surface structure and the deep structure.

Returning to psycholinguistic theory, according to Goodman (1976, p. 480), syntactic information consists of sentence patterns, pattern markers, and sentence transformations.

Sentence Patterns

Sentence production is determined by ordering the parts or the base of a sentence. Words in non-order, such as *ate fish the man the hungry*, appear to make no sense. When placing the same words in order, as in *The hungry man ate the fish*, meaning is restored. In generating a different surface structure but maintaining the meaning, the sentence *The hungry man ate the fish* can be transformed into *The fish was eaten by the hungry man*. In the same way, the base sentence can be transformed by a system of rules or grammar into infinite sets of well-formed sentences, such as *The fish was eaten by the hungry man*; *The man who ate the fish was hungry*; *The fish was eaten by the man who was hungry*; *The man who was hungry ate the fish*; *Who ate the fish? By whom was the fish eaten? Who ate what?* and *What was eaten by whom?*

Pattern Markers

Pattern markers indicate the patterns in a sentence. A pattern is a "set of predictable and describable relations between elements of language, as phonology, word order, or affixation" (Harris & Hodges, 1981, p. 231). A marker, such as a phrase marker, is a "syntactic description of the structure of a sentence"(p. 239).

Sentence patterns cannot be generated without the help of function words. Some of them are *the, was, by, who, of, in, why, what,* and *then*. Function words are those which by themselves or in isolation are hard to define. But when in appropriate company with other words, they predict and describe grammatical functions, as in *the* ball or *a* table (noun function), *in* the house or *around* the barn (phrase function), *when* you come (clause function), *why* are you going? (question function), and it *is* cold (verb function).

Sentence patterns also are marked by inflections. In the two sentences *The man ate the fish* and *The fish was eaten by the man*, the words *ate* and *eaten* are inflections that signal the time and tense of the verb form *to eat*. Other examples of inflections are *fish* to *fishes* to *fishing*, or *part* to *department*. In the latter, affixes, prefixes, and suffixes express syntactic functions by conveying grammatical information. That is, by prefixing *de* to *part*, the verb sense of divide is conveyed, to which the suffix *ment* is added, resulting in a state of being divided, or a *department*.

Caution must be exercised in teaching the inflectional ending -*s*, which can signal pluralism of nouns as well as singularism of the present verb tense, as in *Bob completed the runs* versus *Bob runs*.

Inflection also denotes voice modulations during oral reading, which may signal the meaning to be expressed. This is assisted by punctuation markings within and at the end of sentence patterns.

Punctuation is the system of conventional markings that includes the comma, semicolon, period, exclamation mark, question mark, dash, apostrophe, and parenthesis. Punctuation signals clauses, sentence endings, commands, questions, quotations, possessive noun forms, contractions, and so forth. Punctuation usage assists in making the meaning clearer not only in writing and printing but also in oral reading through the intonation of spoken language.

Another pattern that gives syntactic information is indentation, or the visual pattern of leaving a blank space at the left margin before the beginning of the first sentence to signal the beginning of a new paragraph. In oral reading, an indentation may be marked by a short pause for silence before beginning the next paragraph.

Sentence Transformations

At the end of the earlier section on sentence patterns, various transformations of a base sentence were presented. In each case the surface structure of the given base sentence was transformed or altered into a different linguistic surface structure.

Transformation is a "process or the result of change from one linguistic construction to another according to syntactic rules" (Harris & Hodges, 1981, p. 334). What changes in accordance with the English syntax is the surface structure. *The toy truck is yellow* can be transformed into *Is the toy truck yellow?* Similarly, an arithmetic transformation can be performed without changing values, as in 3 + 4, which is the same as in 4 + 3.

Summary

Syntactic information consists of sentence patterns, sentence markers, and sentence transformations. While sentence patterns are determined by placing words in order of what is to be communicated, sentences cannot be formed without function words, word inflections, and punctuation markings within and at the end of sentences. Paragraphs must be signified visually, usually by beginning them with an indentation. The surface structure of sentences can be transformed without actually changing the deep structure of that sentence.

SEMANTIC INFORMATION

As we have seen when applying transformational rules to a sentence base, different surface structures emerge that "also play a role in determining semantic interpretation" (Chomsky, 1972, p. 107). That is why it seems that "both deep and surface structure enter into the determination of meaning" (p. 110). Deep structure appears to provide grammatical relations and surface structure, the logical elements of word patterns as constituents of a sentence.

Deep structure means meaning, and meaning means semantics. Semantics is the study of meaning or, more formally, the study of the meaning of meaning. Particularly, semantics is the study of "the relations between referents and names, and between concepts and names" (Harris & Hodges, 1981, p. 289). Generative semantics, a newer field in the study of meaning, is concerned with how language systems grow from meaning (Hittleman, 1983, p. 25), with the emphasis on "meaning [which] must precede grammatical analysis" (F. Smith, 1982, p. 74). F. Smith argues that meaning of sentences is not established by putting together meanings of individual words. *The man hunts the lion* and *The lion hunts the man* are exactly the same words in exactly the same grammatical relationships, but the meaning is not the same. What is to be communicated is meaning, so it is meaning that determines the order of words.

But how can meaning become accessible when it is obscured or blocked by words that readers do not know? Meaning must be arrived at under these circumstances through the use of semantic clues, which are definitions, appositives, comparisons, contrasts, and figurative expressions that are added to explain unknown words. In *Bob returned, came back, to the farm*, the appositive *came back* explains the word *returned*. In *Bob was so angry he flew off the handle*, the figurative expression *flew off the handle* helps to explain just how angry Bob was. In *A delta is a land area covered with silt that forms at the mouth of a river*, the definition explains the word *delta*.

Although semantic clues give added information about unknown words, they may not be enough, for example, to explain fully the definition of words and expressions such as *silt*, *mouth of a river*, and even *delta*. Unless readers still can obtain additional nonprinted or nonvisual information, they will not fully understand what *silt* is, what kind of a *mouth* it is and where and how it is formed and under what conditions, and why it is called a *delta*. This semantic information comes from the readers and consists, according to Goodman (1976, p. 480), of experience, concepts, and vocabulary.

Experience

Experience has already been discussed as a source of meaning that rests within the readers. From that discussion it was concluded that the more experiences or nonvisual information readers bring to the printed page, the less they must rely on visual information from print. As in the example given of a delta, when readers know that silt consists of fine earth and sand that is carried and deposited by moving water as a sediment, no further additional printed information is necessary. This information is within the readers, stored in their memories to be retrieved when needed.

Concepts and Schemata

A concept "is not an isolated, ossified, changeless formation but an active part of the intellectual process, constantly engaged in serving communication and understanding, and problem-solving" (Harris & Hodges, 1981, p. 61).

Concepts can be developed when a series of similar experiences converge to form a common result. Individual objects become organized under family names, such as apple, orange, and lemon organized under fruit. The fruit components have similarities that are concrete and factual because they can be seen, touched, and consumed. Forming concepts by putting similar objects, events, or components into classes reduces the need for constant new learning, for identifying anew the world around us. Understanding the relationships from one component to another and among several components within the same concept is not always achieved, even though both concept and components can be named. Within the concept *furniture*, the relationships of chairs and tables may be understood, but the same may not be true of a couch and a shelf.

When all the parts belonging to the concept *furniture* are organized as a collection of facts (data) into a stable whole (structure) to which all members or components pertain and relate (become generic) and are so stored in memory, a generic concept or schema results. "A schema, then, is a data structure for presenting the generic concepts stored in memory" (Rumelhart, 1981, p. 5). Schemata are all our previously acquired knowledge packaged into units. These units of knowledge contain the knowledge itself and the information on how it is to be used (Graesser, 1981; Hacker, 1980; Rumelhart, 1981; Rumelhart & Ortony, 1977).

Schemata interact between and among themselves and assist in thinking. They compare incoming information with that already known and aid in understanding (Hittleman, 1983, p. 42). Schemata are not static entities; they may change with any and all incoming information.

Schemata are the building blocks of cognition and represent knowledge at all levels of abstraction. They are active processes as well as recognition devices whose processing is aimed at the evaluation of their goodness of fit to the data that is being processed (Rumelhart, 1981, p. 13). Schemata have variables that allow us to know and understand what is involved in a simple situation, such as buying a loaf of bread, as well as in a more complex situation, such as teaching a directed reading lesson. Recalling the *delta* definition, we can conclude that, if readers do not have the appropriate *silt* schema together with the subschemata of *fine sands* and *deposits*, they cannot understand the concept that is to be communicated.

Vocabulary

Within the packets of knowledge, or the schemata, there is a repertoire of words or vocabulary that individual readers know and use to sort out words, phrases, and sentences against their schemata. Word meanings, the union of words and thoughts, are dynamic and change over time. The notion that all men are called "Daddy" changes when the relationship of thought to word changes. Thus changes in meaning develop from less to more differentiated to more distinctive.

Vocabulary knowledge may also be measured in breadth and depth. Breadth is the quantity or the number of words a person knows and has some meaning for. Depth is the quality or the understanding a person has of words in using them, and the ability to make them understood by others. Anderson and Freebody (1981) conjecture that vocabulary knowledge will deepen throughout lifetime in the sense that nuances and subtle distinctions of words already acquired develop toward greater refinement in the expression of meaning (p. 94).

How important word knowledge is to reading comprehension is evidenced in the Thorndike study (1973) of fifteen countries with varying languages. In this study, in which over 100,000 students of three different age groups participated, word knowledge was correlated with reading comprehension. The study found that the correlations for the three age groups differed slightly. For the ten-year-old students, the correlation was .71; for the fourteen-year-old students, the correlation was .75; and for the seventeen-year-old students, the correlation was .66.

Since vocabulary knowledge is important to reading comprehension, how should vocabulary knowledge be developed? The answer is simple: in context, not in isolation! As Goodman (1976) reminds us, "vocabulary development outside the context of new ideas and pre-existing language is not possible" (p. 487). Hence, new meaning vocabulary must be built upon the base of the already existing and known vocabulary. As readers forge into unknown territory, unknown words and concepts are encountered. These are tested against the old components of vocabulary and, when required, some of them will either be modified or even discarded.

Summary

Semantics is the study of meaning. Meaning, not words, determines the surface structure of word patterns, and semantic clues can assist in explaining unknown words within sentences. Semantic clues, however, must be supported by stored-up concepts, schemata, experiences, and a sufficient stockpile of words or vocabulary. These combine to assist the reader in extracting the most accurate meaning from the text.

INFORMATION PROCESSING

Information processing is a course of definite actions that are directed toward the specified end of understanding a writer's message. Thus, the ability to process information means to be able to activate the appropriate schemata to find "a configuration of schemata which offers an adequate account of the passage in question" (Rumelhart, 1981, p. 22).

Again recalling the *delta* definition, the *delta* schema activates subschemata of *silt*, *deposit*, *sediment*, and *mouth of a river*. This process begins with the classification of *delta* or the whole geological formation from which the parts are assigned that belong to it. When the process begins with the whole and moves downward to the parts, this is known as *top-down* processing. If, however, the opposite direction is taken, from parts to the whole, this is called *bottom-up* processing. Most often these two processes, bottom-up and top-down, do not occur as two separate ones; rather, they occur simultaneously and interact. Thus lower-level schemata of deposits of moving water may immediately call up higher-level schemata of the famous Nile delta, which in turn interact with lower-level schemata of silt, fine earth, and sand.

The professional literature in reading proposes at least three different models for analyzing how readers may function when processing meaning from print. These theoretical structures are called the bottom-up model, the top-down model, and the interactive model.

Bottom-Up Processing

According to the bottom-up model, processing works on a level-by-level analysis in which the readers work from the graphophonic level through the syntactic level to the semantic level. Such models describe serial or stage-by-stage processing of reading and were introduced into the literature by Geyer (1970), Gough (1972), Gough and Cosky (1977), Laberge and Samuels (1976), and Mackworth (1971).

The theoretical position regarding processing information from the bottom-up may be compared to the approach described earlier in teaching synthetic phonics. In order to arrive at the whole word *cat* and understand it, the process begins with the smallest graphemic unit, the letter, to which a sound or an oral response is attached. Through accurate and sequential processing of letter-to-sound, the whole word eventually is sounded out. If the text is longer than a single word, as in *A cat sat on a mat*, comprehension is accumulated from word to word until the full text is comprehended. Harris and Hodges (1981), in defining bottom-up processing, state that comprehension "is built and governed by the text, and does not involve the reader's inner experiences and expectations" (p. 38).

Thus, processing print in the bottom-up model proceeds in a series of discrete stages involving linking letter features to letter clusters, which are also recognized as spelling patterns. These are linked to words, which must be recognized quickly so that word recognition becomes automatic. Then words and meanings are linked to sentences (Samuels, 1977). Sentences, of course, are linked to paragraphs, and those are linked to full text. Bottom-up processing moves from the subskill of letter identification to the subskill of word recognition, from lower-level decoding to higher-level decoding that ends in comprehension.

When word recognition becomes automatic, it tends to free the readers to attend more fully to extracting meaning from print. Automaticity is said to be the reader's ability to respond to the visual input of words without much attention and conscious effort. Harris and Hodges (1981) state that "automaticity in word attack permits full energy to be put into developing comprehension" (p. 27). Word recognition is processed on the lower, or micro, level, while comprehension is processed on the higher, or macro, level.

Automaticity, as LaBerge and Samuels (1976) explain, is of importance when operating at the macro level. Subskills serving comprehension must be automatic, as well as the transition between them. LaBerge and Samuels conclude that "when one describes a skill at the macrolevel as being automatic, it follows that the subskills at the microlevel and their interrelations must also be automatic" (p. 550). This may explain why less-skilled or even unskilled readers, whose attention is tied to various levels of subskills such as recoding, cannot at the same time shift attention toward comprehension.

The bottom-up models are known also as data- or stimuli-driven models. Otto (1982) explains that bottom-up processing follows the behaviorists' theory of stimulus, response, and reinforcement. When presented with the stimuli or the letters, subsequent responses or sounds follow, which, when correct, are reinforced (p. 15).

The research literature on bottom-up processing indicates that such models are inadequate "because they fail to account for many important empirical results in the reading literature" (Stanovich, 1980, p. 34). Their inadequacy lies in the lack of a mechanism by which semantic processes can act upon syntactic processes; nor can both together as higher-level processes act upon lower-level, or word, processes. Similarly, lower-level processes cannot act one upon another nor upon higher-level processes. Also bottom-up models are said to be "too passive to account for reading, which is both flexible and dynamic" (Downing & Leong, 1982, p. 210).

Top-Down Processing

Processing information through top-down models, in which comprehension is the core of processing print, has been proposed by Goodman (1976), Kolers (1972), Neville and Pugh (1976-1977), and F. Smith (1982).

To understand this theoretical position, readers may think of the experiences and expectations they have had with a cat. Readers bring to the reading experience their concepts of a cat; what a cat does, likes, and so on. With this in mind, when readers encounter the word *cat* in the text, they begin by forming hypotheses based on experience and expectation. These hypotheses are then tested against the text and are confirmed, modified, or rejected in accordance with the text, as in *A cat sat on a mat*. What the readers have hypothesized is what they begin with. Then they work down to the text. Harris and Hodges (1981) define top-down processing in which "comprehension is seen as reader-driven" (p. 332).

In a similar vein, think of children listening for the first time to the story of Red Riding Hood as she walks through the dark forest. Each child will have his or her own expectation of the big bad wolf and what can happen to Red Riding Hood should the wolf come. With each word they hear, their expectations grow. It is not until they hear that the big bad wolf was rather friendly when standing suddenly in front of Red Riding Hood that they can test their expectations against the actual wolf's behavior. The children's relaxing "aah" tells us that they have gladly modified whatever expectations they had.

Top-down models are diametrically opposed to bottom-up models. Top-down models begin with higher-level processing of meaning, directed by hypotheses that must be tested against the text. When a hypothesis is rejected, a new one is set up and tested. Thus, top-down models begin with higher-level processes and proceed downward to lower-level processes of word patterns or even letter stimuli. Top-down models are also known as concept-driven models and are considered to be active, in contrast to the bottom-up models, which are stimuli-driven and considered to be passive.

There are problems associated with using information processing in accordance with top-down models. It may result in meaning expectations, as well as in vagueness of forming concepts that may not be confirmed at the lower level of word stimuli. Anticipating meaning from words as yet not visually analyzed may also result in meaning ambiguity (Wildman & Kling, 1978–1979, p. 133). Anticipated matching of readers' expectations with contextual information may end in mismatching, which calls for new hypothesis testing between thought, language, and text. These procedures may be wasteful of the reader's energies.

Interactive Processing

The features of both top-down and bottom-up processing are combined in the interactive theoretical position, which involves the use of experience and expectation as well as the stimuli of the text. Using the interactive model, a reader might begin by hypothesizing about what can be expected of a cat and then, using the text, verify immediately whether or not the cat *sits* (now) on a mat. Suppose the text tells the reader that the cat *sat*. The beginning hypothesis must be modified accordingly.

Harris and Hodges (1981) define interactive processing as a model in which "comprehension is generated by the reader under the stimulus control of the print" (p. 160). The interactive model attempts to synthesize information processing by using lower- and higher-level knowledge sources. On the one hand, the amount of letter-by-letter analysis used in the bottom-up model is reduced by using the clues offered by the syntactic and semantic constraints in the text. On the other hand, little time is spent in matching or mismatching sensory clues while engaging in hypothesis testing, as in top-down contextual processing. However, when the reader's expectancies and anticipatory strategies fail, plodding through the text letter-by-letter will occur (Wildman & Kling, 1978-1979, p. 160).

The reader may be reminded of Rumelhart's theory (1977) of schemata interaction. Later, based on this investigation of schemata and memory, Rumelhart (1977) also developed what perhaps is the best model of interaction, which assumes that a pattern is synthesized "based on information provided *simultaneously* from several knowledge sources" (Stanovich, 1980, p. 35). These sources are letter extraction; orthographic knowledge; lexical knowledge, such as of words, compound words, and idioms; as well as syntactic and semantic knowledge.

Consider, for instance, the string of words in the utterance *low-flying airplane*. Input information may be extracted by using semantic relationships, that is, by applying the knowledge that, when airplanes land, search, or are in trouble, they will fly low. Syntactic information may be extracted from the context of the larger sentence, which perhaps tells of someone having observed the low-flying airplane. Additional information may be extracted from individual letter features such as *y* and *p* and letter clusters such as *ow*, *fl*, and *pl*, which may contribute to speedier identification of words like *low*, *fly*, and *plane*. Thus, readers may utilize all the various aspects of reading processing, from semantic sources (top down) to individual letter sources (bottom up). At any time, any knowledge source can be called upon by the reader to assist in extracting information from another knowledge source.

When information is received, it goes to what Rumelhart calls a *message center* (Rumelhart, 1977), where it is examined, interpreted, and integrated. That is, the message center keeps account of all hypotheses generated, analyzes them, and accepts or rejects them accordingly. Any rejected hypothesis is removed from the message center, to be replaced with a new one or altered by it (Hittleman, 1983, p. 73).

Interactive models, then, as Stanovich (1980, p. 63) emphasizes, assume that information is processed simultaneously by several knowledge sources and that deficiency or inefficiency in one knowledge source will be compensated for by another knowledge source, regardless of its level of processing. However, a recent study by Freebody and Anderson (1983), tested and failed to find support for an interactive theory such as the interactive-compensatory model of Stanovich. Among other conclusions in their study, they found that there is a performance reduction in reading when "readers encounter words they do not know" (p. 286) and that inadequate comprehension may be due "to a failure of a relevant schema to be activated" (p. 287).

Summary

Comprehension is commonly accepted as the goal of reading. To do this, information must be processed. How information is processed is explained by several theories, including the bottom-up, top-down, and interactive models. While the former two have their own processing features specific to their structures, the latter rests on the assumptions that lower-level and higher-level processes interact and that readers may draw simultaneously from several knowledge sources in order to accommodate contextual processing. There are problems with all three of these theories, and the research literature so far has not confirmed conclusively the mechanisms or effectiveness of any of them.

GUIDING THINKING IN READING

The notion that "reading is thinking" has appeared on and off in the professional literature since E.L. Thorndike in 1917 wrote "Reading as Reasoning: A Study of Mistakes in Paragraph Reading." In it, Thorndike showed the importance of thinking in reading and concluded that reading and thinking belong together.

Reading to inform, to learn, and to enjoy have one common goal: to understand the meaning of printed words. Comprehending a unit of print, whether simple or complex, necessitates thinking. This includes weighing each of the many words in a sentence, considering their organizational and grammatical relationships one to another, and doing the same with sentences in a paragraph and paragraphs in the total printed passage. In fact, thinking is not completed until all mental forces have worked together to produce a final response.

Linked to E.L. Thorndike's early statement on reading and thinking is the development of the generative reading-learning approaches.

Generative Learning

Linden and Wittrock (1981), in a study of ten-year-old, fifth-grade students using the Wittrock model of generative learning, found that comprehension output increases significantly ($p < .01$) when readers relate their knowledge to different parts of the text and to the total text (pp. 48-51). This can be accomplished by attending selectively to and thereby concentrating on the text and its parts, by associating memorized information with that in the text, and by abstracting and inferring information as necessary to achieve fullest understanding. Such achievement may be done for the reader's own satisfaction or, as is often the case in school situations, it may be done to fulfill obligations to pass tests of recall.

In addition, textual information can be supported by constructing imaginary representations in the form of pictures, graphs, drawings, and diagrams. Students can also be assisted in generating textual relationships and associations by learning how to write summaries, form main ideas, construct paragraphs and story headings, draw inferences, arrive at evaluations, and prepare critical comments (p. 45).

How can generative learning be used to increase reading comprehension? When children read, the teacher can ask them to make images in their minds of everything that happens in the passage or the story. Afterward, children may be encouraged to draw pictures of their mental images. This can be followed up by asking them to recall factual information, and the teacher may pose inferential questions, such as, "How can you tell what has happened?"

Later on, the story can be divided into sections, for which children compose oral and then written summary sentences. Finally, children can be taught to use the story to generate analogies or other figurative expressions, such as "all was quiet like a mouse" and "the heart is like a pump." These expressions generate new discussion and lead to new investigations involving further reading. The whole process can be reversed, as well. Summary sentences can be used to synthesize what is like or different about the heart and a pump. This will generate factual and inferential information, which can generate drawings and diagrams to which children imagine titles and captions.

Kinds of Thinking

There are many different kinds of thinking that may be used in the classroom. Piaget (in Furth & Wachs, 1975) holds that intelligence is "constructive and creative" and that intelligence is "but the gradual creation of new mechanisms of thinking" (p. 25). In *Thinking Goes to School*, Furth and Wachs (1975) insist that the teacher's foremost task is to provide "occasions and opportunities" for the children to think and, in doing so, the teacher should provide "the model of a thinking person" (p. 46). Moreover, thinking has "an additional positive influence that is consequently personally rewarding" (p. 47). These words allege that it is the undeniable responsibility of all teachers, including teachers of reading, to make children use their intelligence and to challenge it by moving from simple to complex thinking.

In the following sections we will explore some of the different kinds of thinking, as suggested in the literature.

Categorical and Noncategorical Thinking. The theories of categorical and noncategorical thinking are advanced by Bruner, Goodnow, and Austin (1956). Categorical thinking is successive categorizing. It is needed in problem solving where regrouping of objects or events will lead to final answers. Categorical thinking is also essential in ordering and relating classes of objects or events (pp. 12, 13).

For example, learning about the varieties of housecats and how they relate to the animal kingdom requires understanding of categorical thinking. A variety of cats comprise the domestic species, cat. From there the species leads to the genus of animals to which cats belong, then to the wider circle of family, to the order of mammals, to the class of chordates, and finally to the phylum or the kingdom of all animals.

Noncategorical thinking, on the other hand, relates to expressing thoughts through music, painting, pantomime, and dance. What has been read of events, objects, or persons and how children feel about them can be expressed visually and vocally through the various forms of noncategorical thinking.

Convergent and Divergent Thinking. These modes of thinking are suggested by Guilford (Getzel & Jackson, 1962). Convergent thinking is directed toward one point by eliminating other possibilities and thus arriving at the right answer. What is the color of the toy airplane? To answer this question, the respondent must direct thinking toward one color only, which must be the right one, in accordance with the text.

Divergent thinking, in contrast, requires going beyond a given situation and imagining as many possibilities as there might be by generating new ideas and altering existing ones.

Reflective and Other Kinds of Thinking. The idea of reflective thinking comes from Dewey (1933/1960). It begins with doubting and not being sure. To regain certainty, readers must search, inquire, and try to resolve doubt (p. 12).

Smith, Goodman, and Meredith (1976, p. 128) explain various other kinds of thinking. Autistic thinking is pursued in daydreaming. Wishful thinking manifests itself in imagining what may or may not be feasible, in remembering what was pleasant or painful, in expressing feelings and tastes, and in reasoning by reflecting how similar or different problems are to those solved before.

Question Strategies

It is within the scope of reading practices used in elementary and secondary classrooms to use all kinds of thinking we have just discussed. Teachers may guide students' thinking, and students may guide their own thinking. To assure that thinking occurs, teachers must ask questions, to which students must supply the answers.

The art of asking questions perhaps began with Socrates, who foreshadowed about 2,300 years ago what would become educational practice: "to ask questions whose purposes guide to higher thinking skills" (Taschow, 1978, p. 77). The art of asking questions was also explored by Postman (1979), who believed it was "one of the central disciplines in language education" (p. 154).

Student-Directed Questioning. While question asking is an intellectual tool that is available to the teacher (Taba, 1965), the art of question asking must not rest with the teacher alone but must be transferred to the students (Singer & Donlan, 1980). The kind of questions asked determines the kind of thinking, which determines the kind of answers. Questions, then, influence learning (Guthrie, 1983b), as well "guide the course of knowledge acquisition" (p. 479).

Traditionally, teachers ask the questions, which students are anxious to answer correctly in order to please the questioner. This procedure is not student directed, as teacher-posed questions elicit answers from students who, over time, learn to direct their thinking toward a product predetermined by the teacher—that is, the "right" answer.

Students should be taught instead to generate their own questions so that thinking becomes student-directed (Singer, 1978; Singer & Donlan, 1982). In this way, comprehension becomes active, where responses are emitted, not elicited.

Singer (1978) suggests three steps for transferring the art of questioning from teacher to student: (1) the teacher "models" the questions to be asked, making sure they are appropriate to the subject matter; (2) the teacher teaches students to ask appropriate questions; (3) as students begin to ask their own questions, they are "phased into" the question-asking process and the teacher is "phased out" of it. Nevertheless, the phased-out teacher always should be on the alert and willing to participate with a new guiding question, which will phase in the teacher momentarily. The onus, however, is at all times on the students to generate questions and follow up the teacher's guiding questions with their own additional ones.

In a project study done in cooperation with local school boards, I demonstrated that teaching students to ask questions does improve significantly their comprehension performance (Taschow, 1973). Forty teachers and 771 students in grades one through eight from public and separate schools in Regina and surrounding areas in Saskatchewan participated in this study. The art of questioning was taught first to the teachers, who were given some demonstration lessons in how to involve the students in asking questions. Then, teachers taught questioning to the students until student-directed questioning became an integral part of reading instruction and assessment of reading comprehension.

Content of Questions.   Questioning calls for raising thinking levels (Taba, 1962) so that students are required to use their minds and knowledge in reading and thinking critically (Taschow, 1972a, 1976). Thus, the art of questioning requires knowing which questions are the most important. There is much in the literature to illuminate this point. I particularly recommend Sanders, *Classroom Questions: What Kinds* (1966).

There are many ways to ask questions orally and to present them in writing, and there are many kinds of questions to signify various levels of thinking. After a thorough search through the literature for a list that grouped questions together into different categories representing different thinking levels, I selected the list found in *Reading in the Elementary School* by Spache and Spache (1977). Since, however, these questions were only presented in their interrogative forms without examples, I applied them to a few sentences in a grade-five reader, *Days of Adventures* of the Developmental Reading Series by Bond, Cuddy, and Fay (1962). Later, I revised some of the questions and, at a regional reading conference sponsored by the International Reading

Advanced Information in Reading 115

Association, was privileged to present them as part of a discussion paper concerned with raising thinking levels (Taschow, 1980). The questions organized by categories follow:

1. Memory
    (a) Facts
        What did *the men put up*?[1]
        When did *they put it up*?
        Where did *they put it up*?
        Who *put the buildings up*?
        How many *men put the buildings up*?
    (b) Definitions
        What is meant by *shedlike buildings*?
        What does *Mandan village* mean?
        What meaning did you understand for *stockade*?
        Define *blockhouse tower*.
    (c) Generalizations
        What event(s) led to *putting up the buildings*?
        In what three ways do *the mud houses* resemble *the sheds*?
        How did *snow and ice* affect *the expedition*?
    (d) Values
        What is said about the Mandan village?
        What kind of people were the Mandans?
        What did the Sioux do that the Mandans wouldn't?
2. Translation
        Tell in your own words how *the Mandans lived*.
        How could you restate the concept "peaceful people"?
        How could we make up a play to tell the story?
        Write the story pretending you are *the Mandan chief*.
3. Interpretation
    (a) Comparative:
        How is *a mud house* like *a shed*?
        Compare *the stockade* with *the guard tower*.
        How did *the Sioux* and *the Mandans get food*?
        How does *raising crops* today resemble (or differ from)
            raising crops in 1800?
    (b) Implications
        What will *war* and *defeat* lead to?
        What justification for *the expedition* does the author give?

---
[1] Italics indicate story information used to complete questions or statements.

What is likely to happen when *the Sioux continue to threaten the Mandans*?
What would happen if *the Mandans do not fight*?
- (c) Inductive thinking
  What facts in the story tend to support the idea that *the Mandans are peaceful people*?
  What does the behavior of *the Mandan chief* tell you about him (her)?
  What event(s) led to *the smoking of the peace pipe*?
- (d) Quantitative
  How many times did *the captain ask the chief*?
  How many causes of *the trouble* can you list?
  What conclusions(s) can be drawn from the picture (table, graph)?
  How much did *the captain pay*?
- (e) Cause and effect
  Why did *the chief not answer the captain*?
  How did *the captain* make *it* happen?
  What two *events* led up to *the conflict*?
  What happened when *the chief did not appear*?
  Why did *it come to conflict*?
4. Application
   How can you show that *the Mandan chief wanted peace*?
   What sort of *peace* plans will *the chief* make?
   What could *the people* do to help *the chief*?
   How could *the people* show *the chief* that *they thought of him*?
5. Analysis
   Discuss the statement, "*The expedition got safely away from the unfriendly Sioux.*"
   Some people think that *all Indians are unfriendly*. What do you think?
   The *expedition members* dislike (like) *all Indians*. Are *the members* right or wrong in their feelings?
6. Synthesis
   What other title(s) can you think of for this story?
   What other ending(s) can you think of for this story?
   What might have happened if *the Mandan chief had not acted*?
   Pretend you are *the Mandan chief* who *wants to keep peace*. What might you do to *keep the peace*?
7. Evaluation
   For what reason(s) did you (did you not) enjoy the story?
   What do you think of *the Mandan people* in this story?

Why do you agree (disagree) with the actions of *the members of the expedition?*
What do you suppose *the expedition members* said about *the Indians?*[2]

Suggested Procedure for Teaching Questioning. The preceding question categories were given with the intent of providing a basis for teaching questioning to students. Within the concept of active comprehension, teachers first ask a guiding question that will whet the intellectual appetite and curiosity and will leave plenty of opportunity for the students to ask their own questions.

Students must learn to ask questions in response to the teacher's guiding question. For example, if the discussion centers around a journey up a wild river, the teacher may ask, "What would you like to know about a journey that takes you up a wild river?" This question is broad enough in its content to allow for additional questions to be asked. In contrast, "Who went on the journey?" is too narrow; it ends with the answer, not further questions. A guiding question that is broad enough will prompt students to generate questions that relate and are relevant to the topic. In response to the question, "What would you like to know?" student questions may be: Who did the journey? What is the name of the river? Why is the river called a wild river? Where did the journey start, and where will it end? What kind of a boat was used to journey up the river? Where did the river flow? When did the journey take place? How many people took part in the journey?

In generating such questions, students become actively involved, motivated, and interested in questioning rather than just answering the teacher's questions. When they read the story, they have their own purposes for reading it. At this point, students are phased in and the teacher is phased out of the question-asking process. After sections have been read, additional questions may be posed, until students are satisfied. At this point the teacher phases in again by asking a new question to generate analysis, synthesis, and possibly evaluation questions.

Again, students will read to find and verify responses, which will lead to new questions. These may change the direction of questioning because reading has aroused different interests, curiosity, and awareness.

It should be becoming clearer what the importance is of students asking and generating their own questions. When students pose their own questions, active comprehension does not need to wait for new textbooks especially

---

[2] This list is reprinted by permission of the publisher from G. D. Spache and E. B. Spache, *Reading in the Elementary School,* 4th ed. (Boston: Allyn & Bacon, 1977), pp. 455–457.

prepared for questioning. It must wait only until teachers decide that they are ready for student-directed questioning, until teachers are convinced it is feasible and workable and are genuinely concerned about teaching students to process their own questions on various thinking levels.

As students learn to ask their own questions and learn to generate new questions from a guiding question, they become more and more critical readers, and do not passively accept and recite other answers believed to be correct. Critical readers will doubt, ask, seek, ask more, and verify before accepting or rejecting. As a result, responsible and knowledgeable future citizens emerge who have learned to think and reason independently, which is the foundation of a sound society.

Summary

If "reading is thinking," then it is the responsibility of every teacher to understand and nurture thinking. There are many kinds of thinking, including categorical, noncategorical, convergent, divergent, and reflective. To improve and increase student thinking in the classroom and as a life skill, questions are used to raise thinking levels. Active comprehension is an excellent vehicle through which to initiate and continue student-generated thinking and to transform teacher-directed questioning into student-directed questioning.

CHAPTER 7

Reading in Different Content Areas

Purpose questions for this chapter:
- What are basal readers?
- How is reading in subject-matter textbooks different from reading in basal readers?
- What are organizers in reading, and how can they assist in organizing instruction for reading comprehension?
- What special reading abilities are required in reading textbooks in mathematics, science, social studies, and literature?

READING IN BASAL READERS

Teachers in elementary-school grades are familiar and knowledgeable about basal readers. In fact, most teachers in the elementary schools use basal readers, with all their supplementary wares, as the primary or ancillary sources of reading instruction. Aukerman (1981) points out that "there is an 80 to 90 percent probability that an elementary classroom teacher will be obliged to use them [basal readers] in some way or another" (p. 2). It may also be of interest to know that the term *basal reader* "is strictly American in origin" (p. 6).

What is a basal reader? Aukerman (1981) describes a basal reader as not being one book but rather a whole package of books with supplementary materials that are used to teach reading (p. 6). Harris and Hodges (1981) define a basal reading program or a basal reading series as "a comprehensive, integrated set of books, workbooks, teacher's manuals, and other materials for developmental reading instruction, chiefly in the elementary and middle school grades" (p. 30–31).

Development of Basal Readers

The history of the basal readers goes back to the McGuffy's Eclectic Readers series, published by the American Book Company between 1836 and

1844. The almost-immediate popularity of this series outstripped *The New England Primer* and *Webster's Blue-back Speller* (N. B. Smith, 1965, pp. 103–105).

McGuffy's Eclectic Readers were the first series of readers that consisted of carefully graded and clearly defined readers, one for each grade in the elementary school. Their popularity lasted for about forty years, after which they were replaced by more modern printed basals. But it should be remembered that McGuffy's Eclectic Readers were the ancestors from which all other basal readers, including the current ones, descended.

From the late 1940s to the 1960s the McGuffy's series was succeeded by Betts Basic Readers. These were followed by the predominantly linguistic READ series, which, about 1977, became The American Book Reading Program, with a similar linguistic tone. Finally, a switch back to the traditional basal readers marked the new 1980 American Readers series.

Perhaps the basal readers most remembered by teachers who taught reading and by the students who learned to read are Scott, Foresman's Dick, Jane, and Spot readers, which became another milestone in the trend of the basals from the 1940s to the 1960s.

Scott, Foresman and Company published first the Boyden Readers (1897), followed by the Elson Readers (1909–1914), which became the predecessors of the Dick and Jane basals. Then came the New Basic Readers (1962), succeeded by the current 1981 edition of the Scott, Foresman Reading series.

Another well-known basal reading series has been published by Ginn and Company. Their first readers, the Beacon Readers, came out in 1912 and 1913. They were followed by the Ginn Basic Readers (1948–1949), which were succeeded in 1964 by the revised and expanded edition of the Ginn Basic Reading Program (N. B. Smith, 1965). About 1969, Reading 360 appeared, followed about 1976 by Reading 720, which, after revision, became the Rainbow Edition of 1980.

Basal readers of the 1960s were criticized for artificial language structures, particularly sentence structures, that did not reflect the language children speak (Burns & Roe, 1980, p. 198; Lamb & Arnold, 1980, p. 180). Reading instruction followed the lock-step method, which prescribed in detail what, when, and how to teach reading skills and in what order. Further criticism was leveled toward the portrayal of the all-white middle-class four-member American family consisting of father, mother, and two children, a boy and a girl, who inevitably owned a cat and a dog.

Changes in Basal Readers

What was perceived in the earlier basal readers as the stereotyped American family setting and life, apparently unconcerned with real live people of multi-ethnic origin, and what was expressed in colorless language and tinted dull by overcontrolled vocabulary and sentence structures, changed with the changing outlooks of American society during and after the Vietnam War. These changing attitudes have been considered in the new basal readers published at the end of the 1970s and the beginning of the 1980s. Aukerman (1981) examined fifteen of the basal series of the 1980s and found the following improvements that reflect society's major sociological and economic concerns: better ethnic balance; better balance between male and female members; inclusion of the handicapped and senior citizens; better balance of urban, suburban, and rural settings and of geographic areas; deletion of violence; a more balanced selection of literary styles; vigorous graphic arts components; developmental lesson plans; improved literary quality; and the useful addition of glossaries (pp. 8–11).

Noticeable changes in giving directions to teachers on how to use the basals in reading can be observed when comparing McGuffy's Eclectic Readers to today's current basal readers. McGuffy's included only a few pages of instruction within each reader, describing how to use each reader's content in teaching reading. In contrast, later and current basals have offered increasingly voluminous teacher's editions in which methods and materials are described and prescribed in great detail. The assumption, perhaps dubious, is made that when the prescribed instructional procedures are followed and the various reading materials are used and applied, positive teaching will result and all students will learn to read.

Another advance was the move from only one reader for each grade to two readers for a single grade, followed by current basal reading series, which have multilevel readers without direct grade designation. This change was influenced in part by the so-called "nongraded" school movement.

For instance, the Rainbow Edition of the Ginn 720 has fifteen levels of readers ranging from kindergarten to grades seven and eight. The first-level reader corresponds to kindergarten, with the following four levels ascribed to grade one: two for preprimer, one for primer, and one for first reader.

In the preface of McGuffy's *Eclectic Primer* (1881, 1909), teachers are instructed that "The plan of the book enables the teacher to pursue the Method, the Word Method, the Alphabet Method, or any combination of these methods" (p. iii). In contrast, most current basals begin with the whole-word method and offer, in addition, materials explaining and exemplifying both analytic and synthetic phonics approaches. Again, the Rainbow Edition offers, in separate but ancillary components, decoding activity charts, decoding sound strips, phonics practice books, and other materials (Aukerman, 1981, p. 80).

Yet another indicator of change is the student workbook, which has become a steady companion in the packaging of basal reading series. Student workbooks are designed to reinforce learned reading skills through added practices. To alleviate extra work for reading teachers in composing additional exercises, most basal packages include duplicating masters, extra teacher-directed drills, and independent student skill practices.

Another noticeable feature is the authors who contributed their expertise to contriving the various parts in a basal series. While McGuffy's readers were by single authors, current readers have numerous contributors. The current Ginn Rainbow Edition has one senior author, eight consultants, eighteen coauthors, and a number of classroom teachers and consultants who had a part in developing lesson plans and other materials in the teacher's edition (Aukerman, 1981, p. 79).

There are still other ancillary components, which Aukerman (1981) describes in his book, *The Basal Reader Approach to Reading*. I strongly recommend that prospective and practicing reading teachers consult this book for further valuable information on current basal reading series.

Purposes of Basal Readers

In an attempt to assess the primary goals of basal readers, one may ask what the purposes were of the first basal readers compared to those of current basal readers.

The aims of the first readers, as attested to in the preface of McGuffy's *Eclectic Primer* (1881/1909), were elocutionary delivery and expressive oral reading, no matter if the alphabet-phonetic or word method was used.

McGuffy's *Fifth Eclectic Reader* (1879/1920) reminds teachers that "the great object to be accomplished in reading is rhetorical exercise, is to convey to the hearer, fully and clearly, the ideas and feelings of the writer" (p. 9). Teachers are given additional and precise directions on how to prepare young readers to communicate the writer's thoughts and feelings: "Before attempting to read a lesson, the learner should make himself fully acquainted with the subject . . . and endeavor to make the thought and feeling and sentiments of the writer his own" (p. 9).

McGuffy's *Sixth Eclectic Reader* (1879/1921) states clearly and precisely that, "in reading, we do well to propose ourselves definite ends and purposes. The more distinctly we are aware of our own wants and desires in reading, the more definite and permanent will be our acquisition" (pp. 457, 458). A recent statement on the same matter does not sound much different. Turner (1983) advises: "Approaching a reading task, a child needs to have identifiable and direct reasons for reading" (p. 207).

On the matter of oral reading and understanding, McGuffy's comments are clear and distinct. On the same matter of oral reading and understanding,

Frank Smith (1982) conveys emphatically a similar message that "print cannot be read aloud in a comprehensible way unless it is comprehended in the first place" (p. 71).

Whether two hundred years old or current, basal readers share the same goals: to teach children to read and to teach them to want to and to love to read.

Authors of today's basals also point out how to accomplish the task of learning to read and reading to learn. Suggestions include reinforcing phonics and teaching letter-sound relationships supported by contextual clues. These are assumed to help in word identification and in determining which words fit the context best. Other suggestions single out the teaching of study skills in addition to and together with reading skills, particularly those that are needed in subject-matter areas.

Authors and publishers of basal readers do not leave much to chance in assisting teachers to reach the stated goals. With the help of diagrams and flow charts, each step in the suggested teaching procedure is named, relationships from one to another step are shown, and each step is fully described as to when to do what and how. Although proposed steps in teaching procedures do vary, some commonalities in procedural steps can be identified. They begin with preassessment of a skill to be taught, followed by teaching that skill, which then is practiced and applied. As soon as students are expected to have learned that skill, a postassessment is administered to show skill mastery. Students who have mastered it receive reading materials for enrichment and enjoyment; those who fell short of mastery receive reading materials for reteaching and reinforcing apparent shortcomings.

To further aid reading teachers in meeting the goals, programs may offer other components and strands. Instructional components may consist of the readiness strand, the word-identification strand, the vocabulary-development strand, the comprehension strand, the language strand, and the study-skills strand. To assess what students know before new learning begins and to assess what they should and do know after learning has occurred, preplacement and postplacement tests are included in the basal reader packages. Tests are either in booklets, on duplicating masters, or both.

Basal Readers and Subject-Matter Textbooks

From the preceding discussion of basal readers, it can be safely concluded that basals are not one single book but a whole package of hard- and soft-cover books accompanied by supplementary materials of many kinds. In contrast, a textbook is usually a single book. *The Random House Dictionary* (1968) defines a textbook as "a book used by students as a standard work for a particular branch of study" (p. 1359), and Harris and Hodges (1981) define a textbook as "a book on a specific subject matter used as a teaching–learning guide, especially in schools and college" (p. 328).

These two definitions make it clear that there are some major differences between textbooks and basal readers. How are they different, and how are they similar?

Differences Between Basals and Textbooks. Almost everything that basal packages are in their physical appearance, arrangement, and composition; their instructional intentions and purposes; and their literary components, subject-matter textbooks are not. While basals intend to teach children to read, textbooks assume that students already can read. They differ in the size of print they use and in their choice of vocabulary, sentence length, and in-sentence structure.

Basals have short often fragmentary sentences; other reading materials have longer, more complex sentences. In basals it is assumed that beginning readers can read and understand fragmentary and short sentences more easily than nonfragmentary, longer ones. Research, however, has found that short, fragmentary sentences often are difficult for beginning readers to understand (Malicky, 1975–1976). To ascertain meaning from fragmentary forms of sentences, children must rely to a much greater extent on their ability to infer what is not explicitly stated. Thus, it is much easier to extract meaning from cohesive sentences. Pearson and Camperell (1981) warn that textbook writers "should not be led to false conclusions that writing becomes more readable when complex sentences are chopped in half" (p. 48).

Textbooks feature the actual and sometimes original works of one or a group of authors under a designated editorship. Textbooks give specified accounts of a specialized subject in a special field of study and address themselves to this area and this area only.

Furthermore, textbooks show little or no control over sentence diversification, choice and use of vocabulary words, or the literary expressions with which the often-complex sentences are formed. Special subject areas often come with their own lexical and syntactic idiosyncrasies, to which readers need to bring appropriate semantic and nonvisual information in order to match the context of the intended communication.

Textbook teaching often invites lecturing, where students attempt to take notes listening at the same time to the oral delivery of the message. Textbooks offer no prescribed instructional procedures to be followed and applied. Rather, how textbooks are used before, during, and after instruction and how textbook contents are offered to the students rests with the teachers of each subject area. Individual textbook chapters have no predesigned lesson plans and elaborate practice exercises for students to use in catching up when they need to. Assistance, however, in assessing what students should and have learned comes often in the form of a study guide that accompanies a textbook, or in special questioning sections that follow textbook chapters.

Students who are to read the textbooks and to learn by reading them need abilities in reading that reach beyond those needed in reading and understanding stories in basal readers. Mention must be made that the often-concise, brief, and terse language in which some textbooks are written may be a disadvantage to students who are to read them. Alvermann and Boothby (1982) found in their study that students in grade four who are at the transition stage in reading may "fail to comprehend because of insufficient information," that is, because of "the terseness of some texts" (p. 301).

Advanced reading abilities are essential to reading, understanding, and interpreting tables, diagrams, and formulas; to processing concepts pertaining to particular subjects; and to plucking out, quickly and efficiently, specific, detailed information. Together with advanced reading skills, students need study skills that will assist them in working independently and learning intelligently.

Similarities Between Basals and Textbooks. Similar to both basal and nonbasal reading materials is, of course, the print, which in varying surface structures carries the encoded thoughts of the writer. Easily recognized high-frequency or "service" words facilitate the extraction of meaningful information from print when they are placed within and connected to other patterns of words within sentences and paragraphs. Further, common to reading in basals and nonbasals, yet different in demand and expectation, is the nonvisual information readers bring to the visual patterns of the text. The readers' abilities and proficiencies in bringing together text and personal information serve but one common purpose in reading different materials on different levels of difficulty: to process print and to understand its message. Selective attention, concentration, and willingness to begin, to follow, and to complete a reading task, no matter how simple or complex, are requirements needed in reading all sorts of materials.

Summary

The primary purposes of basal readers are to teach children to read and to encourage them to love to read. These purposes have not changed over the years since basals were first introduced, even though the content and packaging have undergone dramatic change. Basals are very different from subject-matter textbooks in their approach and content, but they share some similarities in the basic way that information is encoded and in the skills the reader must develop to process print and extract its meaning.

CONTENT READING

Whenever people read, they read about something. That something is the content matter of a story, a poem, a book, or any other discourse. The content may be as broad and general in scope as "Controlling the Manufacture of Food" or as narrow and specific as "Incomplete Metamorphosis."

The *content* is the ideas or the subject matter that are found in a book. *Content area* is an organized body of knowledge, also called a discipline, or a branch of instruction or learning (Harris & Hodges, 1981, p. 67). This organized body of knowledge has its own special and technical vocabulary, as in mathematics, science, and social studies. Readers must be able to grasp these vocabularies and match the corresponding concepts with the schemata that represent the generic concepts stored in their memories.

Content-Area Knowledge

The following examples—from plant life in biology; mining in social studies; and points, lines, and angles in geometry—may clarify why content areas need special vocabularies to communicate special knowledge and why readers need to possess special vocabularies to process special knowledge.

In biology, students read that xylem, phloem, and cambium are part of the fibrovascular bundles in the dicot stem. Students learn in social studies that iron ore is smelted from rock and mixed with other minerals to make steel. They learn in geometry that a vertical line is a straight line that is perpendicular to the horizon.

What is the specialized knowledge or nonvisual information that readers must bring to those specialized fields of study in order to understand its content fully?

First, seeing in the biology textbook the technical word *xylem* and then attempting to pronounce it may prove to be difficult if a reader is not certain whether the sound of *x* is that of *eks* in *x-rays*, *z* in *xylophone*, or *ks* in the word *ox*. Similar difficulty may be experienced with the technical word *phloem* if the vowel cluster brings to mind the more common word *shoe*.

Second, nonprinted but specialized knowledge is needed to understand (1) that fibrovascular bundles are an aggregate of strands of special conductive tissues, which in turn are an aggregate of similar cells that form a definite kind of structure in the plant; (2) that phloem is on the outside of the stem, xylem on the inside, and the cambium in between; and (3) what the functions of fibrovascular bundles are in dicot and in monocot stems and how they are different in the two kinds of stems.

Other specialized knowledge in the form of nonvisual information must be brought to the text by the reader who wishes to understand the social studies and geometry examples. Nonvisual and visual information together will assist the reader in knowing what is done in smelting rock and what is a line perpendicular to the horizon.

From these examples, it becomes obvious that word knowledge is a requisite for reading comprehension (Anderson & Freebody, 1981, p. 110) and that difficult vocabulary that is not known may decrease reading comprehension (Freebody & Anderson, 1983, p. 293). Readers who have extensive knowledge of the subject area in question are able to recall larger amounts of information and to give more accurate accounts of the content than those who do not (Spilich, Vesonder, Chiesi, & Voss, 1979). Likewise, readers must have schemata that are relevant to the topic, as these will increase and improve comprehension and recall (Bransford & Johnson, 1973).

Summary

In processing content materials, readers need, in addition to general reading skills acquired in the early school years, advanced reading skills in decoding, lexical access, and text organization (Golinkoff, 1975–1976). The foregoing discussion suggests that less-skilled readers may have to rely to a greater extent on the intermediate steps of recoding, decoding, and comprehension; while skilled readers may move more directly from lexical accessing to text organization (Bradshaw, 1975).

ORGANIZING INSTRUCTION FOR READING COMPREHENSION

As stated often in this book, the primary aim in reading is to comprehend. Yet evidence in the professional literature shows that students are still experiencing serious difficulties in comprehending what they read (M. S. Smith, 1975). This, of course, is experienced in every classroom where reading is taught. Basal readers—in spite of their extensive and expensive hardwares and softwares, which comprise all that should be needed to learn to read and to comprehend—apparently fall somewhat short in what they claim to deliver.

How can it be that what should be taught—reading comprehension—is not taught?

Durkin, in two successive research studies (1978–1979, 1981), found that what is believed to be widespread comprehension instruction in basal and subject-matter reading, particularly in social studies, may in fact be noninstruction in comprehension. Durkin documented that much of teacher effort and time is spent with assessment, not with teaching comprehension. Comprehension assessment focuses on the *product*, while comprehension instruction focuses on the *process* of comprehending (Durkin, 1981, p. 519). Comprehension assessment is directed toward finding out what students should know, do know, and do not know. In an attempt to satisfy these assessments, much of student time is consumed by getting the right answers and completing assignments.

To this obvious and observable dilemma, F. R. Smith (1978–1979), in a reply to the Durkin study, boldly suggested that one of the fatalistic assumptions of teachers is "the all too commonly held view that reading is really separate, different and apart from other things which are taught in schools" (p. 537). Emphasis must be placed on reading as an integral component of all subject-matter study! It is not just another "subject" given in school at a prescribed time. Instead reading cuts across all other disciplines and is needed to study them!

Professional literature and research have advanced certain techniques and strategies that may be used by teachers in instructing and by students in improving comprehension and recall. The techniques we will discuss here are prequestioning, advance organizers, previewing, self-generated questioning, and generative learning.

Prequestioning

Setting purposes most often results in prequestioning. That is, questions are raised before reading begins, to guide students through the reading selection. Marksheffel (1966) advises that "in the beginning, [the teacher] ask several pertinent questions that direct students' reading" (p. 35). Similar directions are given to the teachers by Stauffer (1969b) specifically, "to have pupils read with specific purposes in mind" (p. 96). I also proposed some years ago (Taschow, 1968) and still believe that questioning before reading should belong to the student, who "sets his own purposes and writes them down for his own reference" (p. 31).

Care must be taken, however, that the questions asked before reading are broad enough to leave plenty of room for other questions to develop. Otherwise, as Frase (1968) warned, it may result in rather narrow comprehension because students will read mostly to allocate answers to the prequestions. In doing so, other pertinent information may be overlooked.

What kinds of questions to ask was investigated by Wiesendanger and Wollenberg (1978). They found that when a group of grade-three students were exposed to factual prequestioning, they performed less well in comprehension than when exposed to inferential prequestioning. Under factual prequestioning, they also performed less well than a control group that received no prequestioning. Thus, the level of prequestioning may influence reading comprehension.

Advance Organizers

These are defined by Ausubel (1978), as "introductory material at a higher level of abstraction, generality, and inclusiveness than the learning passage itself" (p. 252). Organizers are "pedagogic devices to help . . . [bridge] the gap between what the learner already knows and what he needs to know if he is to learn new material most actively and expeditiously" (Ausubel, 1980, p. 246). In an earlier study, Ausubel and Fitzgerald (1965) demonstrated that organizers facilitate "learning and retention of totally unfamiliar material for those subjects who have relatively little verbal ability" (p. 297). A prerequisite, however, is that this introductory material be well organized and mastered.

Consider the following example to explain how advance organizers can help students to master new material. The new lesson is about polygons, a geometric figure of five sides. A pedagogic device that will assist students to understand what polygons are and how they can be constructed would be the triangle they already know. Thus, the triangle becomes the advance organizer between something already known about and the new material to be learned. In an orderly way the teacher can add additional triangles to make a five-sided polygon.

Rickards (1975–1976) investigated what happens to comprehension when organizers are placed at intervals before and after segments of text. It was concluded that interspersed advanced organizers yield greater recall of passage information than either interspersed postorganizers or interspersed coordinate prestatements or poststatements (p. 617). Interspersed coordinate prestatements consist of facts directly taken from the related paragraphs and were presented just before every text segment of two paragraphs, while poststatements were of similar content and were presented immediately after every two paragraphs.

Previewing

In previewing a chapter in a book or a book itself, the reader inspects its content by thumbing the pages of the book to get an overview without, perhaps, noting small details.

Graves and Palmer (1981) studied the effects that previewing has on reading. They studied eighty fifth- and sixth-grade students, who were divided equally into high- and low-ability groups. Both groups used previews of about 400 words before reading two difficult stories. The researchers, who had written the previews, read them to the students before reading the actual stories. These previews provided a link between students' existing knowledge and the stories. Significant results ($p < .01$) showed that previewing assists both high- and low-ability students in improving comprehension of the actual text.

In a more recent study, Graves, Cooke, and Laberge (1983) report on the effects that previewing has on reading comprehension, recall, and attitudes when processing difficult stories. Forty students in grade seven who were reading at about third-grade level and thirty-two students in grade eight who were reading at about fifth-grade level were involved in this study. Results indicated students' performance increased significantly not only in factual and inferential comprehension but also in recalling the stories. It also was noted that students liked previewing and found it to be useful.

Self-Generated Questioning

Although self-generated or student-generated questioning has been discussed already in Chapter 6, it cannot be ignored as a self-initiated procedure that assists in organizing knowledge to improve reading comprehension.

André and Anderson (1978–1979) examined the effects when students generated comprehension questions themselves while studying prose materials. Their studies showed significant results from questioning with training and concluded that use of self-generated questions during study is most effective for students with lower verbal ability.

More recently, Cohen (1983) demonstrated that third-graders can be trained to generate questions aimed at the literal level of reading comprehension. The study concluded that "training in self-generating questions can start as early as the primary grades and that this type of training may improve students' comprehension of stories" (p. 775).

Generative Learning

In Chapter 6 I discussed Wittrock's model of generative learning (Linden & Wittrock, 1981). Now we will look at generating learning before, during, and after reading (Craften 1982). In this process, children verbalize what they know about the story before they start to read, thus becoming aware of how they can use information in their heads to anticipate what they are going to meet and how they can make their information useful to the text (p. 294). By anticipating and applying their information, children learn to use their schemata as well as their previous experiences to fit the writer's meanings.

During reading, children's concepts may be altered by receiving new information, which will be checked constantly against current knowledge in order to decide which information is or is not useful to the cause. In the process, difficult words may be left alone until further reading clarifies their meanings, or may be discarded as nonessential to a working understanding.

To show children that difficult words can be put on hold, Goodman and Burke (1980) encouraged them to replace well-known concepts with nonsense words until their reading and background experiences brought meaning to them (p. 295).

After reading, children should apply what they have learned first to writing and reporting and then to more reading and investigating of new but related topics.

Summary

Reading comprehension must be taught as an integral part of study in all disciplines. There are various techniques that may be used by both teachers and students to improve comprehension. These include prequestioning, advance organizers, previewing, self-generated questioning, and generative learning.

ACQUISITION OF GENERAL AND SUBJECT-AREA VOCABULARY

The importance of knowing the appropriate technical words and expressions in understanding content areas has been demonstrated earlier in this chapter. But special and technical words and expressions are also found in stories in the basal readers. Words like *desert, canyon, Indian, postcard, weathervane, rocket, satellite, apartment, building,* and many others may be in the children's listening and speaking vocabularies, but not yet in their reading and writing vocabularies.

Vocabulary load and vocabulary diversity increase when meeting words that are derived from language sources other than English. Content-area textbooks are filled with words and expressions coming into the English language from Greek, Latin, Persian, French, Arabic, Spanish, Italian, Dutch, American Indian, and other origins. A few examples of each are

 Greek: anthropology, graphic, morpheme, phoneme, psychology, thermograph
 Latin: apartment, calorie, career, depart, distribute, moderate
 Persian: check, divan, khaki, lilac, shawl, special
 French: ballet, beauty, finance, menagerie, perfume, village
 Arabic: alcohol, algebra, cipher, magazine (as in storehouse), zenith, zero
 Spanish: castanets, masquerade, potato, rodeo, tomato, tornado
 Italian: buffalo, brigade, model, piano, spaghetti, trombone

Dutch: brand, glad, mart (as in market), uproar, wagon, wind
American Indian: chipmunk, moccasin, moose, pow-wow, tepee, tomahawk

How word knowledge is acquired and how its acquisition is facilitated are areas of major importance in reading comprehension instruction. There are several hypotheses used to explain this process. Anderson and Freebody (1981) summarize the development of word knowledge and its importance in reading comprehension. Based on the available research, they propose three word-knowledge hypotheses: the instrumentalist, the aptitude, and the knowledge hypotheses.

Instrumentalist Hypothesis

The instrumentalist hypothesis assumes that the more words readers know the more they comprehend of what they read. The higher the scores they receive on vocabulary tests, the more words individuals know when they encounter them in the text. In contrast, the lower the score, the fewer words individuals know when they meet them in the text. Whatever the test score may be, once vocabulary knowledge is acquired, "it helps the reader understand text" (Anderson & Freebody, 1981, p. 81).

For instructional purposes, the instrumentalist point of view invites direct vocabulary learning. Readers who want to be successful in reading need systematic instruction in building a large bank of vocabulary, which reading programs must provide.

Aptitude Hypothesis

The aptitude hypothesis contends that individuals who have acquired and have access to large vocabularies comprehend more quickly and perhaps better because they possess superior mental agility. Again, measured on vocabulary tests, individuals who score high are said to have an agile mind, which may lead them to understand more readily than those scoring lower on similar tests. The aptitude position says that large vocabularies assure verbal ability, which "mainly determines whether text will be understood" (Anderson & Freebody, 1981, p. 81).

For instructional purposes, the aptitude point of view may lead to accepting a position that heredity is predominant to learning and little can be done to change the natural endowment readers bring to the reading task. A second position within this frame would be to encourage mental growth. Through greater exposure to language opportunities, efficiency in processing language will increase. When students receive these opportunities, they will acquire greater automatic performance of skills and subskills in reading. Hence, in choosing the second position within the aptitude hypothesis, the teacher "should try to maximize the amount of reading children do," particularly in view of "speed and efficiency of processing" (Anderson & Freebody, 1981, p. 86).

Knowledge Hypothesis

The knowledge hypothesis asserts that vocabulary is a reflection of the individuals' knowledge of their culture. Again, measured on vocabulary tests, high scores indicate that individuals have a deeper and broader knowledge of their culture than those who, while belonging to the same culture, produce lower scores. The knowledge position emphasizes understanding that goes beyond word meanings to include a "conceptual framework or schemata" (Anderson & Freebody, 1981, p. 82).

For instructional purposes, the knowledge hypothesis requires concept building rather than mere word learning. For example, the word *roof* in isolation can form the beginning of the concept *house* by association, as in *a house has a roof*. By associating the words *window* and *door*, a more complete concept emerges, as in *A house has windows, a door, and a roof*. In fact, conceptualizing in word knowledge will enable children to understand sentences that may not contain certain words. Children who know about doors that can be locked will likely understand when they read, *The children could not get out of the house*, which can then be interpreted as the children could not get out of the house because the door was locked.

The knowledge position, then, holds that new vocabulary should be acquired "in the learning of concepts, not just words" (Anderson & Freebody, 1981, p. 87).

Summary

The instrumentalist, the aptitude, and the knowledge hypotheses of word acquisition may be used in teaching general, special, and technical vocabulary, expressions, and idioms. In so doing, an eclectic approach is recommended in which no one hypothesis is followed to the exclusion of the others. Instead, hypotheses should be chosen according to the needs of the learners and the purposes of acquiring word knowledge. As Anderson and Freebody (1981) conclude, "No serious scholar in reading or related fields rigidly adheres to any one of these positions" (p. 89).

TEXTBOOK READING COMPREHENSION

New, unknown, and difficult words and expressions in the multiple fields of reading and learning throughout the elementary and secondary school grades may contribute to overloading readers with unrealistic demands for word knowledge. Some students may not be able to cope. Ability to cope may depend on (1) maintaining or regaining meaning, (2) fitting new words and concepts into existing ones, and (3) being able to work out one's own solution. The demands for vocabulary knowledge in the special study areas of mathematics, social studies, science, and literature will be discussed in this section.

Mathematics

Reading in mathematics and its related branches requires reading skills beyond those usually learned and encountered in basal readers. Symbols like $+$, $-$, $\times$, $\div$, ¼, 3½, .5, and -7 are unlike single sounds and words.

Young readers understand the word *and* when reading, *Mother and Joan go to town*. The same readers, however, may find it difficult to understand the verbal and symbolic *and* relationship in $1 + 1$, as well as when *and* is expressed as *increased by*, *plus*, or *add*. Symbols or mathematical tokens like $<$, $>$, and $\sqrt{}$ need phrase reading, as *is less than*, *is greater than*, and *the square root of*. While the word and concept *square* can refer to the mathematical meanings of (1) a number multiplied by itself or (2) a rectangle in which all sides are equal, it can also refer to a nonmathematical meaning such as square dance.

Reading the teen numbers 13 through 19 begins from the number on the right of the pair and moves to the left, while reading the numbers 21 to 99 follows the usual left-to-right progression. However, confusing directionality may result in reversing figure positions in two-digit numbers, where 42 may become 24.

Other difficulties may be experienced in mathematics' compressed language as in *divide 4 by 5* or *find the square root of 81*, or even when questions are expressed in no-word language, as in $\sqrt{81} = $?

Reading story-problems requires more than recognizing words visually and sounding them out. While most every word within the compressed language counts and must be read, each word must also be related to and interpreted within the context in which it is used.

To ascertain if students understand a story-problem before resorting to number computations, I recommend using these five questions: (1) What does the problem ask for? (2) What information does the problem give? (3) What kind(s) of mathematical computation(s) should be used to get the answer? (4) In what order should these mathematical computations be done? (5) How can the answer be verified? Verbalized answers will show whether or not the correct factual information is available and whether or not the student can relate the facts rationally in order to solve the problem (Taschow, 1972b, p. 313).

Social Studies

Reading in social studies for students in the elementary grades calls for words and concepts and reading-working skills that are not directly encountered and taught through the basal readers. The familiar concept of family will be enlarged to include Eskimo and Indian families, Asian and European families, all connected with specific names of places and countries.

Reading and learning of the similarities and differences regarding where families live, how they dress, what they eat, and what they do, leads to interchanging anthropological and sociological as well as geographic and economic views. Guided by the teacher, children move from home, neighborhood, and community to towns, cities, states, provinces, and countries that are represented on the map and the globe. Reading and learning about themselves and other people and about their country in relationship to other countries will develop their awareness and appreciation of intergroup and intercultural perspectives as bridges to global understanding (Torney, 1979).

Locating names of cities, states, countries, rivers, mountains, and lakes on the map and the globe constitutes basic yet special skills in social studies. These basic skills must grow into advanced skills of reading, understanding, and interpreting contour maps whose lines show the irregularities of land surfaces.

Further, students must learn how to search for and locate information from textbooks, encyclopedias, dictionaries, almanacs, government documents, and historical writings. Students must learn to read, understand, interpret, and communicate information given by tables, graphs, timelines, outlines, and maps.

To fuse these and other skills, social studies requires critical thinking in the pursuit of independent inquiry, analysis, synthesis, and evaluation of day-to-day and long-standing issues in the field (Crabtree, 1983).

Science

Reading in the sciences uses language to construct a precise and systematic way of looking at the world and understanding it.

Common words and their concepts, like culture, family, and zone, lose their generality when used for special scientific classification, in contrast to using the same words in social studies. Bacteria culture is different from

European culture, a dog (canidae) family is different from a Vietnamese family, and a torrid zone is different from a defense zone.

As in mathematics, scientific symbols compress language, and formulas use nonword language. Iron may be expressed as Fe, copper as Cu, water as H_2O, and phosphorous acid as H_3PO_3.

Another phenomenon in science is that new words are coined whenever new frontiers are opened up, as in space and underwater exploration.

Reading in the sciences, as Munby and Russell (1983) have pointed out, "uses language to construct a unique reality, and it is this uniqueness that sets science apart from other disciplines" (p. 167).

Literature

Reading in literature begins with the literary contents of the basal readers, where students read to understand, enjoy, and appreciate stories, fables, adventures, plays, and poems. With this modest literary encounter, much is left for special instruction in reading short stories, novels, dramas, poems, and other literary discourse.

Beginning with vocabulary knowledge, readers must become aware that knowing one single meaning of a word may not suffice in all cases, as in *The actor acted on the stage in act three, scene one*; *He acted behind the scene*; and *The act staged a scene of horror*. Words such as *act*, *stage*, and *scene*, common to literary works, take on different meanings depending on how words are used and positioned within sentences.

Knowing the lexical, direct, explicit meaning of a word—its denotation—and knowing the implied, suggested, nonliteral meaning of a word—its connotation (Harris & Hodges, 1981, pp. 82, 64)—are equally important. A home is a place of residence as well as a place of affection, comfort, and warmth.

Understanding the figurative language of similes, metaphors, allusions, and personifications leads to appreciation of diachronic linguistics, or how the English language changed through time (Burmeister, 1978). In this sense, diachronic linguistics can become an integral part of discussion throughout the elementary grades. Some words have been altered by amelioration, which elevates the meaning of words. A nice person was once an ignorant one, not an amiably pleasant one. Perjoration, on the other hand, has degraded the meaning of some words. A villain was once a simple farm worker or servant, not a malicious person.

Other language changes can be found in the example of the word *channel*, which began as a narrow body of water and has come to mean a selection one makes when watching TV. Specialization is the attempt to make language more precise, as in the expressions *a school of fish* and *a pack of wolves*.

To further comprehension in reading literature, students must learn to compose main ideas; recognize sequences; find details; classify, categorize, and order objects, events, and information; and learn to read symbols, charts, graphs, and maps. Of course, these reading-learning abilities cut across the other subject areas, with critical reading and thinking being no exception. However, the ultimate goal, though different from mathematics, science, and social studies, is to appreciate and enjoy the literary works of the great and world-renowned writers and poets.

Summary

Successful processing of larger segments of print in reading textbooks of various subject areas requires readers to possess large vocabularies of special words and expressions. These vocabulary demands will vary depending upon the subject area. We must agree with Goodman (1976) that "textbook reading, through the elementary years at least, probably requires considerable introductory, preparatory work on the part of the teacher" (p. 486).

CHAPTER 8

Teaching Reading

Purpose questions for this chapter:

- What is the Directed Reading Approach?
- What are other methods similar to the DRA?
- What are linguistic approaches to teaching reading?
- What is the Language Experience Approach?
- What is individualized reading?
- How can I use an eclectic approach in teaching reading?

INSTRUCTIONAL PROCEDURES

Instruction is what teachers are doing when teaching a lesson and imparting information. One who instructs uses methods, approaches, strategies, or techniques. Sometimes these terms are used distinctively, other times interchangeably. To avoid uncertainty (Munby, 1980; Stewart, 1979, 1980) and to let the readers decide for themselves which term to apply to which activity in teaching reading, I will explain each term in accordance with the *Dictionary of Reading and Related Terms* (Harris & Hodges, 1981).

A *method* is an instructional procedure that is well defined and specific and is used for reaching an educational objective (Harris & Hodges, 1981, p. 196). An *approach* is a general instructional procedure that may be used to reach an educational objective (p. 19). A *strategy* is a systematic plan for achieving a specific goal or result (p. 311), and a *technique* is the proficiency needed for a given skilled performance, that is, a systematic method used to handle a complex task such as teaching (p. 325).

Synthesizing the definitions, those who instruct should know appropriate techniques that fit strategies that are suitable to particular methods as well as to general approaches in teaching basal reading programs.

READING IN BASAL READERS: THE DIRECTED READING ACTIVITY METHOD

From the previous chapter, we know already what basal readers are. But what is basal reading? The *Dictionary of Education* (1959) explains that "basal reading is what is fundamental to reading aimed at the systematic development of reading ability by means of a series of books or other materials especially suitable for each successive stage of reading development" (p. 443). While this definition explains what basal reading is, readers also must know what its wider range of systematic development is. Herrick, Anderson, and Pierstorff (1961) expand on this by stating that basal reading is "concerned with all the fundamental habits, attitudes, and skills that are essential to effective silent and oral reading" (p. 166).

About twenty years later, May (1982) explained that basal reading programs use a "continuous-process" approach (p. 278) by presenting a series of stories that systematically increase in difficulty. The ever-more-difficult stories not only help children to learn to read but also to develop fundamental reading habits, attitudes, and skills. This learning is assured by following manuals and guidebooks, which give detailed lesson plans, state special objectives for guiding oral and silent reading, list questions for assessing reading comprehension, and suggest additional materials for reinforcement and enjoyment (Hittleman, 1983, p. 183).

There can be little doubt that basal reading programs are there to teach reading, both orally and silently, so that children can begin in grade one to learn to process print. While this is certainly the purpose or the overall objective, it can be divided into subobjectives that can be identified by smaller and smaller specific targets. Any suggested ordering, however, should not be assumed to represent a hierarchical order, for there is none. Nevertheless, when applying a top-to-bottom access, there is the overall objective of oral and silent reading with the intent to understand the text. This overall objective can be supported by promoting word recognition, comprehension, and the processing of nonvisual information in increasingly larger segments of print in the form of paragraphs and sentences. The main objective then can be divided into the smaller goals of processing print visually and orally. Visually, processing would go from text to paragraphs, sentences, letter clusters, and single letters. Orally, it would go from story to thought units, sound patterns, and single sounds.

With this background in mind, let us now examine in some detail one of the primary teaching methods used with basal readers: the Directed Reading Activity (DRA), also known as the Directed Reading Lesson (DRL). A method, as explained, is a well-defined and specific instructional procedure that is used for reaching an overall educational objective, in this case learning to read orally and silently with the intent to understand.

The three words, *directed reading activity*, spell out precisely what this method is all about. Advice, helpful information, and instruction are *directed* toward the extraction of meaning through *reading*, which must be pursued and accomplished through a vigorous *activity*.

The Directed Reading Activity has been described and discussed in the professional literature and in textbooks on reading beginning with Betts (1946) and has been "a feature of basal readers for decades" (Aukerman, 1981, p. 327).

The method can be traced back about 150 years, when Herbart (Graves, 1912, p. 183) and his disciples devised a teaching method including five formal steps: preparation, presentation, association, organization, and application (Smith & Dechant, 1961). To summarize, preparation involves getting the learners physically, emotionally, and mentally ready to learn. Presentation acquaints the learners with the materials to be acquired. Association connects, merges, and joins the new information, thoughts, ideas, feelings, and images with the already-existing ones. Organization relates the parts to the whole and places them in a systematic organic structure. Application puts to use what has been acquired and how it can be administered practically.

As described by Betts (1957) the Directed Reading Activity also involved five steps: (1) developing readiness, (2) guiding the first silent reading, (3) developing word recognition skills and comprehension, (4) rereading, and (5) following-up the book reading (p. 491). Over the years, the names of these steps have been changed slightly with some shifting in content, as Rubin's (1982) list shows: (1) preparing for reading, (2) guided silent reading, (3) guided oral reading, (4) discussion of material read, and (5) follow-up activities. In the following discussion I shall use the five steps taught to me by students of Betts.

Outline of the Directed Reading Activity

The Directed Reading Activity is suggested in most if not all teacher's manuals of basal series. The outline of the DRA and its steps and substeps is as follows:

I. Reading readiness
  1. Background experiences
  2. New, unknown, difficult vocabulary
  3. Setting purposes
II. Guided silent reading
  1. Students read silently
  2. Teachers observe
III. Comprehension check
  1. Teacher-student discussion
  2. Questioning
    a. Fact questions
    b. Vocabulary-meaning questions
    c. Inference questions

       IV. Rereading
           1. Silent
           2. Oral
       V. Application
           1. Research
           2. Interest
           3. Team
           4. Special needs

   As any method, approach, or model has its strengths and weaknesses, so has the DRA. Its strengths lie in its coherent body of principles and ideas. Its weaknesses are said to lie in the rigidity that results when each step is followed slavishly, which may "negate teacher/pupil originality and/or creativity" (Aukerman, 1981, p. 327).
   This criticism is valid for teachers of reading who do follow each step slavishly, but this is a problem that lies more with the teachers than with the method. Informed teachers of reading know that the potential of the DRA is that it can be adapted and adjusted to teach lessons not only in reading but also in subject-matter areas. The DRA can be adapted to and aligned with cognitive and psycholinguistic development so that reading may be taught at all skill levels. Dasch (1983) has demonstrated that there is a potential for positive change if teachers align "instructional practice with accepted theory without sacrificing the convenience of a basal series, and yet stay within required curriculum content" (p. 431).
   It is my recommendation teachers first must understand the theoretical background of the DRA and then apply it in practice. With experience, they will learn to adapt and adjust the DRA to fit the needs of their situations.

Describing and Interpreting the DRA

   In the following description and interpretation of the DRA, the same numbering as in the preceding outline is used to facilitate the identification of each step.
   I. *Reading readiness.* The overall objective of reading readiness is similar to preparation, Herbart's (Graves, 1912) first formal step—to get the whole child ready to learn a certain task. This objective has three-more subobjectives.
   I.1. *Background experiences.* Getting ready must begin with giving students the opportunity to reflect upon and explore their background experiences; that is, appropriate stored-up information must be retrieved from long-term memory.
   Reflecting and exploring background experiences tells what meaning,

nonvisual information, and schemata students bring to the new learning. At the same time, students become aware of their strengths, or what they know, and of their weaknesses, or what they do not know yet.

Of course, students must be taught to reflect on and explore their own storehouse of knowledge to find out for themselves what they do know and what they can contribute to the matter to be learned (see REIVA, Chapter 2). I have found that children in elementary grades know much more than they usually get credit for. When they reflect upon and explore their background experiences, this knowledge can be demonstrated.

The teacher should begin by modeling this behavior, as follows: Explain that you want to explore your own background experiences. Write a title, topic, or major idea on the chalkboard. Sit down so that all students can see you. Then begin to think out loud, talking as you think. Let the thoughts flow freely, but talk only when appropriate. Begin by systematically sorting out what may or may not apply to the topic. While sorting out the stored-up information, write it down on paper, telling the students why you are doing it—so that what you have recalled may not be lost as other retrievals rush in and crowd out the earlier ones.

Then, practice with the students. They must come to understand that reflecting and exploring is thinking; that thinking must be done individually; that no one can think for someone else; and that thinking needs concentration, silence, and time.

I.2. *New, unknown, difficult vocabulary.* Reflecting and exploring lead to discussing what is known. This verbal interchange provides, without affectation, the opportunity to introduce new vocabulary. Recall Goodman's (1976) recommendation that new words should always be introduced in context, which allows proper pronunciation and enunciation without distortion of the sound patterns. Students listen to the new word in context and check it against their listening and speaking vocabularies. They are then encouraged to use it vocally in their own speech patterns. In this way, new concepts can be formed and schemata built. When the correct sound patterns are in the students' ears, the new word is written on the chalkboard to show the visual letter arrangement. Visual perception of the word helps the students to recognize it when they see it again. While context overrules analysis (Brown, 1982, p. 31) and word-knowledge hypotheses interact, attention is still directed from the background of meaning to the conscious cognitive level of word identification.

Again, it should be emphasized that introduction of vocabulary should be interwoven with, not separate from, context. If new words are introduced in isolation from background experiences and context, this separation disregards the meaning base that students bring to the reading-learning situation and discourages active student participation.

I.3. *Setting purposes.* After new words are introduced, teachers and students are ready to set purposes. Setting purposes means forming questions that will assist in organizing meaning as well as text. This has been discussed in some detail in Chapter 6.

Setting purposes can begin with as short a title as *Birthday Party.* A leading question is formed, one that will generate further questions: What would you like to know about the birthday party? This will challenge students to ask questions of their own, which become the students' own purposes for reading. The emphasis is on the students' purposes, not the teacher's.

Purposes may be written on the chalkboard so students can use them to keep their reading on track.

II. *Guided silent reading.* The stage is set for guided silent reading. Purpose, interest, selective attention, and active involvement will guide students through the segments of print. Generally silent reading should precede oral reading (Betts, 1946, p. 85), as the latter is more complex and difficult (F. Smith, 1982, p. 72).

II.1. *Students read silently.* Students now read silently, eager to test their anticipation of the text by either accepting, modifying, or rejecting the purposes they set. The meaning students bring to the text will assist them in extracting more from it.

In my own experience I have found that all students, even those marked as "low performers," can read, provided they are given the opportunity to grasp the meaning and to gain some certainty about how new words look in shapes and letter clusters. Often I hear teachers say that in silent reading they cannot know whether students read all the words or not. Even if readers do skip some words, I think teachers should not get overly alarmed. How can any teacher know just which words the children really need in order to understand the meaning?

II.2. *Teachers observe.* Silent-reading time should not become an occasion for teachers to attend to administrative chores. While students read silently, teachers should observe students' silent-reading behaviors. Observing should be an intentional search for clues as to how students read. Teachers should watch out for excessive fingerpointing that stops at each word and may or may not be accompanied by excessive lip movement or even audible mumbling or vocalization. Any one or a combination of these actions may signal some sort of difficulty. If the behavior is observed, the teacher may be able to do something about it. If unobserved, however, it may mushroom into more serious reading difficulties.

Students found having difficulties during silent reading should be helped quietly and privately. Such assistance is given without engaging in teaching or reteaching, but by providing the information needed. Reteaching to remove the student's uncertainty is done later, during the application phase. The main objective at this point is to regain and maintain understanding of what is being read. However, the sensitive teacher will take note of the kind of assistance given, so that the student will receive the appropriate help at all stages.

III. *Comprehension check.* When silent reading is completed, students are ready to share what they think they have found out by testing their purposes against the text. The comprehension check should give students the opportunity to react to the reading they have done.

III.1. *Teacher-student discussion.* Discussion will center around the purposes set and extend to further question-investigation and -verification processing (see REIVA, Chapter 2).

In most classrooms, starting and continuing a discussion is almost always left to the teacher's initiative and, in fact, is thought of as being the teacher's role. Discussions thus are started by the teacher, who poses questions that are answered by the students, whose answers are evaluated by the teacher. Mehan, Cazden, Cotes, Fisher, and Maroules (1976) reported that, in a classroom in San Diego, California, 80 percent of the questions were asked and evaluated by the teacher. Kitagawa (1982), referring to the Mehan findings, reported how she shifted the role of questioning from teacher to students in her fourth- and fifth-grade classrooms in Tuscon, Arizona. Just as with purpose setting, explained earlier, teachers can begin with a leading question that is broad enough to let students create and initiate their own questioning. Kitagawa concludes from her experiences that "question creation is a basic process activity, useful with all aspects of the curriculum, which the teacher should make available to the students . . ." (p. 45).

III.2. *Questioning.* In this process, factual understanding should be secured first. Factual information forms the foundation for consciously lifting thinking to higher levels. Teachers model this process by guiding students from factual questions to vocabulary-meaning questions to inference questions.

When details are taken care of on the factual level such that the simple when, where, and who questions are exhausted, discussion can move to questions like, What does this mean? What does one do? How does one know? These will raise the thinking level by inviting students to think of meanings expressed in words and phrases in relation to larger units of print.

Lifting thinking to yet higher levels means guiding students to experience consciously how to answer what is not in print but is beyond it. Answers must be inferred by reorganizing the knowledge that is in the head, not what is spelled out in words. Such questions take these forms: What else may . . . ? How do you arrive at . . . ? How do you think . . . ? How do you respond to . . . ? Such questions require students to build on what is known and can be projected from the given data or premises. Raising thinking levels by involving students as question initiators, even though teacher guidance may be needed, integrates learning with the background experiences that students bring to the reading. Guiding questioning beyond the factual level will encourage critical thinking and evaluation, not just for often-artificial classroom learning but for real-life situations and encounters.

In questioning, language must be considered. When questions are asked, spoken language is used; when questions are written, visual language is used. Both modes of language are different from the social aspect. In regular day-to-day teaching, questions are asked and answered orally more often than in writing. Spoken language differs from written language in three important aspects (Farrar, 1983). First, in speaking, complete sentences are not always needed because gestures may substitute for utterances. Second, oral questions are an instrument of power because they demand a response. Being called upon to answer orally can become threatening to the answerer. Third, an oral question may imply a command, as in "Have you closed the door?" which really means, "If not, *do* it." Farrar advises teachers to be aware of these social aspects of spoken language and "to phrase questions so unthreateningly that students are encouraged to respond and so cleverly that students feel the knowledge was theirs from the beginning" (p. 374).

Discussion and questioning that include raising thinking levels are linked directly with and grow out of the purposes set, as they are tested through silent reading.

IV. *Rereading.* What should be done when, during comprehension check, responses sometimes are found to be different from the facts in the text? Rereading is the answer, as opposed to the usual teacher evaluation of "yes" and "no" or of checking out the answers with the answer key. While these commonly used forms of teacher evaluation appear to save time, they do not advance the teaching of comprehension, active mental involvement, and independent thinking. Product answers, which are either right or wrong, fail to develop the thinking process, or how we arrive at an answer.

Rereading makes the readers go back to the text; locate the information; check it against the given answer; and verify, modify, or reject it. An answer is not an answer until it is verified. Verification must be taught, and through repeated practice from grades one through twelve, it can become a life skill.

IV.1. *Silent.* When an answer is contended, the teacher should not play the all-knowing role and pronounce a yes or no verdict. Instead, students are asked to clarify what they need to know. This amounts to setting specific purposes that bring the uncertainty of the given answer into focus. With these specific purposes in mind, students skim the text to locate the area containing the information needed. This passage is reread silently and matched with the specific purpose.

IV.2. *Oral.* When students think they have found a match, one reader is selected to read aloud only that part of the print that contains the information.

This is the perfect occasion to involve oral reading after silent reading. It is oral reading with and for a special purpose. It is not the "robin-round" oral reading where one student begins to read aloud one sentence, followed by the next student in line. However, this is not to belittle the values of oral reading (Dallman et al., 1982). But oral reading in the form of rereading is guided by a special purpose—to support the verifying process.

V. *Application.* What has been learned through the preceding four steps now leads to application. Some students are ready to move to teacher-guided enrichment activities, while additional practice is needed by students who were observed earlier to have reading difficulties. Special practice activities can come from the various ancillary basal materials or they can be developed by the teacher. This is the occasion for giving functional help, not just drill exercises, to those who have not yet accomplished what is within their reach.

There are various ways in which students can apply their talents.

V.1. *Research.* This may be done by students who can work independently and have the curiosity and inclination to find out more on the topic under study. They can search the library for what they want to read. Later, they may be given the opportunity to report their research findings to their peers. This may spark further curiosity within the class.

V.2. *Interest.* Students may be stimulated to express themselves through painting, drawing, modeling, or writing a play or poem, which they may share with the class.

V.3. *Team.* The cooperative team approach may be initiated for students who have shown some weaknesses in reading, learning, and studying. Students are encouraged to form a team of three or four and, with the help of the teacher and additional learning materials, work together to correct their temporary shortcomings.

V.4. *Special needs.* There are a few students who need special help that cannot be satisfied in a team-helping approach. They need more of the teacher's time and effort. Although in many schools today there are special-assistance teachers or inschool tutors, they often have long waiting lists and do not always reach those who need this special help. At least for a time, these children must rely more than the others on the classroom teacher.

Special exercises are needed but often not found in basal materials. Thus, they must come from the teacher, who often does not have this kind of special knowledge and training. Also, these children may require special-needs assessments, from which special-needs prescriptions and appropriate remediation may be derived.

This completes our description of the Directed Reading Activity, which, when guided by teacher knowledge and experience, is more than a rigid step-by-step method. When properly used, the DRA provides the opportunity for students to evaluate their involvement in learning activities; to know what they want in a learning situation; and to develop their sense of discovering, grasping, and comprehending what is meaningful to them.

Instructional Practices Derived from the DRA

Numerous other text-related instructional procedures have been developed from the DRA. Of these, the most influential in the professional literature will be reviewed here.

The Directed Reading-Thinking Activity. Stauffer (1969a), in *Directing Reading Maturity as a Cognitive Process*, first proposed the Directed Reading-Thinking Activity (DRTA), which begins by identifying individual and group purposes, followed by adjusting the reading rate to the set purposes. While students read silently, teachers observe and, if needed, extend help in adjusting the reading rate to the stated purposes, to comprehension, and to word-recognition needs. After reading, the DRTA focuses on comprehension and finishes with fundamental skill-training activities such as discussion, further reading, additional study, and writing.

Each of the five major steps has many substeps; for instance, there are up to ten substeps under "observing the reading" and nine substeps under "identifying purposes of reading" (Stauffer, 1969a, pp. 41, 42). The main emphasis in this procedure appears to rest on setting the climate for a DRTA and directing its process through the frequent use of three questions: What do you think? Why do you think so? and Can you prove it? (p. 40).

ReQuest. ReQuest stands for reciprocal questioning, which indicates that at least two persons are needed to make it work. Manzo (1969), the originator, reported that this procedure was tested with remedial students with the hope of improving reading comprehension in a one-to-one remediation setting. To guide students through a reading passage, teacher and students read the first sentence silently. The student asks "questions first, then I [the teacher] . . . ask questions" (p. 124). Questions are asked with the book closed, and students are encouraged to ask "the kind of questions a teacher might ask in the way a teacher might ask them" (p. 124).

Guided Reading Procedure. Manzo (1975) advanced the Guided Reading Procedure (GRP), which is built around the four subskills of unaided recall, recognizing implicit questions, self-correction, and organization. Seven steps, intended for application of these subskills, are said to be particularly suited for group teaching and content-area reading.

The GRP begins with readiness by setting a specific content purpose that is followed by reading silently so that a student "remembers all that he can" (Manzo, 1975, p. 290). In step two, students recall all they can, while teachers write on the chalkboard in abbreviated form all that is possible. In step three, whenever students become aware of faulty information or incomplete recall, they are permitted to reread and to correct. In step four, information is organized, perhaps in outline format. This is followed in step five by specific teacher questioning that requires synthesizing of the new with the previous learning, which may contribute to transfer. Step six is one of testing students' short-term memory with conventional teacher-made or publisher-prepared tests of multiple-choice, matching, or true–false questions. The final step, though optional, asks students to deliberate over and manipulate what has been learned and to check periodically their long-term memory (pp. 289–291).

The Experience-Text-Relationship Method. This method, suggested by Au (1979), begins with an experience sequence exploring what children already know about the story to be read. After students have read a text sequence of one to two pages, teachers ask questions and challenge readers to procure the correct answers. The final step is the relationship sequence, in which teachers attempt to "draw relationships for the children between the context of the story discussed in the sequence and their outside experience and knowledge" (p. 678).

Semantic Webbing. Semantic webbing (Freedman & Reynolds, 1980) concentrates on questioning and inquiry. Webbing begins with the core question, which the teacher chooses, followed by the web strands in the form of the students' answers, which are supported by the story information. Finally, the web is tied together by the relationships among the various strands. Six basic steps comprise process webbing (pp. 678–682).

Webbing begins with setting a purpose for reading, which encourages students to decide on a reading-thinking strategy and what part of the story to use. Based on these two prerequisites, teachers ask the core question and elicit responses from the students. Answers, or the web strands, must be supported by the story. If students fail to recall the information, they reread to find supporting details or major ideas. In the last two steps, teachers guide students in establishing interstrand relationships and in applying what they have learned to construct a new web.

Summary

The Directed Reading Activity, with its well-established and well-ordered format for teaching reading, has commanded teacher fidelity through the decades. Although its format is based on sound psychological and educational principles (Spiegel, 1981), moving in a slavish ritual through the five substeps results in meaningless instruction. Consequently many DRA-related teaching practices have been developed that offer variations that can bring life to reading comprehension instruction and help to discourage routine reading-comprehension assessment dominated by teacher questioning.

READING IN LINGUISTIC READERS

Two linguistic reading series feature prominently among the basals: the 1980 Merrill Linguistic Reading Program, published by Charles E. Merrill Publishing Company, and the 1981 Lippincott Basic Reading series, published by J. P. Lippincott Company. The Merrill Linguistic Reading Program is based on the scholarly research of the late Dr. Charles E. Fries, who was one of the best-known linguistic scholars in North America. The Lippincott Basic Reading series is under the authorship of the late Dr. Glenn McCracken and Dr. Charles C. Walcutt.

Auckerman (1981), in describing the Merrill Linguistic Reading Program, concludes that it is "a no-nonsense, highly structured, linguistically controlled, sequential program of instruction, based on language patterns and reading materials exclusively within those patterns" (p. 236).

Linguistic readers emphasize spelling patterns and their phonemic composition. Regularly recurrent patterns of the English language serve as bases to which initial consonants are added. For instance, to the language bases *-at* and *-an* may be added initial consonants like *c, d, f, m, r,* and *s,* with the resulting words *cat, fat, mat, rat,* and *sat,* and *can, Dan, fan, man,* and *ran.* As soon as the words are learned, reading composed of these words can begin, as in *A man ran, A fat cat ran,* and *Dan ran.*

The 1981 Lippincott Basic Reading series introduces five short vowel sounds that permit the use of CVC or consonant-vowel-consonant patterns (see Chapter 4). These patterns comprise the major part of the linguistic approach to reading. By introducing, for instance, *a, e, n, r,* and *d,* CVC patterns can be formed as in *ran, dad, Nan, Dan, Ned,* and *den,* as well as the words *and* and *add.* Once the CVC patterns are learned, little stories can be made, like *Nan and Dad ran* and *Nan and Dan ran.* If special linguistic elements are needed, they are practiced in context, as in *Dan is in the den.*

To increase vocabulary knowledge, linguistic approaches use minimal pairs, substitutions, and phonograms. Minimal pairs are two words that have minimal contrast between them, as in the words *bin* and *pin*, which differ in only the initial phoneme. Further minimal contrast is experienced in the final consonants of the words *rib* and *rip*, and the medial vowels of the words *pan* and *pen* (Durkin, 1978, p. 267). In the substitution method, initial, medial, and final phonemes are substituted, as in the words *can* to *pan, cat* to *cut*, and *fat* to *fan*. Phonograms are vowel-consonant combinations that appear frequently in words. Phonograms like -an and -at were already exemplified. Other phonograms are *-it*, as in the words *bit, fit, kit, pit*, and *sit*; as well as the phonogram *-ight* in *fight, light, might, right*, and *sight*.

However, it should be noted that minimal discrimination, substitution, and phonograms are part of the basic reading skills that are taught in all reading instruction and are not exclusive to linguistic readers.

Linguistically based reading series present controlled, drill-directed phonics instruction as a means for learning to read language patterns. They assume that regular recurrent language patterns give readers, particularly beginning readers, the confidence and certainty they need in knowing that a total spelling pattern represents a certain word and corresponds to a certain sound pattern.

Summary

The purpose of the linguistic reading programs is to control learning to read by sequencing regularly recurrent spelling patterns that correspond to equally recurrent sound patterns. It is believed that these regularly occurring language patterns, beginning with a language base, lead the children to learn to read, spell, and write with ease and confidence.

OTHER APPROACHES TO TEACHING READING

In addition to the methods of teaching reading discussed so far, there are other methods and approaches that can be used to teach reading in the elementary grades. These methods and approaches, with their strategies and techniques, are sometimes in sharp contrast to the basal and related methods because they are less book bound, more dependent on teacher knowledge, and more student centered.

The Language Experience Approach

The rationale for the Language Experience Approach (LEA) is based on Allen and Allen's (1966) assertion that children who write must be able to read. As he put it, "What I can think about, I can say. What I can say, I can write. What I can write, I can read. I can read what I can write and what other people have written for me to read" (p. 21).

The Language Experience Approach is based on the oral language that children use in telling about their experiences and actions. "The mere fact," wrote Piaget (1960), "of telling one's thought, of telling it to others, or of keeping silence and telling it only to oneself must be of enormous importance to the fundamental structure and functioning of thought in general and of child logic in particular" (p. 64). These thoughts are the very underpinnings of the Language Experience Approach. They are its rationale or, as Allen (1973) expressed it, the formula for its implementation (p. 158). The LEA brings children's oral language together with listening and speaking, with reading and writing, and with all verbal or nonverbal communication skills.

The LEA begins with children telling what they have experienced while peers and the teacher listen. Together they discuss and organize the content and dictate the most interesting part of the story to one who can write, usually the teacher. The story is written on a large sheet of paper known as the experience chart, which becomes the heart of learning to read.

While the teacher is writing, students watch how each oral utterance is slowly converted into symbols and how oral sounds look when written down. The emphasis is not on recoding letters and words into sounds; rather, it is on encoding children's thoughts into visual forms. Children actually see with their own eyes how the relationship between oral language (speech) and written language (reading) develops into "talk written down." This visualization brings the realization that personal thoughts, which are not seen, can be organized and expressed in writing, which can be seen, for the child and others to read. The experience chart becomes the basic tool for developing word recognition, word analysis, sight vocabulary, context clues, and comprehension, together with speaking, reading, and writing vocabularies.

These subskills of reading will develop when students begin to use the chart in reading and writing what they have dictated. Writing and reading interact and support each other. Immediate visual feedback is received as each letter is formed in accordance with the whole-word pattern that has been perceived. Writing involves, first, looking intensively at the word as a whole, then at its internal arrangement of strings of letters. The word is imprinted on the mind, enabling the reader to write it down without looking back at the chart. Transforming spoken language into written language involves transforming the total sound pattern into a total visual pattern in which each letter character and each word has its appropriate graphic form and position within a word or within a sentence. Often that means knowing when sound patterns are different or not different from their corresponding visual patterns.

Since vocabulary words are not controlled as they are in the basals, word recognition gains in importance. To strengthen word recognition certainty, words from sentences will be looked at and inspected for similarities and differences in their visual appearance, and they will be listened to in like manner for their sound patterns. However, difficulties in teaching word recognition may arise because there is no sequential subskills chart that will tell which letter, sounds, letter clusters, sound clusters, and words to introduce at what time. Knowing or not knowing this rests with the professional knowledge and experience of the teacher.

When students dictate their stories, they use their language. With no systematic structured language expansion, little or no further development will occur. Therefore, with teacher guidance, speaking, reading, and writing vocabularies as well as syntactic information must be kept on the increase so that students learn to express their thoughts more effectively in oral and written language. That is, in the Language Experience Approach, students must learn the same reading abilities through nonbook-controlled methods that they would learn in the basal reading programs through tightly controlled reading methods.

With these basic thoughts in mind, let us consider the following lesson using the Language Experience Approach.

In our scenario, the children have visited a circus performance. While the children recall their experiences and discuss them, the teacher writes on the chalkboard those utterances that belong to the circus experience. Utterances like tent, circus, clowns, crowd, elephants, lions, and band are written down for further use. Then the teacher guides the students to establish a framework within which the story will be written on the experience chart. The story skeleton may look like this:

Driving to the circus.
What we saw.
How we felt.
Coming back to school.

In developing the story, all students should be involved in composing sentences that belong to the circus, make sense, and are spoken for all to hear. The teacher will write the story on the experience chart, perhaps beginning like this:

Yesterday we went to the circus.
The circus was in a big tent.
Many people were there.
Four clowns came jumping in.
Two black bears danced.

As soon as the first sentence is written, the teacher calls on the child who has said this sentence. The teacher points to the words while the child is attempting to read them aloud. The same procedure is repeated until the story is considered finished. To practice oral reading, first the whole story and then sentences and phrases are read. While individual and group oral reading are encouraged and praised, help is also given in visually recognizing and vocally pronouncing words, phrases, and sentences. These skills are evaluated and improved constantly, in order to assure children's progress in reading.

In sum, the Language Experience Approach is a powerful method (Moffett & Wagner, 1983) that offers children the chance to watch their words being written down, to synchronize spoken words with written words, to remember their own words and those of others that were written down, and to be exposed to the quantity and quality of sentences that make a whole, meaningful story.

Individualized Reading

The individualized reading instruction approach should not be confused with individualizing reading instruction. *Individualized reading* is an organized approach in which reading instruction is adjusted to the students' needs. *Individualizing reading* can be a part of any program (Farr & Roser, 1979) and can be used at any time while teaching reading.

The first attempt to individualize instruction was made in New York around 1890 when students, then called "laggards," who were falling behind instruction were coached to catch up with it. This plan called for two teachers in one room; one teacher to conduct classes, the other to supervise study activities (Betts, 1957, p. 37). Later in 1913, Burk at the San Francisco Normal School devised a plan for individual instruction that was based on individual progress and promotion (Betts, 1957, p. 39). This plan developed in 1926 into the Winnetka plan, which emphasized self-instruction, self-corrective practice materials, diagnostic tests to measure progress, individual subject promotion based on individual achievement and on group and creative activities. Later, in the 1950s, Jeanette Veatch and Philip Acinapuro (1966) became the major proponents of this approach.

The principles of self-selecting, self-seeking, self-pacing and self-evaluating (Zintz, 1975, p. 106), not only reflect the objectives of fifty years ago but are also the hallmarks of today's approach to individualized reading. "Individualized" implies that there are no special reading materials needed, no prescribed step-by-step skill sequences, no controlled language in terms of vocabulary and sentence structure and length, and no teacher's manuals to follow.

Instead, materials used are the books in the school library and classrooms, which the students select themselves. Subskills to reading are taught when children need them and, as in the Language Experience Approach, depend on teacher knowledge. Teacher-student conferences, teacher record keeping, and special time arrangements are part of the common-sense instructional and managerial classroom organization used in this approach.

To use individualized reading, the four principles listed above must be observed. Let us discuss each one briefly.

1. *Self-selecting.* Individualized reading evolves around a large collection of reading materials that must meet students' interests and wants as well as their learning needs. Children's books on family life, adventure, travel, mystery, boys and girls, fairy tales, legends, games, and more must be readily available to make this first principle, self-selection, possible.

   However, teachers have a role to play in student's self-selecting. Teachers must assist in matching reading materials to students' reading abilities. While students will select what they like to read, sometimes liking supersedes reading ability, which may jeopardize the self-selecting principle.

2. *Self-seeking.* While reading what was self-selected, children will meet new words that may be difficult. They need to seek out additional information in dictionaries, glossaries, encyclopedias, and other reference materials. Self-seeking, the second principle, is particularly important when the teacher is unavailable to the students during student-teacher conference periods. Otherwise, students will receive help when they ask for it.

3. *Self-pacing.* Self-pacing, means pacing one's own progress and achievement at a more-or-less steady rate from one student-teacher conference to the next. During each conference, teacher and student plan explicitly what to read, write, practice, study, and accomplish. Although the teacher keeps the student record, the student knows exactly what will be expected in the next conference.

   In this way, the teacher can assist students to self-pace according to ability. Since students are not encouraged to compete with peers by being segregated into average, above-average, and below-average groups, self-pacing allows students to respond to their individual abilities and progress in processing print.

4. *Self-evaluating.* While in conference, teachers assist students in evaluating their own progress and achievement, which is recorded in separate folders. It contains the work accomplished and in progress, the reading goals to be attained, word recognition and comprehension skills mastered and yet to be learned, materials read, and whatever special information will need attention in future conferences. Self-evaluating, the fourth principle of individualized reading, makes students aware of what they know and of what they have yet to learn in order to reach their set goals.

Of prime importance in individualized reading, however, is what students understand and recall about ideas, events, and characters met in the reading materials and how they can relate their ideas to what they have read. Teachers will encourage children to dramatize, draw, write, and use other creative means to express, enjoy, and appreciate what they have learned and how they feel about it. Proponents of individualized reading argue that, if children continue to grow in reading comprehension by understanding, interpreting, and integrating what they have read, there should be no need to teach reading skills in isolation.

In sum, individualized reading may be an alternative attractive to teachers because it focuses on the individual, yet it demands the quantity and quality of reading materials necessary to meet readers' interests and needs. It calls for extensive and careful teacher planning and record keeping and for the willingness to meet each student in a highly organized conference session. It calls for teachers who themselves are avid readers, who know how to teach the reading subskills when they are needed, and who have that personal commitment to individualized reading that becomes not only the mover but also the inspirer.

Individualized reading places additional demands on an already-demanding school day and a busy teacher. To alleviate this, a modified individualized reading approach is suggested that makes use of small-group settings of three to six students, grouped differently for different purposes. Allen (1983, p. 48) suggests that students in small groups can still select their own reading materials, set their own reading pace, seek information, and evaluate their progress and achievement.

Summary

In contrast to the linguistic reading series, the Language Experience Approach and individualized reading instruction have no prescribed, sequenced readers or teacher's guidebooks that direct instruction in teaching reading. Both approaches depend instead on teacher knowledge and willingness to take on the responsibilities of planning, organizing, and teaching reading in a mutually enhancing environment in which teacher and students are learning partners.

ECLECTIC APPROACHES TO TEACHING READING

It is beyond the scope of this book to describe additional approaches to teaching reading in the elementary classrooms. However, we must ask whether or not there is a best method for teaching reading that is appropriate for all students in any given classroom. The simplest and most obvious answer is that, of course, there is no one best method. A similar statement could be made about the many basal reading series: There is no one that is best for every student. A more feasable and workable answer is to try an eclectic approach.

What is an eclectic approach to reading? It is "any approach or method of teaching reading that draws upon and combines other . . . approaches or methods" (Harris & Hodges, 1981, p. 98). From experience in and knowledge of teaching reading, the teacher selects desirable aspects from a number of methods and combines them into an instructional procedure (Burns & Roe, 1980b). Rubin (1982) suggests "that the best reading program is one that incorporates an eclectic-pragmatic approach . . . [in which] teachers use skill and ingenuity to mold any approaches into a workable whole" (p. 280).

Eclecticism requires teachers who are competent and courageous, who make choices and decisions based on the understanding that no one single method and no one single book can serve the diversity of student capabilities—individual and collective—found in any given classroom. Eclectic approaches enable teachers to grow beyond clinging to manuals and guidebooks that limit their freedom to choose. Finally, considering the widespread differences in reading abilities and interests and in languages used in today's classrooms, it appears reasonable to suggest that eclectic approaches in teaching reading to beginning and advanced readers may stand up the best under the test of time.

Assessing Ranges in Reading Abilities

Not all students in any given grade read equally well, even though they are in the same classroom. Teachers should know the ranges of reading achievement within their grade or classroom. As students progress through the grades, the range of their reading abilities within a single grade widens. Betts (1957, p. 583) reported that, for example, in grade five some students may be able to read materials only at the first- and second-grade levels, while a few others may read at a twelfth-grade level. A formula that I picked up years ago and have used on many occasions can assist teachers in calculating approximate reading ranges in grades one through twelve. The calculation is as follows:

$$\text{reading range} \cong \text{grade level} \pm \frac{\text{grade level} + 1}{2}$$

For example, what is the approximate reading range in a fourth-grade classroom?

$$4 \pm \frac{4+1}{2} = 4 \pm \frac{5}{2} = 4 \pm 2.5$$

which approximates a reading range from 1.5 to 6.5.

How, then, can some students in grade four be expected to read in a book designed for this grade level, when they can read only at about a second grade level? The inevitable answer is to try to use an eclectic approach that includes multilevel reading materials.

An Example of an Eclectic Approach

This is a brief account of a practical application of an eclectic approach that I demonstrated in the summer of 1982. Two groups (N = 14, N = 13) of young students devoted three hours a day for two weeks of their summer holiday to learning to read better. These students, boys and girls, ranged from grades two to eight and were accepted on a first-come, first-serve basis. Approximate reading abilities ranged from grade three to about grade eleven. Eclectic teaching approaches were used, including multilevel reading materials that had been checked out with readability formulas. Readability was of some importance, since no school books were used throughout the two weeks. As I was told later, the young readers appreciated this highly. Emphasis at all times was on reading-comprehension instruction.

A session began with deciding on a topic to study. The children reflected on it and explored their own experiences (see REIVA, Chapter 2), as appropriate and applicable to the study theme. At times, an experience chart was used to record some of their invaluable ideas. Whenever necessary, vocabulary words were introduced. This was particularly important, since the different reading materials did not control for any words.

I showed the children how to set purposes. First, we did it together; later, they did it on their own. In the beginning, they also found it more convenient to write down their own purpose questions to forestall forgetting. To verify their anticipations, children read silently.

At times, active comprehension was interspersed with semantic webbing, ReQuest, or other additional techniques that included rereading whenever needed to support verification of the hypotheses. Results led to further reading, which sometimes was accomplished by moving the group to the library for further investigation of unresolved questions. At the same time, library resources opened up new avenues for broadening and deepening knowledge and awakened new curiosity.

At the end of the two-week session, twenty-seven young readers said, "We really did learn a lot." Joined by their parents, they asked a question I was hard pressed to answer, "Why couldn't reading be taught in our schools as it was here?"

Summary

Combining several instructional approaches into an eclectic approach to teaching reading is a more likely way to reach all the students in a single classroom than is the use of one routine alone. Knowing the wide range of possible reading abilities within the group of students in a given classroom helps one to comprehend why some students have difficulties and others are bored with being compelled to read in a single book. There are many ways that individual student needs could be addressed by the sensitive teacher using an eclectic approach. Experience has shown that students appreciate the difference.

Part III

READING IN THE READER'S CONTEXT

CHAPTER 9

Toward Independent Reading

Purpose questions for this chapter:

- What should I know about oral and silent reading?
- What is SQ3R, and how can it be used for reading and learning?
- What are some other study techniques, and how do they compare with SQ3R?
- How can knowledge that students possess be put to use?
- How can spelling be taught, other than by memorizing words?
- How will computer-assisted instruction influence learning to read and reading to learn?

GROUPING

Pestalozzi (1746–1827) began graded schools in which children were divided into classes according to age and achievement and in which one teacher was in charge of a single class. The Pestalozzian school arrangement soon influenced the American school system (N.B. Smith, 1965, p. 83), which, in turn, hastened the development of graded reading series.

Graded readers that were used in correspondingly graded classes initiated grouping according to how students performed in reading. With the introduction of the first reading tests in the 1920s, ability grouping began.

Hiebert (1983) reports on research of ability grouping and finds that functional answers on grouping are still outstanding. There are, as yet, no definite answers to questions such as, How much teacher time should be allocated to groups of students differentiated by high and low ability? How much time should be allocated to oral reading and silent reading? How should reading practices be paced, and how would pacing influence reading achievement? What are the alternative patterns of teacher-group interactions concerning types of questions, time waited for responses, mutual feedback, teacher and peer responses to reading miscues, and interaction of group time (pp. 249/250)?

While these questions await further investigation, immediate interest and concern focuses on research findings of what happens to student members once they are assigned to high-, average-, and low-ability groups. Membership in any of these groups appears to be permanent, with only occasional changes after the first month of school (Grant & Rothenberg, 1981; Pikulski & Kirsch, 1979; Weinstein, 1976).

Grouping also affects teacher time and reading instruction given to the students in high- and low-ability groups. Hiebert's study (1983) draws attention to the fact that students in low-ability groups get more instruction of oral reading and decoding than students in high-ability groups, who receive the most silent reading and meaning-related activities (p. 236). Likewise, teachers who instruct poor readers in low-ability groups direct attention more to graphemic and morphemic word information and to word pronunciation than teachers who instruct good readers in high-ability groups, who direct attention more to syntactic and semantic information (p. 239). Differentiating the quantity and quality of teaching in each group will contribute to the ever-widening gap between poor and good readers. This gap must also be perceived in terms of the social context of reading instruction. Teachers need to become sensitive to how graded reading instruction affects students, how teachers make a difference in what happens in reading instruction within and across groups, and how students perceive and react to reading instruction. How do the readers read orally, and how do they read silently?

Summary

The idea and practice of grouping began with Pestalozzi in Switzerland and soon spread to and influenced the American school system. As a result, graded classrooms needed graded reading series, and after the introduction of the first tests to assess reading performances, ability grouping started. Research has shown that ability grouping appears to differentiate, if not to discriminate, among and between readers once they are placed in the various ability groups. Not only is the debate of the educational and social implications of ability grouping on teachers and students still acute and ongoing, but it is also intensified by the ever widening gap that appears to distinguish instruction, performance, and accomplishment of poor and good readers.

ORAL AND SILENT READING

Of the two modes of reading, oral and silent, oral reading is used predominantly, at least during the first three grades in elementary school. As Barnitz (1980b) asserts in *Reading Research Quarterly*, beginning readers have acquired significant language competence and oral language facility before entering grade one. Kameenui and Carnine (1982) claim that students have mastered recoding and decoding skills by the time they move from grade three to grade four, but they may not yet be fluent readers. Schallert, Kleiman, and Rubin (1977) point out that structures and functions of written language are known to interfere with comprehending a given passage.

Nevertheless, research in reading comprehension is inconclusive in determining which mode of reading is superior to the other. Proponents of either oral or silent reading have shown comprehension of both to be superior, while nonpreferential studies have shown no difference between oral and silent reading comprehension (Juel & Holmes, 1981).

Oral Reading

From the very beginning of early American life, reading was oral reading or pronouncing words. In school oral reading as explicated in the McGuffey's Eclectic Readers was a rhetorical exercise. In the home the Bible was read aloud mornings and evenings at family prayers. Oral reading often was simply pronouncing words, where not all words were understood. This still may be the case: All too often, readers follow a bottom-up phonological model in which sounds are put together and meaning is lost. Juel and Holmes (1981) contend that "readers may stop processing [meaning] after achieving phonological recodings"; moreover, "with attention focused on the pronunciation of individual words, less comprehension could occur" (p. 547).

Oral reading was once said to be done "to hear them [children] read" (Gray, 1963, p. 55), and the same appears to be true in present-day reading instruction when children take turns reading orally. When sounding out becomes of primary importance, reading as a thinking process is relegated to an inferior position and pronouncing will distract the word pronouncers from following the writer's thoughts (Taschow, 1971, p. 16).

Oral reading must be prepared for in advance, so that the reader has secured meaningful understanding and can fully attend to the oral delivery. Only then can the oral reader reach out to the listeners or the audience to communicate the message with certainty, fluency, and speed. This will make it possible for the listeners to partake in the message by hearing the sound patterns of the words and interpreting their meanings.

Verbal delivery should always be a utilitarian part of reading that is practiced at all grade levels in our schools. Oral reading in schools, often teacher guided and teacher modeled, is essential to reading drama and poetry and to communicating textbook information in all subject areas. But oral reading is also a real-life skill. It is needed, for example, in public meetings when reading minutes and other announcements or in business when discussing company memos, regulations, and contracts. Above all, oral reading is essential for parents, who should read to their children in order to awaken their awareness of how the printed word can be said aloud and acquire meaning.

Yet the value of oral reading may be marred by round-robin reading in school. It may not instill in the students the love for reading orally, silently, or both. Oral reading for the sake of making noise and hearing someone read is not oral reading at all! Spache and Spache (1977) have aptly summarized twelve advantages and disadvantages of oral reading (pp. 245–254) and suggest about thirty ways to use oral reading (pp. 254–256). They are recommended for all students of reading. Perhaps now we should reconsider the words of Huey (1908), written about eight decades ago: "In preparing for life we are instructed almost exclusively in reading aloud, and have not troubled ourselves to ask whether habits learned in reading aloud may not be hurtful in reading silently" (p. 10).

Silent Reading

Since Huey (1908), silent reading has been recognized as a necessity and oral reading as a desirable accomplishment (p. 342). To prepare for oral reading, the readers read silently first, because, as Betts (1946) maintains, silent reading precedes oral reading (p. 85).

The mechanical process of calling out words or, as has been aptly said, "barking at the print" was greatly refuted by E. L. Thorndike (1917) in his influential study, *Reading as Reasoning*. The beginning of the last paragraph of this momentous investigation gives testimony to the often-neglected place, then and now, of silent reading: "In school practice it appears likely that exercises in silent reading to find answers to given questions, or to give a summary of matter read, or to list the questions which it answers, should in large measure replace oral reading" (Schubert & Torgersen, 1968, p. 57).

Readers read silently to learn, to study, and to comprehend. In silent reading, readers are holding dialogue with the authors by thinking while processing print. This is not accomplished in a mechanical, passive, and indiscriminating way; rather, it is done by being actively involved in reorganizing, understanding, and evaluating thought. Silent reading should be a part of every reading lesson, beginning in grade one and including remedial instruction (Wilson, 1981).

Placing emphasis on silent reading means explaining, practicing, and learning what readers do to process print silently. Students at successive grade levels must experience that different materials place different demands on readers because of increasing complexity of syntactic and semantic information, which demands more complex cognitive processing. Students must learn that silent reading can be processed faster than oral reading and that extracting meaning is silent reading's main concern, to be accomplished by thinking while reading.

There may be thinking without reading, but there is not reading without thinking. During the last fifteen years I have taught improvement courses in reading for adults from all walks of life. Their real problem in reading is not difficulty recognizing and pronouncing words; rather, as I express it to them, it is their need to "read with their minds," not with their eyes or mouths. That is, they must think while reading, and follow the thoughts not the words. Inevitably, they ask why they did not learn this in school. Many participants, some not too long out of school, tell me that they never learned to read silently for meaning.

From Oral to Silent Reading

Oral reading is still the predominant mode used by teachers in the primary grades to teach reading and to make students read. What matters, then, is the transition from oral to silent reading. This transition is not brought about by telling students when we read today we will not pronounce or say the words out loud. Instead, functional and transitory exercises must be implemented that guide students from oral to silent reading.

Within a given passage, students can look for words they already know how to pronounce and match some of them with corresponding pictures from a pile of different picture cards. Students can search for words given by another student or the teacher, to find how many times these words appear in the story. They also can look for words with specific phonic elements in initial, medial, and final positions, and look for phrases beginning with *at, on, in,* and the like. In addition, written instructions can be given for the students to follow or act out, as in *Come to me, Take two sticks and give them to Peter,* or *Take the pencil.* Sentences can be written on the board, first to be read silently and then to be talked about. Written or typed notes that require answers can be distributed, read silently, and then answered orally. These notes can state simple problems, as in *Peter has five sticks. He gives them to Mary. How many sticks has Peter?*

Silent reading gradually extends to finding additional information, preparing a paragraph to be reread aloud, writing a poem, or preparing parts of a play for choral reading. These and many other various ways make children aware that reading is the means of getting thought from print and not just the pronouncing and naming of words. When children learn to verbalize in their own words what they have read silently, they also begin to realize that print and speech are different.

Young students, of course, will insist on reading aloud their favorite stories or parts of them. In the beginning this may be done largely from memory, but, with increasing practice in silent reading, more and more cues will be picked up from the printed page. In time, this will lead to more and more silent reading, which should be followed up with retelling and discussing main ideas, details, facts, and anticipations of what may or should happen next.

These school practices must not fail to transfer silent reading into life reading. Even before entering grade one, children have observed their parents reading silently all sorts of printed materials and have also learned not to interrupt adults who are practicing the art of thought getting and thought manipulating through print. Beginning in grade one, students should experience silent reading as the kind of reading adults normally do.

Newspapers, public announcements, TV guides, posters, and more should be part of silent reading. This is the only way that reading becomes lifelike and meaningful and can be perceived to have utilitarian value. This is the real sense of reading, which may otherwise be missed if it is teacher imposed and textbook bound.

There are many other differences between oral and silent reading, some of which are worth mentioning briefly here, but it is beyond the scope of this book to discuss them in detail. Vocalization refers to oral reading and is heard and can be observed. Subvocalization is something like mental pronunciation, in that it cannot be heard but can be perceived by observing the speech muscles during silent reading. Eye movements are different in both modes of reading; for example, eye fixations in oral reading are usually of longer duration than those in silent reading. Also, in oral reading, the eyes are slightly ahead of the voice. Waiting for the voice to catch up with the eyes, which see more than the voice can say at the same time, may result in more regressions than in silent reading.

Summary

There are two modes of reading, oral and silent, and both must be learned and practiced during reading instruction in school. Yet, one mode must not be taught or learned to the exclusion or neglect of the other. Oral reading enjoys the company of listeners, while silent reading retreats within the individual reader. While oral reading is used to share enjoyment and information with others, silent reading is used to understand and hold dialogue with the author. Research as yet has not shown one mode to be superior to the other (Juel & Holmes, 1981, p. 546), leading to the tentative conclusion that "good readers comprehend well in both modes, while poor readers comprehend poorly in both" (p. 565).

TOWARD INDEPENDENT STUDY

Although consideration of whether oral or silent reading results in superior comprehension must be left with the researchers for further investigation, in the meantime individual readers must decide which mode or combination of modes is best suited to their purpose of extracting meaning from print. If and when to use a top-down, bottom-up, or interactive-compensatory approach depends on the readers and their background experiences and the text difficulty.

What matters, however, is not that research studies are still inconclusive but that teachers of reading know the different approaches to processing print. When teachers have this knowledge, they can expose their students to many avenues to reading from which students will choose those that fit best their learning and cognitive styles. There are many learning-study techniques and strategies both teachers and students should know.

To study is to engage actively in attentive and thoughtful examination of events, subject matter, or problems, "with a view to gaining knowledge or skill" (Harris & Hodges, 1981, p. 313). Studying is a purposeful activity in which one applies oneself to the task of thinking-through with the intent to search, ascertain, and learn.

The professional literature cites many study techniques that may be used to assist students in accomplishing a desirable quantity and quality of learning. Skillful use of a study technique enables readers and listeners to extract information that satisfies general as well as specific purposes. Although there are varying study techniques, they appear to have common factors that include following directions, selecting and organizing information that needs to be retained, and interpreting graphs, tables, and other visuals.

SQ3R and Other Study Techniques

The Survey, Question, Read, Recite, Review (SQ3R) method of study was introduced into the literature by F.P. Robinson in 1946 (Robinson, 1961). Since then, this study method has been used widely in reading and in content-area textbooks. This study method also became the basis from which other study approaches were developed.

In the SQ3R, Survey, the first component, directs the readers to read the title and subtitle; look at the pictures, graphs, diagrams, and other visuals and view each description and explanation; and inspect the introduction, summary, and questions. This survey is a way of organizing part of the material by previewing it (H. A. Robinson, 1983).

In theory, the Question component follows the Survey. In practice, however, questions begin at the moment when surveying begins. The title, subtitle, and headings are turned into questions. For instance, the title of a primer story may be "Fun with the Wind." This title is turned into questions that will give direction to the mind when the passage is read later. To prevent forgetting them, the questions may be written down. Some questions may be, Who had fun with the wind? How did the wind have fun? What kind of fun can the wind have? What did the wind do to someone to have fun?

Closed questions, such as, Did the wind have fun with the childen? should be avoided because they yield yes or no answers and lead nowhere unless a second question is asked to replace the first one.

If this primer story has subtitles and pictures, surveying them will elicit further questions, which lead eventually to the first R, or Read. This stands for silent reading, which readers do by themselves. During silent reading, the reader's mind may form new questions that were not raised before.

Often stories extend over many pages. The Survey and Question phases can be used to lead readers to read just the highlights, searching for the information they need rather than ploughing indiscriminately through the story, word by word and page by page.

When the first R, or Read, is completed, the second R, or Recite, takes over. Recite here does not mean to repeat, word for word, from memory, the way one would recite a poem. Reciting involves physically covering up the reading passage by turning the book face down or by closing it, then sitting back and thinking, reflecting mentally on what has been read. Reciting in the form of thinking means organizing and reorganizing the content into units of thoughts, ideas, or information.

Recall for a moment the third step of the DRA, which is the comprehension check. What the teacher does in the DRA, through discussion and questions, the learners do for themselves in the reciting phase of the SQ3R. When information is found to be lacking during reciting, questions cannot be answered fully, so readers must return to the first R, or Read. Returning to Read also may mean returning to Question. These steps are about equal to rereading in the DRA, which is used to clear up uncertainty.

The last of the three R's is Review. After a chapter, a story, or a passage has been worked through in terms of intermittent and interacting surveying, questioning, reading, and reciting, the total work is reviewed. Reviewing serves to summarize, reorganize, and admit worthwhile information to memory.

The five steps of the SQ3R, just like those of the DRA, have been altered over time to make way for new and extended strategies. One change has been the SQ4R. The fourth R stands for Reflect and focuses on reorganizing, manipulating, and associating thoughts and ideas with regard to existing knowledge. The PQRST—Preview, Question, Read, Summarize, Test—is a study method particularly designed for reading science materials. The

SQRQCQ—or Survey, Question, Read, Question, Compute, Question—is recommended for reading problems in mathematics. Another offspring of Robinson's original study method is the OK5R—Overview, Key ideas, Read, Record, Recite, Review, Reflect. The PARS is a study method that stresses Purpose, Ask questions, Read, Summarize. Finally, REAP stands for Read, Encode, Annotate, Ponder. Whereas Encode means to put the writer's ideas into your own words, Annotate means to write these into notes for yourself or another, and Ponder means to think about the reading and perhaps to discuss the writer's thoughts with others (Tonjes & Zintz, 1981, pp. 248–249).

Research Results with SQ3R and Other Study Techniques

The SQ3R was developed from the SQR—Survey, Question, Read—method, which was the longest used and most successful "how-to-study" program at Ohio State University (Robinson, 1961, p. vi). By adding two additional R's to the SQR, the SQ3R resulted.

Adams, Carnine, and Gersten (1982) investigated the efficacy of utilizing systematic instruction in teaching study-skills strategies to fifth-grade students by using the SQ3R study method. Some of the results and their implications led to the conclusion that students who are taught the SQ3R study strategy perform significantly higher than those not trained in it (p. 49). The authors confirm that fifth-grade students without systematic instruction "do not appear to know how to study effectively" (p. 51). Also, Durkin's (1978–1979) research found the near nonexistence of study-skills instruction in social studies classes in grades four to six.

Jenkins and Pany (1981) report on studies that focus on the use or nonuse of particular study skills in the middle elementary grades. They found that students who are given title and paragraph headings answer about 43 percent more comprehension questions correctly than do students who read the same passages without the headings (p. 169). The report also notes that pictures appear to improve reading for understanding when they are used in the sense of advance organizers, headings, and subheadings, provided that students read for new information (p. 171). Inconclusive and sometimes even controversial findings are reported when purpose questions and statements are used to facilitate comprehension of text. While forming questions before reading a passage has not consistently increased reading comprehension, questions interspersed before and after segments of print have aided performance. But then, as these researchers conclude, other studies do not find similar improvements (p. 185).

No doubt, additional research is still needed to prove empirically the assumption that students make gains when using the SQ3R or any other study technique (Crewe & Hultgreen, 1969; Spenser, 1978).

Summary

Various study methods or techniques have been developed to help students learn to study independently. The techniques discussed here were the SQ3R and its modified approaches. However, pertinent research has indicated no strong empirical support for any of the study methods.

CORRELATES OF USING KNOWLEDGE

The previous discussion made it clear that, in order to learn, students must be exposed to study methods and made to practice and apply them. Possessing knowledge is beneficial only when one is aware of how to activate this knowledge and put it to use. Some of the correlates of knowledge, or those physical and mental forces that enable knowledge to be put to its proper use, will be discussed in the following sections.

Habits

Forming good learning habits is placing, organizing, and arranging information, ideas, and thoughts in one's own mind. In doing this consistently, behavior patterns or habits form and are achieved gradually without further outside motivation (Lerner, 1981, p. 402). Through regular use, habits become almost-involuntary practices that develop into a prevailing quality of mental character and disposition. Study habits are observable in that they show consistent ways of using study skills, whether they are used effectively or not.

How effective study skills are will be assessed not so much by the teachers or externally designed tests, but by the users, the students, who are not simply mechanisms but active participants. What students experience in learning by using or not using study skills and how they interpret these experiences will ultimately determine the degree of formation or nonformation of study habits.

Metacognition

As part of the process of becoming independent in reading and learning, students must become aware of how their minds function when they are remembering, retrieving knowledge, extending attention, concentrating, focusing on simple and complex reading-learning-thinking tasks, and processing information. Knowing how one's mind functions when called upon to execute thinking processes awakens one's ability to monitor, restrain, and direct cognition. This ability is referred to as metacognition (Babbs & Moe, 1983; Brown, 1980).

Stewart and Tei (1983) explain that metacognition is a person's awareness and understanding of how to use the knowledge or cognition that this person possesses (p. 36). Fluent readers possess the skills they need to extract meaning from print, which again implies cognition. But when readers are aware of and have control over knowing when, how, and why to use these skills, they are using metacognition (p. 37). Metacognition is being able to assimilate, accommodate, and equilibrate new knowledge with prior knowledge so that new cognitive disequilibrium (Lawton, 1982, p. 248) will ferment new learning.

Concentration and Self-Discipline. Although students may have learned to direct their cognitive functioning toward various mental activities, no full measure of accomplishment will be achieved without having learned to concentrate and to exercise self-discipline. Self-discipline is "the ability to mobilize and commit themselves" (Etzioni, 1982, p. 184) to concentrate on cognitive achievement.

Of course, concentration and self-discipline contradict relaxation, and students and teachers should recognize this obvious contradiction (Rubin, 1982, p. 173). In concentrating, children must learn to focus on relevant information and ignore distractions or irrelevant information. To disregard distractions is an important ability, especially when students are expected to engage in self-teaching activities in science, social studies, reading corners, and self-teaching centers. While students are expected to work only with materials designated for the task, other materials close by act as distractions and may interfere with concentration.

In concentrating, readers give exclusive mental attention to what they are doing or were asked to do. In relaxing, the effort to concentrate is diminished to the extent that learning is reduced or stopped and replaced with enjoyment or fun. Can readers concentrate on reading while simultaneously relaxing and having fun? What truth is there in the often-heard educational slogan, "reading is fun"? How can this be reconciled with the seemingly contradictory demands of concentration and relaxation?

Perseverance. It is obvious that learning to concentrate depends more on the inner state of mind than on external circumstances, although the latter can either promote or inhibit concentration. To prevent the latter, readers and learners need also the ability to coordinate, activate, and direct all those mental and physical forces that are necessary to accomplish a set goal (Düker, 1975, p. 11). It is not motivation or the lack of it that may disturb the reader from without and from within; rather, it is the lack of perseverance in engaging in and completing a certain task.

Perseverance can be taught by beginning with activities that are easy and so structured that students can experience and recognize unaided success at tasks they had considered to be too difficult or even impossible for them (Brandt, 1977, p. 951). Cultivating perseverance, or the will to learn, will result in the ability to perform independently.

Lack of perseverance or the will to perform a certain work, on the other hand, will negatively influence concentration, physical and mental energy, and decision-making efforts. Lack of perseverance results in disappointment and eventually in failure. Quite the opposite, however, is experienced when a task that formerly was insurmountable, such as extracting meaning from a given passage in print, can be completed successfully. This change may well result in a change in the student's self-image and self-confidence and will increase energy and perseverance, perpetuating a cycle that supports concentration and the willingness to pursue more independent and deliberate activities.

Cognitive Styles

What is attainable is attained in accordance with students' own cognitive styles. Cognitive styles are ways in which individual learners perceive, conceptualize, and organize information (Wittrock, 1978, p. 90). Cognitive styles explain how, not what, an individual learns (Good & Stipek, 1983, p. 29) and are distinguished by such concepts as risk taking, field dependence, field independence, categorizing, and scanning behaviors (Bruner, Goodnow, & Austin, 1956). Different cognitive styles distinguish students' cognitive preferences for what they want to learn under what conditions. Cognitive styles explain conceptual levels of concrete and abstract thinking. They explain conceptual tempo, or how fast or slow responses are given; and they explain psychological differentiation, or how dependent or independent students are in their task performances.

Field-dependent students prefer to work with others in group settings and to interact with the teacher, whom they try to please. They rely on the teacher's encouragement and praise, seek detailed instructions for what to do and how to do it, and like to be told explicitly what the performance outcomes are to be and how to reach them. Indeed, they may insist on the latter.

In contrast, field-independent students prefer to work by themselves or in small groups. By using individualized approaches that fit their styles, field-independent students, if allowed to do so, structure their own learning tasks and appear to be better equipped at doing so (Good & Stipek, 1983, pp. 32–33).

Learning Styles

Learning styles, in contrast to cognitive styles, are the ways in which individuals respond to their environment—the sociological and physical stimuli that surround them (Dunn, 1981). Learning styles are the students' preferred ways of learning (White, 1983, p. 842), and they are the aggregate of students' opinions about the ways they learn (Dunn, Dunn, & Price, 1981). Learning styles describe the educational conditions under which students most likely learn and how much structure they need to learn best (Hunt, 1981).

How learning situations are structured for students is another aspect of learning styles. Research suggests (Holland, 1982) that students who are the motivated, persistent, and responsible learners may work best in the least structured environments.

The ideal practice to follow in reading instruction and other subject areas would be to match students' cognitive and learning styles to teaching styles. To achieve this, teachers must observe students and how they work, reflect on their performances, and adapt their teaching styles accordingly.

Spelling

When learning through listening or reading has occurred, its results are usually elicited through questioning and discussions as well as through written notes and reports. Whether reports are oral or written, brief or extended, meaning dominates over sound (Templeton, 1983, p. 10), and meaning prevails where there is a conflict between pronunciation and meaning (F. Smith, 1982, p. 143).

Meaning determines the choice of words, and choosing written words can be performed only by using the alphabetic system of written language. Writing connects with spelling, which is "the process of representing language by means of a writing system or orthography" (Harris & Hodges, 1981, p. 305). In writing, to be conventionally correct, the writer must know the series of letters in sequential order that reflect the meaning of the chosen words.

But producing words in writing can be different from verbalizing them, as in *caught, thought, light, pain*, and *pane*. The pronunciation of a word often is not the same as its spelling. What is important in learning to spell is learning the underlying forms—the lexical spellings—to which English orthography corresponds quite closely (Chomsky, 1973, p. 100).

If learning to spell is to be achieved by associating sounds directly with letters, spelling in the English language becomes a problem. Learning to spell should begin instead with acquiring knowledge of how the English alphabet reflects meaningful language.

Gentry and Henderson (1980) suggest that teachers in the primary grades should encourage students to write creatively and independently by manipulating and discovering words and by comparing their writing with standard orthography. The same writers also maintain that how children spell what they write should not be measured against conventional spelling standards. This advice implies deemphasizing English standard spelling and instead counting on teachers' willingness to respond appropriately to nonstandard spellings (pp. 112–117). This means not only allowing children to spell the words as they think they should be spelled but also, at least temporarily, accepting nonstandard spelling. Psycholinguistic research indicates that the invented spellings are part of students' knowledge domain and provide clues for the teachers as to what is already known about letter-sound correspondence (Hittleman, 1983, p. 261).

Teachers, of course, need to assist children in learning to spell by letting students experience the difference between phonetic and abstract word representation. Needless to say, cognitive development combines with cognitive and learning styles in helping some students to learn faster than others. The faster-working students' efforts in accomplishing abstract representation should not be stifled by waiting for the slower-working students to catch up.

Research by Beers (1980) on how cognitive development relates to spelling and reading abilities recommends a strong sight vocabulary as beneficial to later phonics instruction because it provides a broader base of knowing words from which generalizations can be made. It also concludes that the practice of learning to spell words in isolation is questionable, that reading and spelling should be integrated, and that weekly spelling quizzes in which words are memorized appear of little value unless these words are part of the daily reading lessons (pp 82–83).

A five-stage procedure for spelling has been suggested by Gentry (1982). Students in preschool and primary grades progress through these stages, with each one representing a different conceptualization of English orthography. The first stage is the precommunicative stage, in which single symbols or letters from the alphabet are used to represent words and several letters are used to represent a message, which can also be pronounced by the precommunicative speller. The second stage is the semiphonetic, prephonetic, or invented spelling stage in which letters are used to represent sounds that match their letter names, as U (*you*) SE (*see*), and U (*you*) R (*are*). The third stage is the phonetic stage, in which all the surface sound features are represented, as in KOM (*come*) and KAK (*cake*). The fourth stage is the transitional stage, in which students adhere to the basic conventions of English orthography; and the last stage is the correct stage, in which students spell correctly those words designated for their level.

For poor readers in the middle grades, research suggests that spelling instruction should be subordinated to vocabulary learning because word meanings appear to be more effective facilitators of higher spelling accuracy than the teaching of spelling mechanics (Blair & Rupley, 1980, p. 762).

Emphasis always should be placed on teaching spelling together with meaning, for spelling is meaning. When this is ignored, problems occur, as in the rote memorization of how words are to be spelled. Recent literature supports this position. Templeton (1983) advises that "words that are related in meaning are often related in spelling" (p. 9). What this statement says can be observed in words like *please* and *pleasant*, *explain* and *explanation*, *medicine* and *medical*, *nation* and *national*, *nature* and *natural*, and *crime* and *criminal*. When, however, each word pair is pronounced, the sound changes. When each is inspected visually, the underlying abstract orthographic representation—the spelling—shows little change.

In this sense, Templeton writes of "spelling/meaning patterns in words" (p. 9) "in which English spellings can directly represent the words' meanings" (p. 14) and in which the spelling/meaning connections are used systematically to develop word knowledge.

Computer-Assisted Instruction

Becoming independent readers and learners may well be hastened by a new educational tool that already has had an unequivocal impact on today's society and hence its schools. As the saying goes, "the computer age is here," and schools must prepare students to become computer literate. There is no doubt that methods and materials derived from computers will impact on the teaching of reading, from processing and exercising word identification to word and sentence comprehension.

What, then, is the current state of affairs regarding computer-assisted reading and learning?

I myself look at computers and their manifold software as a means of assisting teachers with instruction in reading, instruction which still is done mainly by the teacher. This contrasts with computer-based instruction, in which the teaching is done chiefly by the computers. Different again is computer-managed instruction, in which the computer is programmed to identify reading difficulties and provide recommendations for improvement.

The bulletin of the Department of Education's Program Development Branch in the Province of Saskatchewan announces that the wave of computers in education is here and suggests the following program (*Chronicle*, 1983) to introduce computer literacy. In grades one through six, computer literacy will be taught in informal settings; and students in grades seven through nine will be exposed to formal learning about computers, leading to full-credit courses in computer science for students in grades ten through twelve.

While the computers themselves are the hardware, the software is the instructional programs, including drill activities for spelling and word recognition. Materials like these may be used on an individual basis for students who can work above the average class level, as well as for those who experience difficulties and need additional support. Computers can assist teachers (Rubin, 1982) in asking questions after students have read a passage. With the help of desk terminals, all students in the class can "key in" their individual answers, which are received by the teacher's computer, which gives not only the answers but also a pattern of the answers (p. 331).

Carver and Hoffman (1981) used a PLATO IV computer that was programmed to read and reread a prose passage for high-school students at about a grade-five level in reading ability. The computer program, or the software, for PLATO was especially developed and called Programmed Prose. "Repeated readings," or successive rereadings of short passages using a computer-controlled feedback system, showed a gain of about three grade levels, from five to eight, on one measure of general reading. That is, repeated readings of materials will improve students' ability to perform similar reading tasks but will not improve reading ability in general (p. 389). Computers apparently can assist teachers in assisting students who otherwise would need extra teacher time and effort to provide feedback and check performance.

H. A. Robinson (1983) points out that, in using computers to run and respond to a program, students must follow rules and directions precisely. In the process of composing programs, computers test and challenge students' abilities in writing, reading, and thinking (pp. 265–266).

Nolen (1980) reports on a spelling computer that talks. This automatic drilling device pronounces a word clearly and asks the user to spell it. As soon as the word is spelled, letters are converted into audible speech patterns. Praise is heard when the word is correctly spelled. Then the spelling score is computed and displayed, after which a new word is given (p. 538). Although these spelling computers display visual representations accompanied by sound correspondences, teacher guidance is essential so that children receive help in misspelled words. Nolen warns that teachers must not "turn their teaching functions over to automated devices" (p. 539).

Word processors with high-quality printers that delete unwanted lines, add others, correct misspellings, combine sentences, reset paragraphs, and add punctuation are no longer strangers in schools. Word processors are used for composing sentences and larger segments of print, for checking spelling, and for reading practice through revising and improving the text.

Microcomputers are used not only in schools but also in adult basic literacy education, in studying reading and writing skills. Special programs are available for spelling practice as well as for completing and building sentences that develop into action stories.

Computer hardware and software may be, and perhaps are already, the wave of this decade and, as McLuhan expressed it, "the central nervous system of our society" (Dupuis & Askov, 1982, p. 23).

Summary

In order to become independent readers and learners in school and in later life, students must become aware of not only the knowledge they possess but also how to process it by directing their physical and mental forces toward the best possible achievement. To this end, they must form good study habits, dependent on such factors as metacognition, especially concentration and perseverance, as well as their cognitive and learning styles. To achieve independent spelling, it is recognized that spelling and meaning must be connected, while teaching techniques that match sounds with letters must be avoided. The importance and potential of computers for school use and particularly for teaching reading and spelling cannot be overlooked, especially considering the enormous impact that computers are having on our society as a whole.

CHAPTER 10

Different Readers

Purpose questions for this chapter:
- What are the deficit and difference positions in language learning?
- What are the additive and subtractive kinds of bilingualism?
- What are some language divergencies that may interfere with teaching reading to non-English-speaking or limited-English-speaking students?
- How can ethnolinguistic differences be applied positively to the teaching of reading in a monolingual classroom environment?

WHAT THE RESEARCH LITERATURE SAYS

The issue of students being different and with it showing wide ranges in abilities to read was attested to and discussed as early as 1924 as evidenced by *The Report of the National Committee on Reading* (Gray, 1925). In the following years, Durrell (1937) affirmed that individual differences not only exist but also that children of the same age differ in their abilities, interests, and habits in reading and that the range of individual differences increases in reading under an excellent instructional program (p. 325). The Detroit *Curriculum Guide in Reading* (*Curriculum*, 1950) recognized that there were widely differing needs represented in the city's schools and that there was no one method nor one set of materials that would meet these differences (p. 13). DeBoer and Whipple (1961) contended that, while individualized instruction in reading was on the upswing, the same could not be noticed in the subject-matter areas, in which students read most of the time (p. 60). H. A. Robinson (1964) asserted that, while the term *individual differences* had been in use for a number of years and at least educators talked about it, visits to schools did not reveal essential teacher efforts to meet individual differences (p. v). About twenty years later, Fenstermacher (1983) reaffirmed that although there appears to be agreement that people do differ, there seems to be no agreement in "how people differ and what, if anything, should be done about their differences."

With the recognition of differences, educational treatments have been developed to alleviate them, although this appears to be neither an answer nor a solution, particularly not when cultural and lingual deviations are treated as if they were inferior to the dominant culture and language. What should be considered is how accessible teaching in general, and teaching of reading in particular, is to all students. Also to be addressed is how undiminished achievement of success can be assured for all students and how individual differences can contribute to enhancing and enriching teaching and learning for all students.

Factors Related to Language Differences

Recent literature concedes that all children must have the opportunity of an education made available on equal terms (Fischer & Sorenson, 1983, p. 78). It is not often, however, that life realities coincide with what literature suggests and law requires. We have to pause a moment and reflect on the fact that all students and teachers in our schools come from a variety of different language and cultural backgrounds.

In the United States, diverse cultures and languages can be traced to the first recorded modern-language classes, given in the German language in 1702 in Germantown, Pennsylvania (Bartel, 1976), in the French language in New York in 1703 (Watts, 1963), and in Spanish in 1766 (Leavitt, 1959–1961). On the Canadian scene, approximately one-third of the population traces its culture and language to Anglo-Canadian, one-third to French-Canadian, and the other third to diverse cultures and languages from various countries (McLeod, 1981, p. 12).

After World War II and as an aftermath of the American involvement in the Vietnam War, the traditional ideal of the American melting pot was replaced with that of a pluralistic societal structure. In Canada, the emphasis on assimilation, which meant to anglicize the culturally and linguistically different groups, was replaced with that of pluralism prompted by the awareness of French-Canadian nationalism.

The pluralistic societies on both sides of the border not only envisioned but resulted in multicultural and multilingual societies. However, the English language and perhaps its culture is at least thought of as the dominant one. Speakers of other languages—those not born into and descended from the Anglo-American or Anglo-Canadian speech communities—were regarded and labeled as "different." Being different meant to be different in language and culture, which in turn meant to be a member of a minority group.

Being different, of course, could mean only being different in the eyes and ears of the beholders. Being different begs the question: From whose point of view is one different? There is no satisfactory answer to this question.

When individual A says that B is different because of language and color, then B can equally say that A is different because of language and color.

Being different or diverse in language brought about two positions that at the time of this writing are not yet resolved. Both theoretical positions must be discussed, at least briefly, so that the readers may become aware of them and better understand the various misconceptions that they carry—labels like verbally deprived, culturally different, culturally disadvantaged, educationally deprived, disadvantaged, underprivileged, lower socioeconomic group, lower class, and more.

No attempt will be made to define all these terms. Harris and Hodges (1981) explain by citing M. A. Vernon that "these terms seem to be used more-or-less synonymously to refer to children whose cultural environment appears to be less favorable to their cognitive development than that of middle-class white Americans." They also cite Y. A. Goodman: "Cultural deprivation is an impossibility—unless we all agree that all people are culturally deprived in certain situations and at certain times" (pp. 75/76).

If the word *deprive* means to remove or withhold something from, then being *culturally deprived* means that an individual is removed from his or her culture, which would result in being without a culture. It stands to reason that no human being, rich, poor, or in between, of whatever color, race, speech, and creed, is without a culture to provide the base for living (Lamb & Arnold, 1980, p. 48).

Similarly, *verbal deprivation* would mean being dispossessed of or experiencing a loss of spoken words. Whenever people are being transplanted, perhaps suddenly, into a different speech community, they find themselves in a minority surrounded by a majority of people speaking other languages and following different customs. The members of the minority group may be observed as unable to function "as expected" by the members of the majority group and from their perspective may be said to be culturally and verbally deprived. However, the same people will not be perceived as being verbally and culturally deprived when returned to their original context or when interacting within their own family.

Nevertheless, deprivation of the predominant culture and language may lead to being disadvantaged in educational development, in employment opportunities, and in the socioeconomic stature of housing and public life.

Let us now discuss the two different theoretical positions regarding being disadvantaged, as reflected in the literature of the last two decades. They are known as the deficit position and the difference position.

The Deficit Position. This position is based on the concept of verbal deprivation, which mainly plagues people of lower socioeconomic status who are members of minority groups that speak little or no English. Children of parents who speak little or no English are reared in home environments less compatible with those of middle-class American or Canadian families and their children. In addition to being verbally deprived (Bereiter & Engleman, 1966), they also are culturally deprived (Deutsch, Katz, & Jensen, 1968).

Deficit positionists assert that poor children have language problems. Since these children understand a minimum of school language—distinguished from the vernacular of the street—they are ill-equipped to follow classroom instruction. They are found to encounter difficulties in understanding oral and written language. To assist these students in achieving minimum language competence, special programs are designed to remove existing deficits.

Intervention programs such as Head Start and other enrichment programs offer direct and indirect experiences and activities through trips and visits, films and tapes, and games, all designed to correct impaired sensorimotor and cognitive development.

Of further importance to the deficit theory are Bernstein's (1973) concepts of restricted and elaborated language codes. The restricted language code is more context bound and reflects the social structure of the working class. The elaborated language code is less context bound and reflects the social structure of the middle class.

Both codes reflect differences in the way children use language in describing a specific context (Bernstein, 1973, p. 27). Thus, a picture card showing an apple may elicit a stereotyped, simple, short, and nonspecific response of *an apple*, a response that is cleary context bound, that is, dependent on the picture card to be understandable. An elaborated language code, on the other hand, would be less context bound, that is, freed from the picture card and proliferating complex verbal structures. From the perspective of code development, children from both social strata learn first the restricted code of ordinary conversation. Then children from the middle strata advance to learning the more elaborate code, which Bernstein claims is essential for coping with the instructional language and the learning tasks in school.

The Difference Position.   Although the proponents of the difference position agree with those of the deficit position that children from poverty families are failing in schools and that something must be done, the point of departure is what should be done. While the deficit theorists place the unreadiness for school on the children, the difference theorists charge the schools with being not ready for the children.

Stewart (1973) calls for a change of terms, from *substandard* English to *nonstandard* English. Labov (1973) calls for an end to the concept of verbal deprivation, for it "has no basis in social reality" (p. 153). Their research results show that, although speech variations are language differences, they are otherwise normal and well-developed linguistic or dialect systems whose speakers apply sentence-making rules automatically and consistently. Baratz (1969) asserts that language differences such as the dialects of black, Cajun, Appalachian, and Hawaiian English-speaking people are "well-ordered, highly structured, highly developed systems" (p. 88).

In reading the literature on difference theory it becomes clear that the methodological inadequacies in our schools' teaching procedures fail to teach these children to read effectively. In turn, the educational system (Baratz, 1973) treats reading failure "as if failure were due to intellectual deficits of the child" (p. 11). This modern myth of verbal deprivation has expanded rapidly and become accepted in the school systems. Labov (1973) points out that this modern myth "is particularly dangerous, because it diverts attention from real defects of our educational system to the imaginary defects of the child" (p. 154).

Cazden (1972) asks us to consider whether or not there is a single variety of English used by educated speakers throughout this country. The answer, of course, is that there is no single standard in pronunciation, that regional variation in "accent" exists and usually is accepted without social stigmatism (p. 144). Why not accord speakers of other languages and dialects the same courtesy?

Downing and Thackray (1975) conclude from their review of the literature that "the truth is that working-class children are highly competent in their language" (p. 40). Irrespective of language differences, both divergent and standard speakers undergo the same language development. In this sense, Barnitz (1980a) explains that language differences should not be held against children, nor is there a need to reject their "linguistic heritage as a means of teaching reading in Standard English" (p. 785) just because "many experienced teachers are not aware of sociolinguistic facts and how language relates to reading instruction" (p. 779). Correcting divergent speakers in overt fashion and consequently treating their language differences as defects will lead to "heightened cognitive confusion in the literacy learner" (Downing & Leong, 1982, p. 279).

Contrary to the verbal deprivation theory, evidence has been levied to show that nonstandard forms of English or dialects are rule-governed systems with their own patterns of sounds, syntax, and semantics, which are acquired naturally by their speakers.

Differences from the standard forms of English are regular and consistent, not erratic and erroneous. Black speakers, who often delete the auxiliary verb *to be* from their speech, use this form consistently. What is considered standard English, as in *She is coming*, is expressed in black English as *She comin'*. Yet perhaps we should remind ourselves that what commonly is called standard English is really just another dialect. However, it also happens to be the most commonly used dialect in present-day American society and is the preferred language of communication for the majority of Americans.

Summary

Although research acknowledges that people differ in their abilities, interests, and habits, there is little or no agreement as to what should be done about the differences. Two approaches to resolving language differences are represented by the deficit position and the difference position. The former is based on the concept of verbal deprivation, which holds that culturally different children are not ready for school. The latter acknowledges that children from poverty-stricken homes fail more often than other children in school, yet this theory holds that the schools are not ready for these children. Literature strongly recommends, however, that language diversities should not be held against the children, nor should any language be viewed as inferior because it is not the preference of the majority.

TOWARD MORE ACCEPTABLE FORMS OF ENGLISH

As Shuy (1973, p. 339) observed, there is a linguistic continuum, which has a topmost dialect, or acrolect (Greek *acro* means highest), and its opposite, the bottommost dialect or basilect (W. A. Stewart, 1965). English speakers around the world fall between the two extremes but cover only a portion of the continuum. As each individual occupies a place on it, the positions of most speakers of the English language do overlap. Speakers within the overlapping portions understand each other, even within given language variations. However, the farther speakers move away from the overlapping portions toward the extremes of the linguistic continuum, the more they move toward the nonstandard forms of the language that constitute a social dialect.

No doubt, school efforts are directed toward moving the divergent English-speaking students, or those recognized as being speakers of nonstandard English, toward what teachers recognize as being an acceptable or standard form of English. Outside school, teachers may have an ally in television and radio programs that encourage speakers of nonstandard English to become standard speakers through listening to that language (Dupuis & Askov, 1982, p. 74). However, listening to these programs does not always guarantee that students will use more acceptable forms of English in speech and writing.

Bidialectism

Gillet and Gentry (1983) suggest a four-step procedure intended to lead children speaking nonstandard dialects to early exposure to and experience with standard forms of English. The Language Experience Approach, discussed previously in Chapter 8, is used as the vehicle for building bridges between the two forms of English.

In the first step, children dictate the story, which the teacher writes down without modifying or correcting their language. When reading the dictated story, children can make the connections between oral and written language that matches their own speech patterns, and they also are encouraged to use their language as equal to and as worthy as any other. In the second step, the teacher prints—or, more accurately, reprints—on chart paper the same story by introducing a standard English version. This is done by using as many words as possible from the children's first production, while simultaneously employing sentences, organizational patterns, and different words with which the children should become familiar. Reading the teacher's revised story follows, with the students joining in until they can read the newer version by themselves. In the third step, children compare both stories, talk about the changes, and are encouraged by the teacher to revise their original sentences. It is during the revision that children move from the extreme of the linguistic continuum to the overlapping portions of standard English. This movement encourages fluent reading and word recognition on sight, particularly of the new words. In the last step, sentences are transformed and generated by substituting different words and verb and noun inflections, and by building word banks, exploring vocabularies, and composing more complex sentences from simple ones.

While these four steps suggest how to lead students from nonstandard to standard spoken and written forms of the English language, it is important to realize that at no time are students told, either directly or indirectly, that their speech is no good, bad, or wrong; nor at any time are they conspicuously corrected. Rather, a second dialect has been added, resulting in bidialectalism, which, when properly nurtured, will enable students to converse in and use both dialects equally well. The first dialect has not been eradicated by learning another one. A more acceptable dialect, which overlaps on the linguistic continuum with an even more acceptable or standard form of the English language, has been added. It is a form of English that has its own linguistic features, ones that are recognized and valued by the school, the teachers, and the larger speech community.

Bilingualism

While bidialectalism is one way of teaching less-divergent English, another way, perhaps much more frequently found in our schools, is bilingualism, in which another language, usually a second language, is learned in addition to a native language already known by the speaker.

A cursory look at Europe tells the story of how the demand for and exchange of labor across national boundaries in the past two decades has challenged the host country's cultural, socioeconomic, and educational structures. Funcke (1982) reports that, between 1961 and 1980 about four million workers and their families migrated to West Germany. In addition to finding accommodations and making adjustments to the host country's day-to-day living conditions, learning to listen, speak, read, and write the country's language became one of the major and immediate requirements. Often this created unequal and unfavorable circumstances. The immigrants, particularly "children and adolescents who live in a foreign country under foreign social and economic conditions, must also struggle with a foreign language and culture. The goal of social and employable integration is not assimilation, but the unconditional acceptance into the German society" (Blüm, 1982, p. 185, freely translated by H. Taschow). The educational struggle becomes one of learning a second language.

On yet larger, intercontinental dimensions, political upheavals have sent refugee migrants around the globe, mainly to the United States and Canada, where they form and live in minority groups. While newcomers usually have to struggle to overcome various socioeconomic difficulties, they also face the often-insurmountable task of learning a second language. Reading numbers and computational notations like 4+5 appears easy, when compared to the tough job of learning to speak, read, and write in the language of the host country. While migrants do not stop thinking in ways that express the deep structure of their own vernacular, the words are missing with which to express that same meaning through the surface structure of the new language.

Thought and language are intimately related, and one speaks or writes what one thinks. Second-language learners think first in their mother tongue what they want to communicate, encoding meaning through the choice of familiar words, sentence structures, and semantics. Then translation into the second language may be attempted by trying hard to match words from the first language with those of the second, rather than by matching meaning. While word-to-word language translation may be successful, meaningful understanding may not, as in the headlines *Red Sox Score Victory over Blue Jays*, or *Stocks Hit Bottom*. What learners of a second language must come to understand is that the surface structure of their language cannot be translated directly into the surface structure of another language. This points to the fact that written language is not made comprehensible by being translated into speech sounds (F. Smith, 1982, p. 81).

The next obstacle confronting the neolingual is understanding what is said and then concocting a reasonable reply that conforms to the English sound system. Spontaneous talk, the everyday common talk, is not like a written sentence. While vocabulary and grammatical forms are the same, the purposes of spoken and written language are not.

Imagine being in a country whose language is Spanish. You have learned from the book to say, ¿Como está usted? You are sure of its pronunciation because of the pronunciation key from which you learned it, but you say it and you are not understood! Intonation, accent, or simply how the utterance is said reflect the sounds and accents of the newcomer's, not the host country's, language. Oral language—speaking—immediately marks the foreigner or the stranger in a new country.

What should newcomers do with the language that is their own, in relationship to the new language that is not their own but must be acquired? Should newcomers forget their mother tongue in favor of the new language? Should they use their language as a base for learning the new language? Should they learn the new language just enough to get along in public life and on the job?

Here we discover what Lambert (1972) calls the two kinds of bilingualism: additive and subtractive.

Additive Bilingualism. Additive bilingualism is a new approach to language teaching and learning whereby the native language is fully retained while the acquisition of the second language is an added achievement (Gradisnik, 1980, p. 125, 126). The learners who learn to listen to, speak, read, and write the second language are all members of a same-speech community who have been reared in this language. This new approach began with Lambert in Canada in the 1960s. It is referred to as a program of "immersion." It was started in an elementary school in St. Lambert in the Province of Quebec in 1966. English-speaking children were immersed in the French language as a second language, which for the first two or three grades was used as the medium, not the object, of instruction. At the end of grade four, the results showed that the French-immersion students were at the same level in English performance as the English-speaking students in the English control group, whose medium of instruction was solely the English language. In addition, the students in French immersion had achieved favorably in French when compared to their French-speaking counterparts (Gradisnik, 1980).

Tucker (1980) explains in reviewing research on bilingual education in Canada that immersion in French as the second language starts from the very beginning of school, that all children speak English as their mother tongue, live in English-speaking families and neighborhoods, and speak virtually no French upon school entrance. Tucker warns, however, that the results from the Canadian immersion studies should not be interpreted to mean that "minority group youngsters in the United States, Canada or the third world should be immersed or submerged in the target language" (p. 3). Certain conditions must be met that make immersion possible. These conditions are supplied by the social settings of family and peer group, where the home language is highly valued, where literacy is actively encouraged, where the mother tongue is maintained, and where it can be assumed that children will succeed.

At the time of this writing, many public schools in Saskatchewan offer numerous French-immersion programs beginning in kindergarten for children whose dominant language is English. Some of these English-speaking students, I have found, are having difficulties processing the French language in speaking, reading, and writing. Questions have been asked: Do these students have difficulties because of learning French? How is it being taught? Would these students have similar difficulties in the English language while being in the same grade at the same time? Answers, however, are not yet available. Parents and some teacher appear to be concerned and are beginning to ask for help. Parents are wondering if they have made the right decisions in putting their children in the immersion classes. Teachers teaching French immersion wonder if remedial teachers for the French language are needed, as they are for the English language.

Subtractive Bilingualism. In subtractive bilingualism, the native or first language is replaced to a great extent by the second language, such as when the language of the minority group is replaced by the language of the majority group. As discussed earlier, whenever people or groups of people who already belong to one speech community move into a speech community other than their own, these people find themselves in a minority. Learning the new language of this new speech community can result in subtractive effects on the newcomers' native language.

Subtractive effects are observed more when children of different ethnolinguistic minority groups are in classrooms where the dominant language is the only one used for instruction and where school administrators, teachers, students, and parents are noncommittal and indifferent toward speakers of other languages. This effect results in monolinguistic instruction, which Lambert (1980) calls the "steamroller effect of a powerful dominant language [which] can make foreign home languages and cultures seem homely in contrast" (p. 3). It is observed further that subtractive effects may result in low-level achievement in both languages when the native language is suppressed because it is incompatible to some degree with the majority language.

When, however, bilingual education is fostered out of respect for the interests and civil rights of minority groups, or when bilingual education is even enforced by law, it sometimes is either refused or grudgingly complied with. The mostly nonbilingual teaching staff often feels threatened in the sense that bilingualism creates an "elite" and with it promotes "separatism." According to the Academy for Educational Development and the Edward W. Hazen Foundation (Academy, 1982), the impact of bilingual instruction is typically transitional. As soon as students understand English well enough to follow all-English instruction, teaching in the non-English language is discontinued, and instruction in non-English language skills may be suspended (p. 3), which would also indicate a subtractive effect on the minority language.

To overcome both minority- and majority-group language anxieties, the Academy and the Hazen Foundation (Academy, 1982, pp. 3–4) recommend working toward

1. An overall shift in emphasis to a language-competent society . . .
2. Full mastery of English as an essential aspect of "language competence" in U.S. society . . .
3. Real competence in English and another language . . .
4. Parent–school system partnership [and] . . . parental encouragement . . .
5. More bilingual programs [that] . . . include English dominant students . . .
6. Increased attention to the economic advantages of multilanguage competence . . .

Differences Among Second-Language Learners

Not all non-English speakers or students will be able to approach second-language learning under the same social and personal conditions. Economic status; personal feelings of self-worth, pride, and security; family; peer encouragement or pressure; and cognitive and learning styles all will influence and affect, if not determine, the non-English speaker's attitude, desire, and willingness to learn a new language.

Attitudes. Attitudinal considerations work both ways between those who learn and those who speak the language. Attitudinal reciprocity is seen in how the second-language learners of the minority group perceive the members of the majority group, who already are experienced speakers of this language, and in how the majority group, in turn, perceives the learners. Reciprocity is seen in the level of desire among the learners for participation in and acceptance of the different ethnolinguistic settings of the speakers, and in how they, in turn, desire to participate in and accept the different cultural settings of the learners. Learners should be helped, if necessary, to develop positive feelings toward the speakers, who, in turn, should be concerned with, care about, and, if possible, relate personally to the learners (Chamot, 1981, p. 3).

Such an attitude has been developing in West Germany, where the Minister of Labor and Social Services invites both learners and speakers of the German language to have positive feelings toward each other, to participate in and to accept different ethnolinguistic conditions, and to practice tolerance in overcoming language barriers (Blüm, 1982).

Concern with the integration of speakers of other languages is an issue of state, provincial, national, and international magnitude. The battle of language and cultural integration will not be won in the legislative branches of national governments but in the schools of each society. Speakers and learners in general and educators and students in particular must learn to respect one another as persons and members of pluralistic societies whose cultures contribute to fuller and richer lives and enhance insights into the nature of humankind. By observing how learners go about processing the new language, preferred language learning styles can be identified so that instruction can maximize them.

Language-Learning Styles. There are three basic types of language-learning styles: beading, braiding, and orchestrating (Ventriglia, 1982). They relate to how individual learners acquire the target language and, consequently, how they will apply it to the actual tasks of speaking, reading, and writing.

Orchestrators listen intensively to sounds and intonation patterns of the language to be learned, in order to become aware of how the new sounds are used to form sentences, phrases, words, and syllables. Orchestrators want to be certain that they produce the new sounds correctly before pronouncing them publicly. They depend upon an oral pronunciation model, usually the teacher. Listening to sounds also brings awareness of intonation patterns, from which the meaning of the utterances may be derived.

Beaders, like orchestrators, listen carefully; but beaders learn words and their meanings first. Then, beaders string words together like beads, to make phrases and sentences. In contrast, braiders acquire chunks of words and phrases, often without conscious analysis, and then try them out to see how and if they work.

Instructing Second-Language Learners

The approach to teaching English to non-English speakers in America has gone through three named phases: (1) Teaching English as a Foreign Language (TEFL), (2) Teaching English as a Second Language (TESL), and (3) Teaching English to Speakers of Other Languages (TESOL, which also stands for Teachers of English to Speakers of Other Languages) (Alatis, 1980, pp. 88, 89).

The TESOL methodology is practiced in adult education classes throughout the world. TESOL professionals treat speakers of other languages in a positive manner and teach TESOL methodology as an *additive* approach to bilingual education.

Language Continuum. Robinett (1972) suggests a goal-directed language continuum. Non-English speakers who are learning English as a cultural acquisition are placed on the beginning of this continuum, followed by those learning English for specific functional purposes. In both instances, the native or first language is still dominant over the second language to be learned. When the learner's goal changes so that English becomes the language of instruction in school as well as the language of communication in public life, then the English language is used integratively, thus lessening the dominance of the first language. If learning continues to even greater proficiency, both the learner's native language and new language reach equal status, making language switching more viable. That is, the individuals who possess two languages can use them interchangeably depending on a given situation.

Input Hypothesis. An approach that is designed to assist monolingual teachers in making second-language learning for minority students in their classrooms even more effective is the input hypothesis advanced by Krashen (1980). The input hypothesis suggests that, in acquiring a second language, new linguistic patterns will be understood only when the amount of input is just a little beyond the current level of language proficiency. When, for instance, new linguistic input is too far beyond the learner's present language proficiency level, what is heard will be noise and what is seen will be meaningless. At the opposite end, when linguistic input is at or below the learner's proficiency level, there will be no new language acquisition. Furthermore, new learning must always contain meaningful information first, rather than advanced grammatical structures, which can and should be provided through input that is relevant to lifelike learning. Overemphasis on often-meaningless and repetitive drills should be avoided, since they have little communicative function.

Similarities and Differences Between Languages. Chamot (1981) reports of similarities as well as differences between the first and the second language (pp. 1–3). For both languages, meaning appears to be the key, for what is meaningful is put together and need not imitate sentence models. Just as listening plays a major part in learning the first language, so is it important in learning the second one. Before children speak, they want to be certain of what they want to say. In addition, learners want to put the second language to use by trying out what the new language can do for them. Readers may recall the brief account of language development in Chapter 1. As soon as the child knows a word, this word can be used in a functional sense in the second language, like *la tasse* in French or *die Tasse* in German.

Differences in the acquisition of the second and the first language lie in the fact that the first one is informally acquired through the preschool years, while the second one must be learned through instruction. Chamot (1981) points out that there are qualitative and quantitative differences in the ways a one-year-old child and a seven-year-old child learn a language. Older learners appear to be more mature and have different social needs, and their cognitive system is more developed. Another difference lies in the desire to learn a second communication system when a first system has already been acquired. On the other hand, the first linguistic system can assist the second one because the learner already knows how language works. What teachers should take advantage of, however, is "what children already know about language through their first language so they can make successful transfers and correct generalizations to the second language" (p. 3).

Further differences in second-language learning can be seen in the motivations for studying it. Why is a second language learned, and what will it be used for? Is a second language learned for socializing, for gaining academic accomplishment, or for both? Proficiency in second-language learning may and will vary accordingly.

Second-Language Proficiencies. Cummins (1980) distinguishes between proficiency requirements for communicating socially as compared to those needed for academic accomplishment. He distinguishes between Basic Interpersonal Communicative Skills (BICS) and Cognitive/Academic Language Proficiency (CALP). BICS defines the second-language proficiency to which one will aspire when one wants to interact socially with others of that same tongue, as, for example, when visiting France.

When the second-language learners reach the type of proficiency where knowledge and concepts already deposited in the first language can be transferred to the second language, learners have reached what Cummins (1980) calls the threshhold level leading to CALP. This level is the proficiency that is needed to achieve in school subjects and in taking tests. Cognitive levels and conceptual knowledge mark this proficiency and make transfer from one language to another possible.

Summary

Modern migration caused by political upheaval or other factors has not only contributed to American and Canadian multicultural and multilingual societies but also has greatly affected the monolingual school systems. The variety of English dialects and non-English languages thus imported have brought consternation to and sometimes resistance from the white, middle-class, conservative, monolinguistic school systems. Over the years, many approaches have been developed to help monolinguistic teachers understand and instruct children with different ethnolinguistic backgrounds.

PLURALISM IN MONOLINGUAL INSTRUCTION

Reading instruction in elementary schools is generally conducted by assuming that all students, though from varying ethnic backgrounds, bring the same or similar experiences to the receiving end of teaching reading. What reading instruction is concerned with matters little, so long as all readers achieve the prescribed outcomes as directed by teachers whose orientation to the reading process is mostly monolingual. Readers who fail to achieve because of divergent cultural-lingual backgrounds and instructional mismatching become candidates for remedial or tutor-assisted reading instruction.

What must be realized in today's reading instruction is that the background experiences of the members of the white, middle-class, North American, English-speaking community are not the same as—and often are not even similar to—those of the members of other speech communities. Sometimes these differences are masked and not readily observable. Even when children speak some English and want to be like their Anglo-American peers, it does not indicate that, in fact, they are like them. Instead, these children may hear and also speak another language at home and live according to other customs because of their parents' wish and sometimes because of parental inability to adjust to the majority culture. All of this, in turn, adds to background experiences that are different from those of their peers in school, different from those who successfully read in English-language textbooks and partake in and follow school instruction.

Cultural Schemata

Schemata, as discussed earlier, direct human thinking and assist in interpreting the meaning of what individuals know and have experienced. In this sense, cultural schemata are tied to the individual's upbringing, speech community, and culture.

Cultural schemata, then, are with all of us. They provide the framework for what we understand and how we interpret various reading passages. Cross-cultural studies on reading comprehension have shown that the background knowledge readers have about the materials to be read may constitute an important source of individual differences in understanding (Sheffensen,

Joag-Dev, & Anderson, 1979). These researchers conclude that a distinct possibility exists that "some portion of the difficulties that United States minority children often have in learning to read with comprehension is attributable to mismatch between subcultures and the majority culture whose viewpoint predominates in the material children are given to read" (p. 28).

Additional empirical evidence comes from research by Reynolds, Taylor, Steffenson, Shiren, and Anderson (1982), who explain that cultural schemata can influence how members of different cultures interpret what they read and that cultural bases account for individual differences in the readers' responses. After 105 eighth-grade students, some black and some white, have read a passage dealing with a form of verbal ritual insult, known as "sounding" or "playing the dozens," results have shown that there is a clear cultural difference of the role cultural schemata play in reading comprehension. When one of the black male participants in the study was told afterward that "white children understood the letter [the reading passage] to be about a fight instead of sounding, he looked surprised and said, "What's the matter? Can't they read?" (p. 365).

Another research study, in which the results are perhaps attained more directly from actual classroom teaching and teacher-student interaction, is that of Tharp (1982), who reported on the Kamehameha Early Education Program (KEEP). Through KEEP, effective instruction in comprehension was given to Polynesian-Hawaiian children who had a potentially high risk for educational failure. KEEP incorporated six instructional practices that are believed to be critical elements to success in teaching reading to multicultural and multilingual students. These are (1) active instruction of comprehension, (2) classroom organization into small groups, (3) child motivation, (4) continuous monitoring and feedback of student achievement, (5) individualized diagnostic/prescriptive instruction, and (6) a quality-control system (pp. 519–521).

Further research on effective instruction of comprehension through the KEEP program found that "instructional practices are compatible with the culture of the students" (p. 523) and that the "KEEP program with its six instructional features differs significantly from the public school classes attended by our control subjects" (p. 521).

Some Recommendations

Teacher instruction in learning to read and in reading to learn must be directed toward and include all students in any given elementary classroom. No matter how ethnolinguistically different, all students should be receivers of and interactors in appropriate instruction in reading, instruction that gives them ample opportunity to express themselves in accordance with their cultural schemata. Based on the discussions in this chapter, some recommendations for English as the target language of instruction in reading are in order:

1. Develop listening and speaking abilities that are adequate for beginning formal reading instruction. Otherwise, bilingual and bidialectical students' efforts in learning and teacher's efforts in teaching may lead to frustration and failure.
2. Involve background experiences from both the minority and the majority students, so that varied cultural schemata are an integral part in the pursuit of learning to read.
3. Learn about and be knowledgeable of differences between the target language and other languages. Thought and language are closely related, and for all young learners the most accessible schemata are those of their parents and siblings.
4. Integrate reading instruction pertaining to word recognition, sight words, decoding, and recoding into the larger context of comprehension. A suggested approach may be the Language Experience Approach, in which students are able to identify with and move from speech to print to establish relationships between the two, and in due course, to move from meaning to reading subskills.
5. Start building vocabulary and concepts by incorporating cross-cultural reading materials within the school-adopted reading program. This will allow ethnolinguistically different students to identify with their own culture and heritage and simultaneously acquaint and enrich their peers with another culture.
6. Do not treat "different" pronunciations as errors that must be corrected. Respect and accept students' courage and efforts in speaking and reading orally in the target language. Know that they will make "errors" because they will transfer phonological and syntactic features of their native linguistic system into the one they are required to learn. Instead, say the proper pronunciation for one utterance at a time, so that it can be repeated and used in different sentences.
7. Encourage all students to accept ethnolinguistic differences as divergent from, not interfering with, the target language; and treat language divergencies always as an opportunity to enrich all reading-learning situations.
8. Become aware that reading comprehension in the target language must be understood in the wider perspective of cultural and sociopsychological divergencies that are inherent in all readers and learners. Avoid teaching reading comprehension in the often-narrow perspective of school directives that are to be executed in the even-narrower classroom enclave.

Summary

American and Canadian school systems are still steeped in traditional and conventional ways of administering education by conducting classes in the language of the majority of school children. Much has yet to be accomplished in actually adapting and extending classroom instruction to all children as members of today's pluralistic societies. Much needs to be changed in monolingual-directed classroom instruction in general and reading in particular to accommodate the immense diversity of the cultural schemata that directs human thinking and makes, in turn, meaningful learning possible. As long as the viewpoint of the thinking-cultural schemata of the so-called English majority predominates over the thinking-cultural schemata of the so-called minority subcultures, mismatching of learning-reading instruction will continue to plague the school systems. Many otherwise able children with divergent ethnolinguistic backgrounds will continue to be assigned to remedial instruction where their true potential to learn will not be developed. Eight recommendations to the monolinguistc teacher suggest ways to make all children of English speaking and non-English speaking parentage full members and partakers in learning to read and reading to learn.

CHAPTER 11

Evaluating the Readers' Reading

Purpose questions for this chapter:
- What are summative and formative evaluations?
- What are some characteristics of norm-referenced tests?
- What is criterion-referenced testing?
- How is informal assessment different from formal assessment?
- What is a cloze procedure?
- How can I use an informal reading inventory?

USING ASSESSMENT FOR EVALUATION

When a student reads orally, the teacher can appraise the oral reading performance. Over a period of time, the gathered data provide quantitative measures that can be used to assess strengths and weaknesses in reading.

The results of appraisal, assessment, and measurement can form the basis for evaluation. The *Dictionary of Reading and Related Terms* (Harris & Hodges, 1981) defines evaluation as "judgment of performance as a product or process of change" (p. 108). Changes that result from students' performance in sight-word recognition, in fluent oral reading, and in multiple-choice tests given after silent reading can form the basis for evaluating achievement and growth in these areas.

Change in reading achievement is measured most often by using either formal or informal testing procedures. In its broad application, evaluation is targeted toward the students and measures how much they have learned and consequently improved as a result of expected learning.

Measuring through testing is usually done after completion of learning tasks near the end of the school year. Through posttesting, or testing after learning, the outcomes of learning can be obtained. This kind of assessment is known as summative assessment, as it sums up what students have learned after the learning is over. The data received through testing can be used to assist in evaluating the reading program or any part of it.

While summative evaluation is important to the overall reading program, more important to the classroom teacher is formative evaluation, which assesses reading-learning performance while it is in progress. Formative evaluation is based on a number of ongoing dimensions. The teacher needs to determine how many of, to what degree, and how well the instructional goals have been accomplished. The students need to become aware of to what extent they have achieved their goals. Since neither "teacherproof" nor "studentproof" nor "materialproof" instructional procedures exist, formative evaluation must look at teacher, students, and materials during the actual reading-learning processes. It also must examine reciprocal feedback between teachers and students and analyze how well reading performance measures up against the standards of reading established by the school system.

Evaluation, then, can be either summative or formative in nature. Evaluation that views the reading performance of students in a classroom, a school, a school system, a province, a state, a nation, or several nations, for the purpose of classifying students into high, average, and low achievers, tends to be summative in nature and not to be concerned directly with how reading was taught and how individual students performed. Evaluation that views reading from the point of teaching and what is going on during instruction tends to be formative in nature (Martin, 1983, p. 114). The question then arises: At what time is what kind of evaluation appropriate for what kind of purposes?

Individual Assessment

Individual readers' performances can be sampled every time they read, recognize words orally, and answer questions orally or in writing. Each sample then can be compared with the previous one, and an ongoing evaluation can be started at the end of each school year. Similarly, when tested at the end of each school year, year-end samples of individual students' reading performances can be compared and quantitative progress evaluated.

Evaluation can provide individual students with information about their own performance, reflecting any efforts to improve. Ongoing performance assessments can reflect a whole spectrum of individual student inclinations and mental dispositions toward active or passive involvement in the reading-learning task.

Through this kind of evaluation, teachers also can gain insights into their own teaching of reading. That is, if "properly used, evaluation should enable teachers to make marked improvements in their students' learning" (Bloom, Hastings, & Madaus, 1971, p. v). In this sense, results of individual assessment can indicate how well instruction—through presentation, explanation, and structure of content—reaches the students; how well short- and long-term goals and objectives are accomplished; and how instruction is affected through strengths and weaknesses in preparing and delivering reading lessons.

Classroom Assessment

In group performance, ongoing evaluation provides students with measures of their own accomplishment, compared to total peer accomplishments. Although these also are concrete, quantitative measurements, they lend themselves to comparing achievements with other or all members in a group or class. When the achievements are expressed in numbers, students who have received higher numbers are perceived as being better, smarter, or brainier than the less-fortunate ones who have attained lower numbers on this test at this time under these circumstances. In this way, these measures can be misleading because of misinterpretation by students and sometimes teachers.

Group measurements in reading performance, however, supply classroom and subject-matter teachers with information that can be important in the planning of future instruction, in guiding individual and group reading, and in teacher-student feedback.

The outcome of the ongoing, formative group evaluation should be directed by the teacher particularly toward his or her own teaching. Evaluation outcomes should prompt teachers to ask themselves if the teaching pace is too fast or too slow; if voice articulation is clear, audible, monotonous, or interesting; if usage of words and sentence structures is appropriate to the student schemata; and if instructional approaches are suitable to the learning styles and cognitive styles of the students.

When formative evaluation continues as a supporting factor during instruction, the use of diagnostic or analytic teaching may result in marked improvements in students' learning.

Diagnostic Teaching. Diagnostic teaching is the fusing of diagnosis and instruction into a single teaching process. According to Guszak (1978), diagnostic teaching requires a specially trained teacher, called a diagnostic reading teacher, whose special and unique skills should prevent failures in reading (p. 1). Thus, in teaching reading from a diagnostic point of view, the teacher looks for factors within the student that contribute to or produce failure and then tries to find reasons for these factors.

In my opinion, however, diagnostic teaching is inadequate in that it addresses only those who do not read well and assesses their reading performance in accordance with a failure conceptualization.

Analytic Teaching. Analytical teaching of reading, in contrast, addresses and assesses all students' reading performance. It consists usually of a five-step procedure (Hittleman, 1983, p. 88). In *describing*, teachers observe how students read but make no judgments of their reading behaviors. Describing leads to placing students into a plan, structure, or schema of the reading process, known as *classifying*. *Inferring* the quality of performance in the various reading tasks is done by using a set of guidelines. These can be applied to individuals as well as to groups of students and are consistent with the plan of the reading process. In *predicting*, the fourth step, decisions are made regarding how the observed reading performance needs to be modified, and hence, what planning should follow to integrate any modification. In the end, planning and modifying needs to be confirmed through *verifying*, the last step, which determines whether or not the planning was effective in regard to the individual student's reading performance.

School Assessment and Beyond

Assessment in reading achievement is also the concern of the school principal and all the other teachers in that school. Single-classroom assessment may extend into a schoolwide assessment that will tell more about the general state of reading. At this point, reading assessment becomes summative in nature. Assessment is done once a year, usually near the end of the school year. Results of a schoolwide assessment provide information to principals and other administrative personnel about the direction and adequacy of students' development in reading. Development is seen in terms of total student performance within each classroom. Performance also may be separated into high, low, and average achievement, depending upon how the results are to be used by the administrator of school units and districts. Since schoolwide assessment is repeated each year, accumulated results provide a basis for long-term summative evaluation. This will show, for instance, how total results in vocabulary and comprehension performance fluctuate over the years and what directions the performance takes. When each school district establishes similar bases for assessing reading achievement, summative evaluation can extend beyond schools to become statewide, provincewide, to national and international in scope.

An example of a schoolwide reading evaluation is the Taschow and Cicansky (1982) three-year report on French immersion instruction. For provincewide reading evaluation, a good example would be the Tuinman and Kendall (1980) *British Columbia Reading Assessment*. An example of a nationwide reading evaluation would be the Micklos (1982) report on reading achievement. For international reading evaluation, I would suggest the Thorndike (1973) fifteen-nation study on the relationship between vocabulary knowledge and reading comprehension, and the Collins and Demos (1983b) fourteen-country report on trends and needs in beginning reading instruction.

Summary

Assessing reading performance leads to evaluation by which individual and group samples may be compared. These are expressed in numerical or quantitative measurements that can be designated as high, average, and low performance. Assessment can be either summative or formative, and evaluation can be directed toward individual, classroom, and schoolwide performance. It can even extend to state, provincial, national, and international evaluation. Assessment results can provide teachers with the feedback they need to modify their methods, perhaps by including diagnostic or analytic teaching of reading.

FORMAL TESTING

Formal testing in reading means to assess students' reading performance. To say, however, "assess reading performance," is somewhat preposterous, yet it is applied most often to the process of evaluating reading. It would be more accurate to speak of the different dimensions of reading that are to be assessed and by which kind of assessment instrument. Teachers should look for answers to questions like, What are students' reading scores in vocabulary, comprehension, and reading rate achievement? What does the test measure, and how are the scores obtained? How do the scores of one student compare with other students in class? Answers to these and other questions can be obtained from the results of formal assessment instruments.

Standardized Reading Tests

One way to find out what students do in various facets of reading is to administer one of the many standardized reading tests on the market today. All standardized tests, including the reading tests, that have been commercially produced are listed and critically reviewed with related information in the volumes of Oscar K. Buros' (1978) *Mental Measurements Yearbooks* or MMYs. These are reference volumes that have been published periodically, not annually since 1938. A smaller edition, entitled *Reading Tests and Reviews*, also edited by O. K. Buros (1975), deals with reading tests and related information only.

The word "standardized" as used in the phrase *standardized reading tests* does not mean that there is a certain set standard or a specified goal that students must reach or accomplish. Rather, the expression *standardized* indicates that there is a uniform method of administering the parts or subtests of the test, of scoring and recording the answers, and of transforming and translating the raw scores into understandable and usable results. The procedures are fully described and written out for the teacher in the test manual that accompanies the test booklets for the students. The test manual also notes how thoroughly the test—as a whole and in its parts—has been experimentally researched. It tells how much time is to be given to complete each subtest, what the test's and subtests' reliability and validity are, how to score the test, what kinds of scores or norms can be obtained, how to obtain them from accompanying statistical tables, and how to interpret the test scores.

Norm-Referenced Tests. Standardized reading tests, also known as norm-referenced tests, usually are of the survey type; are given to students in a classroom; and are designed to sample proficiency in vocabulary, comprehension, and reading rate. Each subtest has its own predetermined length of time during which answers to the presented test items must be given. Length of time is printed in the manual and must be adhered to and strictly complied with. The possibility that a student could answer more questions when given more time clearly is not the point in any standardized instrument.

The first yield of answers from a test is known as the *raw score*, that is, the actual number of correct answers that a student has produced by marking the appropriate spaces on the scoring sheet. A raw score is the first quantitative indication of points earned by the student on this particular subtest. When added, the total points on the whole test represent the *total raw score* attained at this time on this test. If, for instance, there are 100 words in a vocabulary subtest and a student has marked fifty-four items of the 100 words, and if the fifty-four items are correct, the student's raw score is fifty-four. However, the raw score is not the one most often obtained on standardized tests.

Raw scores are converted into *derived scores* or *norms* and are commonly reported as grade-equivalency, percentile, and stanine scores.

Criterion-Referenced Tests. Another type of standardized test, in addition to the norm-referenced test, is the criterion-referenced test. While norm-referenced tests are used to assess students' performance in relation to that of the normal population used in standardizing, criterion-referenced tests assess students' mastery of specific tasks. The former are used for comparison; the latter tell what an individual reader is able to do. A score on a norm-referenced test shows placement in relation to a group; a score on a criterion-referenced test shows placement in relation to a set of goals or standards. For instance, a specific score may be obtained by measuring the students' ability to pronounce consonant-vowel-consonant trigrams (CVCs) in grade two.

In constructing criterion-referenced instruments, test makers assume a hierarchy of reading skills that must be achieved in succession, with one particular skill being mastered before moving on to the next. The *Wisconsin Design for Reading Skill Development*, for example, published by National Computer Systems, Minneapolis, Minnesota, is an objective-based approach to reading that includes assessment through criterion-referenced tests (Morrison, 1979, p. 35).

This assumption of hierarchy, however, is not necessarily valid. Samuels (1976) suggests that, while subskill mastery may be essential to achieving skill in reading, "the sad truth is that the task is so complex that a validated reading hierarchy does not exist" (p. 174). Bourque (1980), in comparing two models of methodologies used for establishing hierarchical relationships, used the criterion-referenced test data from several phonics and structural-analysis skill sections selected from a reading skills battery. When reading experts were asked to establish the hypothesized hierarchy, Bourque found that "these experts' opinions were less stable than the hierarchies based on the empirical data obtained with either model (Downing & Leong, 1982, p. 25).

Teachers and students of reading, at least for the present time and until empirical evidence provides the contrary, must observe in relation to criterion-referenced test data that research "has not upheld the distinctness or increasing difficulty of such hierarchical levels" (Radebough, 1983, p. 601).

Using Reading Tests. While standardized reading tests are frequently administered, their use does not always agree with the purposes for which the tests were developed. The purposes of any norm-referenced and criterion-referenced test should be clearly stated in the manual. Webb (1983) suggests that the stated purpose of the test should indicate how appropriate the test is for use by the classroom teacher. To use a reading test just because it is said to be the best on the market or has been used over the years and served well the school's expectations may not represent sound educational practices.

When using test and subtest scores obtained from norm-referenced reading tests, comparisons are invariably made of reading achievement between and among students, classes, and schools (Baumann & Stevenson, 1982, p. 528). In making comparisons, teachers must be aware that reading survey tests provide global measures of achievement only. They do not provide specific diagnostic information. Results from reading survey tests are best used as screening scores for group placement and for referring for further diagnostic evaluation. Test scores should always be considered in conjunction with a student's academic potential, test-taking ability, and performance in the current reading program.

A further concern in using standardized reading tests is administering a test that does not fit a student's reading ability. This is a malpractice that is widespread throughout school systems, and its shortcomings are rather obvious.

Recognizing these shortcomings, Gunning (1982) suggests out-of-level testing, which means assigning "tests on the basis of the students' reading ability rather than on the basis of grade placement" (p. 903). As discussed earlier, multilevel reading materials have been developed to overcome individual differences in reading abilities, so out-of-level testing seems to be the sensible way to match testing with instruction. It should be clear that grade-level testing "yields erroneous information, can be frustrating to children [for] whom the test is a mismatch, may mask achievement gains, and worst of all, may prevent some children from getting the help they need by falsely minimizing or even hiding the severity of their reading problems" (p. 905). The positive aspects of out-of-level testing are confirmed by L.L. Smith et al. (1983) in their research with fourth-and fifth-grade remedial readers in compensatory reading programs. Their studies suggest that out-of-level testing may give a more reliable estimate of reading achievement.

Summary

Assessment is done through group and individual testing, including the norm-referenced reading tests and criterion-referenced reading subskills tests that are widely used in today's elementary schools. Norm-referenced tests are standardized reading tests that assess and compare student performance in vocabulary, comprehension, and reading rate. The results are expressed in raw scores from which grade-equivalence, percentile, and stanine scores are obtained. Criterion-referenced tests, which assess what an individual can do, are based on the assumption that reading consists of a known hierarchy of subskills that must be mastered in sequence. This assumption has not upheld by research.

INFORMAL TESTING

Informal or nonstandardized assessment responds to the need for information that is lacking or cannot be obtained from standardized tests. Both kinds of assessment are important and supplement and complement each other. How and why students do what they do during reading and learning is left to informal assessment.

Teachers, as I have been assured by many, believe they have to use informal assessment during the teaching of reading to assure themselves that students have read and that they have understood through reading. As part of informal assessment, teachers probe with oral and written questions. On demand, students read orally, to prove that they can read all the words and at the same time understand the sounded-out word patterns.

Informal assessment generally can be a very valuable complement to its formal counterpart. Like formal assessment, it can provide samples that can be compared later in evaluating either group or individual performance. Informal assessment also can be ongoing and may yield raw scores or earned points. But otherwise, informal assessment lacks most of the characteristics of standardized test construction, such as a norming population and normative data. Informal assessment procedures can be very vague, as with the use of round-robin oral reading to test how well students read. The procedures also can be precise, as in testing the hearing of the same sound.

Informal assessment instruments are usually composed by the teacher, who decides on their content, scoring, and interpretation as well as on the date and time of administration. Teacher-made tests may have an edge over standardized tests in that they may reflect better the actual teaching purposes because they intend to test what has been taught in this particular classroom and what students can be expected to know. Examples of such intruments are the in-between quizzes and the longer unit tests given after a course of instruction has been completed.

These teacher-made informal instruments can be supplemented by the cloze test and the informal reading inventory. Since both are well-recognized and recommended by most authorities in the field and since they are widely used by teachers of reading in classrooms to assess students' reading proficiency, these two instruments are discussed here in regard to what they are; how they are constructed, administered, and scored; and how teachers and students benefit from the results.

The Cloze Procedure

In 1953 Wilson L. Taylor developed the cloze procedure, which is a technique for constructing tests. Rankin (1959) pointed out that cloze tests are neither difficult nor expensive. Therefore teachers can prepare enough of them to do frequent sampling and comparing of individual performance and progress in reading.

Since the 1950s, cloze test techniques and their validity and importance have been discussed, disputed, and researched, as evidenced by Schneyer (1965), Rankin and Culhane (1969), Ohnmacht and Fleming (1972), and, more recently, Cziko (1983) and Duffelmeyer (1983). These teaching instruments have been used to test improvement in students' language abilities as well as knowledge of vocabulary. Mateja (1982) reports on a cloze procedure applied in music, and Propst and Baldauf (1979) report using it to test English proficiency of students for whom English was a second language. Cziko (1983) emphasizes that it appears that the cloze procedure "is here for a long stay of widespread use in education as a measure of reading comprehension and general language proficiency," and that "we need to make a serious effort to learn how to make the best of it" (p. 364).

The term *cloze* is derived from the gestalt concept of *closure*, which means to fill in the missing gap or to complete a structured whole, such as to fill in a missing (deleted) word in a sentence. The reader then must anticipate meaning from the given context and supply the correct word by writing it in the blank space. Taylor (1953) defines the cloze procedure as a method of "intercepting a message from a 'transmitter' [a sender], mutilating its language patterns by deleting parts, and so administering it to 'receivers' that their attempts to make the patterns whole again potentially yield a considerable number of cloze units" (p. 416).

To make a cloze test, no expertise in test construction is required. By following a set of procedural steps, anyone can construct a cloze test.

Preparation, Administration, Scoring, and Interpretation. To prepare a cloze test, start with the beginning portion of a book, chapter, story, or passage that you plan to use for instruction (Rankin & Culhane, 1969, p. 195). First, select a 275-word passage, then delete every fifth word to a maximum of fifty words, making sure to start and finish the selected passage with a complete sentence. Finally, type up the cloze test and leave an underlined blank space in place of each deleted word. Spaces should be always of equal length disregarding the length of the deleted words in the passage.

Distribute the cloze test to the students and instruct them to (1) fill in the blank spaces by writing down the words they think will best fit the meaning of each sentence and the whole passage; (2) write with a pencil so it will be easier to erase and change a word when they think it should be changed; (3) try hard to fill in every blank; and (4) not be concerned about time as there is no time limit for completing the text.

When completed, students return the tests for scoring. The teacher (1) marks every word that is not the same as the one deleted from the chosen passage (no synonyms are accepted), (2) totals up the unmarked correct responses, (3) calculates the percentage of correct responses, and (4) determines the level of a student's performance.

There are various suggestions for interpreting the scores. Rankin and Culhane (1969, p. 197) indicate that when 61 percent or more of the deleted words—30 words or more—are correctly replaced, the reading materials are probably at the student's *independent reading level*. Students will benefit from such materials when reading independently. When 41 percent or more of the deleted words—20 words or more—are correctly replaced, the reading materials are probably at the students' *instructional reading level*. Students will benefit from such reading materials, but only with teacher guidance. Assistance will be needed with background experiences, readiness, unfamiliar words and their structure and usage, concept building, purpose setting, and comprehension. When 40 percent or less of the deleted words—20 words or less—are correctly replaced, the reading materials are probably at the student's *frustration level*. Students will not benefit from them, and other avenues of learning must be found.

Cloze as a Teaching Device. As a measuring instrument, the cloze procedure has been and still is widely researched. Nonetheless, the cloze procedure has been used as a means to improve reading comprehension and language abilities. Cloze tests can be administered before beginning and after completing certain reading tasks. By finding the differences between preperformances and postperformances, gains or losses can be determined (Rankin, 1965, p. 137). Students can discuss why certain words fit the blank spaces while others do not, what kinds of words they are, and how meaning from surrounding words in the sentences can assist in determining the missing words. When unable to decide which word fits best, students should be urged to read on before choosing a word, to consider the preceding and succeeding meanings of the passage, and to call on their background experiences in order to avoid wild guessing.

Cloze procedures can be constructed with various types of deletions. The preceding discussion reflects a type called "every-nth" deletion, which is done without regard to grammatical form. The nth-word deletion appears to be well suited for students' showing their mental capacity for understanding structural meaning of syntax. Another type of deletion is known as "noun-verb" deletion, or deleting words in regard to grammatical form. Variations may include deletion of adjectives, adverbs, pronouns, conjunctions, and so on.

By using the every-nth procedure, as in deleting every fifth word, the spaces are fixed. By using the "random" procedure, word-deletion spaces are not fixed. In fact, exercises in sentence completion use mostly random procedure, as can be seen in workbooks.

A sample cloze procedure is illustrated in Figure 11.1. Directions should be modified according to purpose and grade level and may be read orally by the teacher while followed silently by the students. Questions should be clarified before starting. Remember, this is a power test and has no time limit. Note that this small sample does not contain the required fifty deletions; nevertheless, it shows how a cloze test would look with the beginning and ending sentences unmutilated.

Before moving on to another yet more comprehensive sampling procedure, it should be remembered that, while the construction of the cloze test

Evaluating the Reader's Reading

FIGURE 11.1.   Sample Cloze Procedure

Student Name:_____ Grade:_____ Date:_____

<u>Directions</u>: In this story, every fifth word has been left out. Read quickly through the story to get the general idea. To fill in the proper words that are missing, you must anticipate the meaning of the writer of the story. Write the appropriate word, one word only, on each blank line.

The Shoemaker

In the house there was a shop where a little old man made shoes. A little old woman _____ him. They were happy _____ they had made many _____.

One night the little _____ man....

Late that day the _____ man went out to _____ more leather to make _____ shoes. When he got back, he didn't have time to make the shoes.

---

is relatively uncomplicated, its value, like that of all other informal testing, is related directly to the objectivity and competence of the examiner.

Informal Reading Inventory

Another instrument used to bridge the gap between the contents of standardized reading tests and the contents of the reading curricula is the informal reading inventory (IRI). Like the cloze procedure, the IRI reflects the specific reading content employed in a particular classroom; and unlike normative tests, the IRI has greater utility in assessing students' strengths and weaknesses, aiding placement in reading programs.

Informal reading inventories began with Wheat (1923), who recommended that the first weeks of each school year should be spent by having students read orally and silently from several books that vary in level of difficulty. This, in essence, is the very core of an IRI. The lead given by Wheat was picked up by Betts (1946), who is credited with being the first to describe the technique of an informal reading inventory. The following discussion of the IRI is based on Betts' description, with minor adjustments as research has warranted them over the forty years of ongoing practice with the IRI.

First, however, let us take a look at some of these research implications. As is the case with most informal instruments that may be applied to reading instruction, some or all of the concepts involved in the IRI still await empirical validation. Perhaps the first two studies, also cited in Betts (1946), are that of Young (1936), who investigated the relation of reading comprehension and retention to hearing comprehension and retention; followed by Killgallon (1942), who investigated relationships among factors in pupil adjustment to reading situations. Later, H.L. Beldin (1970) reviewed historical and research aspects of informal testing, and Powell (1971) used a validity study to probe the reading levels of the information reading inventory. Pikulski (1974) delivered a critical review of the IRI. In the 1980s, Fuchs, Fuchs, and Deno (1982) produced a reliability and validity study of curriculum-based IRIs; and McKenna (1983) reviewed the extant literature and discussed the important issues related to the Informal Reading Inventory.

In 1965, Johnson and Kress published a manual for developing and using IRIs, a book that, as Clymer wrote in its introduction, clearly and distinctly bridges the chasm between theory and practice. IRIs are constructed instruments that can assist classroom teachers and clinicians alike in learning and understanding more about students' levels of reading achievement, capacity to achieve, and specific strengths and weaknesses. Let us now consider the steps involved in administering the IRI.

Isolated Word Recognition. An IRI begins with teacher-student rapport and is followed by assessing the student's proficiency in recognizing words in isolation. These words are taken from known word lists or from glossaries found in basal readers or current textbooks. There are about twenty words in each list, beginning with preprimer to sixth level. Each stimulus word may have two responses: an immediate or flash response and a delayed or untimed response. The immediate response indicates the student's ability to recognize words on sight, while the delayed response shows the ability to work out words by using phonics and structural subskills when given additional time. In recording responses, a zero (0) is given for no response and a checkmark (✓) for a correct response, and when both responses in flash and untimed are incorrect, this checkmark (✓) is used. When the stimulus word is pronounced incorrectly, the examiner writes the response on the blank line. Figure 11.2 shows a sample IRI procedure; note that the explanation column has been added only for the readers of this text, as it does not appear otherwise.

Correct responses in each column are totaled, with 90 percent in the flash column constituting a minimum score that, when received twice in succession, signals the discontinuation of word recognition and the beginning of the reading inventory. If word recognition ends at the third level, then the reading inventory starts one level below, or at the second level.

In sum, word recognition in isolation assesses three specific factors: (1) the ability to recognize words immediately, (2) the ability to work out

Evaluating the Reader's Reading

FIGURE 11.2. Sample IRI Response Record for Isolated Word Recognition

Name		C.A.	Date
Pre-Primer Level			
Stimulus	Flash	Untimed	(Explanation)
1. you	√		correct immediate response
2. on	an	√	incorrect in Flash, correct in Untimed after working out
3. it	0	√	no response in Flash, correct after working out
4. come	came √		incorrect response but immediately corrected
5. here	0	her	no response in Flash, incorrect response in Untimed
6. what	that	want √	Flash and Untimed incorrect

words, and (3) the level at which to start the reading inventory. Following the assessment of word recognition in isolation, students proceed to oral and silent reading of words in the context of longer passages.

Preparation of the Reading Inventory. From a basal reader series that students are not using in their current reading program, a teacher should select two passages for each level, beginning with preprimer to level eight. Similar selections can be made when graded series of subject-matter textbooks are used. One selection is for oral reading, done on sight, without preparation; the other is for silent reading, with parts to be selected for oral rereading. Each selection increases in length of words as reading progresses through the levels. For preprimer to third reading level, selected passages range in length from 30 to 50 words; for levels four to six, from 50 to 100 words; for levels seven and eight, from 100 to 150 words; and for students in grades nine to twelve, passages range up to 200 words. However, length of materials must be controlled sufficiently to avoid student fatigue in performance.

When the selections have been chosen, questions are constructed for each reading passage. Since the purpose of the questions is to sample student ability to recall and reorganize facts and to explain vocabulary meaning and make inferences, questions must address themselves to these abilities. Ten questions are suggested, of which three ask for facts, three for vocabulary, and four for inferential understanding. The teacher asks the questions orally, and students answer orally. Two copies of each selection on each level should be prepared: one for the teacher that includes questions; the other for the student without questions.

Oral Reading at Sight, Comprehension. The student is asked to read orally the designated passage. Since the student has not had the opportunity to look over or read the passage before reading orally, this kind of practice is known as oral reading at sight, or ORS. As the student reads, the teacher or examiner listens to pronunciation, hesitation, intonation, and fluency. Errors are marked immediately (see Figure 11.3), resulting in a score that reflects word recognition (W/R) in context. Only one error is counted per word; hence five errors within a 50-word passage would result in an ORS score of 90

FIGURE 11.3. Sample IRI Response Record, with Symbol Explanation, for Word Recognition in Context During ORS

1. Sample sentence from reading passage: Mother goes to town to buy groceries.
2. Sample sentence as read by the student: My mother went to the towns buy to . . . gro-gro-groceries.
3. Sample sentence as marked by the teacher to show the student's response:

My ^Mother ~~goes~~ went to ^the towns to buy // groceries.

Symbols	What they mean
∧	insertion, place caret and word where inserted
~~goes~~ went	substitution, cross out word and write new word over it
//	hesitation, a slanted line before the word equals about a second
___	repetition, part of or whole word
◯	unknown word, teacher says it
s	addition, underline added sounds
~~s~~	omission, cross out omitted sounds
⌒	inversion, words changed in position
⌣	running on sentences, ...went to town. We got...

percent. When ORS is completed, the student closes the booklet, and the teacher asks the ten predesigned questions and records the given answers. If eight out of ten answers are correct, the comprehension score is 80 percent.

Silent Reading and Oral Rereading. Silent reading on the same level follows ORS. As the student reads silently, if difficult or unknown words are encountered, the teacher pronounces them and the student continues reading. However, the teacher records these words by circling them in the text booklet. While the student reads silently, the teacher watches for excessive lip movement, head movement, fingerpointing, subvocalization, and other disturbing symptoms. After completion, a silent-reading score is obtained, and the student is asked the comprehension questions.

Oral rereading (ORR) follows the silent reading. This time the teacher asks the student to read orally a small portion of the passage the student has just read silently. The teacher may say, "Find the part of the story that tells us how the boy felt about his first airplane ride." The student first locates, then reads aloud this portion. The teacher listens, checks for word recognition errors, and observes whether the student performs better in oral rereading than in oral reading at sight.

The student proceeds through increasingly more difficult levels of reading passages until oral and silent reading and comprehension performances reach the frustration level. Then student reading ceases, and the student listens to the teacher read.

Listening Comprehension. The last part of the IRI is known as listening comprehension or probable capacity. The teacher reads aloud from the selected passages, and the student listens and again answers ten questions, which are scored by the teacher. When a reading level is reached in which the student answers less than 70 percent of the questions correctly, the listening comprehension portion of the IRI is terminated. At this point the IRI is complete, and the teacher can compute the student's total scores.

Interpreting the IRI. Based on the scores a student obtains at each level of increasingly more difficult passages, a teacher can determine the student's independent, instructional, frustration, and listening-comprehension levels. The scores to use in determining these levels are given in Table 11.1

The independent reading level may be described as that level at which readers can read on their own and are able to engage in extensive reading activities. Care must be taken, however, that the vocabulary load of specific words and their concepts does not become a barrier to independent reading. Materials should be at or near the readers' levels.

The instructional reading level may be described as that level at which

TABLE 11.1. IRI Scores to Use in Determining Reading Levels

Word Recognition (W/R)	Comprehension	Reading Level
99-100%	90%	Independent
95%	70%	Instructional
90% or less	50% or less	Frustration
none	70%	Listening Comprehension or Probable Capacity

learning begins. Teacher guidance and assistance are essential to improvement in graphophonic, syntactic, and semantic information processing; in reading certainty, fluency, and speed; and in reading attitude and interest.

The frustration level in reading may be described as being the level at which readers are unable to extract meaning from print. Reading materials are beyond their abilities. Difficult reading materials on the one hand and lack of preparedness on the other hand may lead to excessively disturbing symptoms that may contribute to even greater frustration. Readers at this level need extensive help from the teacher, which may exceed not only teacher time but also teacher expertise. Additional assistance from personnel trained in reading may be desirable.

The listening-comprehension or probable-capacity level may be described as being the highest level at which listeners still comprehend what is read to them. For instance, poor readers, in upper-elementary and junior and senior high schools may "switch" from getting information through reading to getting it through listening. Dedicated parents have been known to read textbooks to their children, so that they can follow instruction in school. The probable-capacity level also reflects the level that can be achieved in reading, provided proper instructions are given. When a substantial difference exists between instructional and listening comprehension levels, rapid improvement can be realized that will bring the student back to the instructional level.

In sum, IRIs can and do indicate students' levels of achievement as well as specific strengths and weaknesses in oral and silent reading and its comprehension. IRIs provide reading materials that students read at successively higher levels until the level is reached at which they can no longer read adequately. Without reference to what other students do and achieve in reading, an IRI reveals the reading performance of the individual reader, whose needs become the basis for further teacher guidance, instruction, and assistance.

Some words of caution, nevertheless, are in order. To remain in tune with classroom instruction and instructional materials, IRIs need to be revised and reconstructed frequently. This is not apparent when using commercially published IRIs. These are based on materials not used in actual instruction. There is a tendency to "standardize" the contents of the IRIs, as was done with those by Sucher and Allred (1971), Woods and Moe (1977), Burns and Roe (1980a), and Silvaroli (1982).

Another caution concerns the reading levels. An instructional reading level that is obtained from general reading materials of a basal reading series may change when the same students are observed reading in inventories constructed from graded textbook series in social studies, science, mathematics, health, and other subject matters. Special vocabulary decreases ease of readability, and difficult or even unknown concepts overdraw schemata availability. Also, more complex sentence structures and longer paragraphs may well overload the processing capacity for extracting and carrying meaning from beginning to end.

Summary

Informal tests are teacher-made instruments. They are a valuable complement to their formal counterparts in that they add important information, not to be attained otherwise, to a thorough understanding of students' proficiency, comprehension, and behavior during reading. Two widely used informal teacher-made instruments are the cloze procedure for use with a total classroom population and the informal reading inventory for use in a one-to-one teacher-student setting. While the cloze asks students to complete mutilated language patterns to form a structured whole, the IRI requires students to demonstrate capacities in reading, responding, and listening. Informal instruments are here to stay, and can and do provide adequate means for revealing students' strengths and weaknesses in reading. Their benefits, however, depend on how thoroughly those who use teacher-made instruments understand them.

REFERENCES
ABOUT THE AUTHOR
INDEX

References

Abrams, J. C., & Kaslow, F. Family system and the learning disabled child: Intervention and treatment. Journal of Learning Disabilities, 1977, 10, 86-90.

Academy for Educational Development and the Edward W. Hazen Foundation. A new direction for bilingual education in the 1980s. Focus, March 1982, No. 10.

Adams, A., Carnine, D., & Gersten, R. Instructional strategies for studying content area texts in the intermediate grades. Reading Research Quarterly, 1982, 18:1, 27-55.

Agnew, A. T. Using children's dictated stories to assess code consciousness. The Reading Teacher, 1982, 35:4, 450-454.

Alatis, J. E. TESOL: Teaching English to Speakers of Other Languages. In the 79th Yearbook of the NSSE, Part II, Learning a Second Language. Chicago: University of Chicago Press, 1980, 88-103.

Allen, R. V. The Language Experience Approach. In R. Karlin (Ed.), Perspectives on Elementary Reading. New York: Harcourt Brace Jovanovich, 1973, 158-166.

Allen, R. V., & Allen, C. An Introduction to a Language Experience Program, Level 1. Chicago: Encyclopedia Britannica Press, 1966.

Allen, S. Using small groups in an individualized reading program. Reading-Canada-Lecture, 1983, 2:1, 47-51.

Allport, G. W. Becoming. New Haven and London: Yale University Press, 1963.

Alvermann, D. E., & Boothby, P. R. Text differences: Children's perception at the transition stage in reading. The Reading Teacher, 1982, 36:3, 298-302.

Anderson, R. C., & Freebody, P. Vocabulary knowledge. In J. T. Guthrie (Ed.), Comprehension and Teaching: Research Reviews. Newark, Del.: International Reading Association, 1981.

André, M. E. D. A., & Anderson, T. H. The development and evaluation of a self-questioning study technique. Reading Research Quarterly, 1978-1979, 14:4, 605-623.

Anselmo, S. Improving home and preschool influences on early language development. The Reading Teacher, 1978, 32:2, 139-143.

Asbell, B. The case of wandering IQs. Redbook Magazine, August 1967, pp. 32-33, 112-118.

Au, K. H. P. Using the experience-text-relationship method with minority children. The Reading Teacher, 1979, 32:6, 677-679.

Aukerman, R. C. The Basal Reader Approach to Reading. New York: John Wiley, 1981.

Aulls, M. W. Developing Readers in Today's Elementary School. Boston: Allyn & Bacon, 1982.

Ausubel, D. P. In defence of advance organizers: A reply to the critics. Review of Educational Research, 1978, 48, 251-257.

Ausubel, D. P. Enhancing the acquisition of knowledge. In the 79th Yearbook of NSSE, Part I, Toward Adolescence: The Middle School Years. Chicago: University of Chicago Press, 1980, 227-250.

Ausubel, D. P., & Fitzgerald, D. Organizers, general background, and antecedent learning variables in sequential verbal learning. In R. C. Anderson & D. P. Ausubel (Eds.), Readings in the Psychology of Cognition. New York: Holt, Rinehart and Winston, 1965, 290-302.

Auten, A. Reading and writing: A mutual support system. Journal of Reading, 1983, 26:4, 366-369. (a)

Auten, A. The ultimate connection: Reading, listening, writing, speaking--thinking. The Reading Teacher, 1983, 36:6, 584-587. (b)

Babbs, P. J., & Moe, A. J. Metacognition: A key for independent learning from text. The Reading Teacher, 1983, 36:4, 422-426.

Baratz, J. C. Language and cognitive assessment of Negro children: Assumption and research needs. American Speech and Hearing Association Journal, 1969, 11, 88.

Baratz, J. C. Teaching reading in an urban Negro school system. In F. Williams (Ed.), Language and Poverty, Chicago: Rand McNally, 1973, 11-21.

Barnitz, J. G. Black English and other dialects: Sociolinguistic implications for reading instruction. The Reading Teacher, 1980, 33:7, 779-786. (a)

Barnitz, J. G. Syntactic effects on the reading comprehension of pronoun-referent structures by children in grades two, four and six. Reading Research Quarterly, 1980, 15:2, 268-289. (b)

Baron, R. W., & Baron, J. How children get meaning from printed words. Child Development, 1977, 48, 587-594.

References

Bartel, K. J. German and the Germans at the time of the American Revolution. *Modern Language Journal*, March 1976, 60, 96.

Bartlett, E. J. Selecting an early childhood language curriculum. In C. B. Cazden (Ed.), *Language in Early Childhood Education* (rev. ed.). Washington, D.C.: National Association for the Education of Young Children, 1981, 33-75.

Baumann, J. F., & Stevenson, J. A. Using scores from standardized reading achievement tests. *The Reading Teacher*, 1982, 35:5, 528-532.

Beers, C. S. Relationship of cognitive development to spelling and reading abilities. In E. H. Henderson & J. W. Beers (Eds.), *Developmental and Cognitive Aspects of Learning to Spell*. Newark, Del.: International Reading Association, 1980, 74-84.

Beldin, H. L. Informal reading testing: Historical review and review of the research. In W. Durr (Ed.), *Reading Difficulties: Diagnosis, Correction and Remediation*. Newark, Del.: International Reading Association, 1970.

Bereiter, C., & Engelmann, S. *Teaching Disadvantaged Children in the Preschool*. Englewood Cliffs, N.J.: Prentice-Hall, 1966.

Bernstein, B. A sociolinguistic approach to socialization: With some reference to educability. In F. Williams (Ed.), *Language and Poverty*. Chicago: Rand McNally, 1973, 25-61.

Betts, E. A. *Foundations of Reading Instruction*. New York: American Book Company, 1946, 1957.

Biglmaier, F. Methodische Struturmodelle für das Lesenlernen. In *probleme des lese-schreib-erstunterrichts*. Komission für erziehungswissenschaft mitteilung II, deutsche forschungsgemeinschaft, DFG. 5407 Boppard (West Deutschland): Harald Boldt Verlag, 1979, 36-46.

Blair, T. R., & Rupley, W. H. New trends in spelling instruction. *The Reading Teacher*, 1980, 33:6, 760-763.

Blass, R. J., Jurenka, N. A., & Zirzow, E. G. Showing children the communicative nature of reading. *The Reading Teacher*, 1981, 34:8, 926-931.

Bloom, B. S., Hastings, J. T., & Madaus, G. F. *Handbook on Formative and Summative Evaluation of Student Learning*, New York: McGraw-Hill, 1971.

Blum, N. Integration bedeutet nicht Assimilieren. *Buildung und Wissenschaft* (Bonn, Bundesrepublik Deutschland), 1982, 11:12, 185-186.

Bond, G. L., Caddy, M. C., & Fay, L. C. *Days of Adventure*. The Developmental Reading Series. Chicago: Lyons & Carnahan, 1962.

Bourque, M. L. Specification and validation of reading skills hierarchies. *Reading Research Quarterly*, 1980, 15:2, 237-267.

Boutwell, M. A. Reading and writing process: A reciprocal agreement. *Language Arts*, 1983, 60:6, 723-730.

Bradshaw, J. L. Three interrelated problems in reading:

A review. Memory and Cognition, 1975, 3, 123-134.
Brandt, E. P. Investigations into ways of developing willpower. Contemporary Psychology, 1977, 22:12, 951-952.
Bransford, J. D., & Johnson, M. D. Consideration of some problems of comprehension. In W. G. Chase (Ed.), Visual Information Processing. New York: Academic Press, 1973.
Broadbent, D. E., & Gregory, M. Visual perception of words differing in letter digram frequency. Journal of Verbal Learning and Verbal Behavior, 1968, 7, 569-571.
Brown, A. L. Metacognitive development and reading. In R. J. Spiro, B. C. Bruce, & W. F. Brewer (Eds.), Theoretical Issues in Reading Comprehension. Hillsdale, N.J.: Lawrence Erlbaum Associates, 1980.
Brown, D. A. Reading Diagnosis and Remediation. Englewood Cliffs, N.J.: Prentice-Hall, 1982.
Bruner, J. S. Some processes on instructions illustrated with reference to mathematics. In the 63rd Yearbook of NSSE, Theory of Learning and Instruction. Chicago: University of Chicago Press, 1964.
Bruner, J. S. Studies in Cognitive Growth. New York: John Wiley, 1966.
Bruner, J. S. Beyond the Information Given. New York, W. W. Norton, 1973.
Bruner, J. S. Toward a Theory of Instruction. Cambridge, Mass.: Belknap Press, 1978.
Bruner, J. S. On Knowing Essays for the Left Hand. Cambridge, Mass.: Belknap Press, 1979.
Bruner, J. S., Goodnow, J. J., & Austin, G. A. A Study of Thinking. New York: John Wiley, 1956.
Burmeister, L. E. Reading Strategies for Middle and Secondary School Teachers (2nd ed.). Reading, Mass.: Addison-Wesley, 1978.
Burns, P. C., & Roe, B. D. Informal Reading Assessment. Chicago, Rand McNally, 1980. (a)
Burns, P. C., & Roe, B. D. Teaching Reading in Today's Elementary Schools (2nd ed.). Chicago: Rand McNally, 1980. (b)
Buros, O. K. Mental Measurement Yearbooks (8th ed.). Highland Park, N.J.: Gryphon Press, 1978.
Buros, O. K. Reading Tests and Reviews. Highland Park, N.J.: Gryphon Press, 1975.
Buurman, R. D., Roersema, T., & Gerrisson, J. F. Eye movement and the perceptual span in reading. Reading Research Quarterly, 1981, 16:2, 227-235.
Carillo, L. W. Fonyx. The Reading Teacher, 1976, 30:3, 280-282.
Carver, R. P., & Hoffman, J. V. The effect of practice through repeated reading on gain in reading ability using a computer-based instructional system. Reading Research Quarterly, 1981, 16:3, 374-390.
Cattell, J. Mc. The time it takes to see and name objects. In Mind, 1886, 11: 63-65. From a long article in Philosophische Studien, 1885, 2: 635-650.

Cazden, C. B. Child Language and Education. New York: Holt, Rinehart & Winston, 1972.
Chamot, A. U. Applications of second language acquisition research to the bilingual classroom. Focus, September 1981, No. 8, 1-8.
Chomsky, C. Reading, writing and phonology. In F. Smith (Ed.), Psycholinguistics and Reading. New York: Holt, Rinehart & Winston, 1973.
Chomsky, N. Syntactic Structures. The Hague: Mouton & Co., 1957.
Chomsky, N. Aspects of the Theory of Syntax. Cambridge, Mass.: The MIT Press, 1965.
Chomsky, N. Language and Mind. New York: Harcourt, Brace and World, 1972.
Chomsky, N., & Halle, M. The Sound Pattern of English. New York: Harper & Row, 1968.
Chronicle Supplement Program Development Branch, Development Division. Saskatchewan Education. Regina, Sask.: Government of Saskatchewan, 1983.
Cohen, R. Self-generated questions as an aid to reading comprehension. The Reading Teacher, 1983, $36:8$, 770-775.
Collins, C., & Demos, E. S. An international study of the elements of beginning reading instruction. The Reading Teacher, 1983, $36:8$, 814-818. (a)
Collins, C., & Demos, E. S. Trends and needs in beginning reading instruction in 14 countries. The Reading Teacher, 1983, $36:9$, 900-904. (b)
Crabtree, C. A common curriculum in social studies. In the 82nd Yearbook of NSSE, Part I, Individual Differences and the Common Curriculum. Chicago: University of Chicago Press, 1983, 248-281.
Crafton, L. K. Comprehension before, during, and after reading. The Reading Teacher, 1982, $36:3$, 293-297.
Crewe, J., & Hultgreen, D. What does research really say about study skills? In G. B. Schick & M. M. May (Eds.), The Psychology of Reading Behavior. Milwaukee, Wis.: The National Reading Conference, 1969, 75-78.
Crowder, R. G. Psychology of Reading. New York: Oxford University Press, 1982.
Cummins, J. The construct of language proficiency in bilingual education. In J. E. Alatis (Ed.), Current Issues in Bilingual Education. Washington, D.C.: Georgetown University Press, 1980.
Curriculum Guide in Reading. Detroit: Public School of Detroit, 1950, 13-14.
Cziko, G. A. Another response to Shanahan, Kami and Tobin: Further reasons to keep the cloze case open. Reading Research Quarterly, 1983, $18:3$, 361-364.
Dallman, M., Rouch, R. L., Char, L. Y. C., & DeBoer, J. J. The Teaching of Reading (6th ed.). New York: Holt, Rinehart & Winston, 1982.
Dasch, A. Aligning basal reader instruction with cognitive stage theory. The Reading Teacher, 1983, $36:4$, 428-434.
Davis, J. Quotable. The Reading Teacher, 1982, $35:5$, 610.
DeBoer, J. J., & Whipple, G. Reading development in other

curriculum areas. In the 60th Yearbook of NSSE, Part I, Development in and through Reading. Chicago: University of Chicago Press, 1961, 54-74.
DeStefano, J. S. Enhancing children's growing ability to communicate. Language Arts, 1980, 57, 807-813.
Deutsch, M., Katz, I., & Jensen, A. R. (Eds.). Social Class, Race, and Psychological Development. New York: Holt, Rinehart & Winston, 1968.
Dewey, J. How We Think. Lexington, Mass.: D.C. Heath, 1933, 1960.
Dictionary of Education. C. V. Good (Ed.). New York: McGraw-Hill, 1959.
Dinkmeyer, D., & Dreikurs, R. Encouraging Children to Learn: The Encouragement Process. Englewood Cliffs, N.J.: Prentice-Hall, 1963.
Downing, J. Reading--Skill or skills. The Reading Teacher, 1982, 35:5, 534-535.
Downing, J., & Leong, C. K. Psychology of Reading. New York: Macmillan, 1982.
Downing, J., & Thackray, D. V. Reading Readiness. London: University of London Press, 1971.
Downing, J., & Thackray, D. Reading Readiness. London: Holder & Stoughton, 1975.
Duffelmeyer, F. A. The effect of grade level on cloze test scores. Journal of Reading, 1983, 26:5, 436-441.
Düker, H. Untersuchungen über die Ausbildung des Wollens. Bern: Verlag Hans Huber, 1975.
Dulin, K. L. Reading and the affective domain. In S. Pflaum-Conner (Ed.), Aspects of Reading Education. Berkeley, Calif.: McCutcheon Publishing, 1978.
Dunn, R. Teaching in a purple fog: What we don't know about learning style. NASSP Bulletin, March 1981, 65, 33-36.
Dunn, R., Dunn, K., & Price, G. E. Learning styles: Research vs. opinion. Phi Delta Kappan, 1981, 62:9, 645-646.
Dupuis, M. M., & Askov, E. N. Content Area Reading: An Individualized Approach. Englewood Cliffs, N.J.: Prentice-Hall, 1982.
Durkin, D. Teaching Them to Read (3rd ed.). Boston: Allyn & Bacon, 1978.
Durkin, D. What classroom observations reveal about reading comprehension instruction. Reading Research Quarterly, 1978-1979, 14:4, 481-533.
Durkin, D. Reading comprehension instruction in five basal reader series. Reading Research Quarterly, 1981, 16:4, 515-544.
Durkin, D. Teaching Them to Read (4th ed.). Boston: Allyn & Bacon, 1983.
Durrell, D. D. Individual differences and their implications with respect to instruction in reading. In the 36th Yearbook of NSSE, Part I, The Teaching of Reading: A Second Report. Bloomington, Ill.: Public School Publishing, 1937, 325-356.
Durrell, D. D. Letter-name values in reading and spelling. Reading Research Quarterly, 1980, 16:1, 159-163.

References

Durrell, D. D., & Murphy, H. A. A prereading phonics inventory. *The Reading Teacher*, 1978, *31*:4, 385-390.

Elkind, D. Cognitive development and reading. In H. Singer & R. B. Ruddell (Eds.), *Theoretical Models and Processes in Reading* (2nd ed.). Newark, Del.: International Reading Association, 1976.

Elkind, D. *Children and Adolescents* (2nd ed.). New York: Oxford University Press, 1977.

Emans, R., & Harms, J. M. The usefulness of linguistically-based generalizations. *The Reading World*, 1973, *13*, 13-21.

Emig, J. Writing as a mode of learning. *College Composition and Communication*, May 1977, *28*, 122-128.

Epstein, H. T. Growth spurts during brain development: Implications for educational policy and practice. In the 77th Yearbook of NSSE, *Education and the Brain*. Chicago: University of Chicago Press, 1978.

Erdmann, B. & Dodge, R. *Psychologische Untersuchungen ueber das Lesen auf experimenteller Grundlage*. Halle: Max Niemeyer, 1898.

Etzioni, A. The role of self-discipline. *Phi Delta Kappan*, 1982, *64*:3, 184-187.

Ewing, J. M. The place of attitudes in the reading curriculum. In E. Hunter-Grundin, & H. U. Grundin (Eds.), *Reading: Implementing the Bullock Report*. London: Ward Lock, 1978.

Farr, R., & Roser, N. *Teaching a Child to Read*. New York: Harcourt Brace Jovanovich, 1979.

Farrar, M. T. Another look at oral questions for comprehension. *The Reading Teacher*, 1983, *36*:4, 370-374.

Fenstermacher, G. D. Introduction. In the 82nd Yearbook of NSSE, Part I, *Individual Differences and the Common Curriculum*. Chicago: University of Chicago Press, 1983.

Fernald, G. M. *Remedial Techniques in Basic School Subjects*. New York: McGraw-Hill, 1943, 35-46.

Fischer, L., & Sorenson, G. P. Legal bases of individualization. In the 82nd Yearbook of NSSE, Part I, *Individual Differences and the Common Curriculum*. Chicago: University of Chicago Press, 1983.

Forester, A. D., & Mickelson, N. I. Language acquisition and learning to read. In R. E. Shafer (Ed.), *Applied Linguistics and Reading*. Newark, Del.: International Reading Association, 1979.

Fox, S. E. Assisting children's language development. *The Reading Teacher*, 1976, *29*:7, 666-670.

Frase, L. T. Effect of question location, pacing, and mode on retention of prose material. *Journal of Educational Psychology*, 1968, *59*, 244-249.

Freebody, P., & Anderson, R. C. Effects of vocabulary difficulty, text cohesion, and schema availability on reading comprehension. *Reading Research Quarterly*, Spring 1983, *3*, 277-294.

Freedman, G., & Reynolds, E. G. Enriching basal reader lessons with semantic webbing. *The Reading Teacher*, 1980, *33*:6, 677-684.

Frostig, M. & Horne, D. *The Frostig Program for the Development of Visual Perception*. Chicago: Follett, 1964.

Fuchs, L. S., Fuchs, D., & Deno, S. L. Reliability and validity of curriculum-based Informal Reading Inventories. *Reading Research Quarterly*, 1982, 18:1, 6-25.

Funcke, L. Humanitäre Principien nicht aus dem Auge verlieren. *Buildung und Wissenschaft* (Bonn: Bundesrepublik Deutschland), 1982, 5, 71.

Furth, H. G. Reading as thinking: A developmental perspective. In F. B. Murry, H. R. Sharp, & J. Pikulski (Eds.), *The Acquisition of Reading*. Baltimore: University Park Press, 1978.

Furth, H. G., & Wachs, H. *Thinking Goes to School*. Toronto: Oxford University Press, 1975.

Gentry, J. R. An analysis of developmental spelling in GNYS AT WRK. *The Reading Teacher*, 1982, 36:2, 192-200.

Gentry, J. R., & Henderson, E. H. Three steps to teaching beginning readers to spell. In E. H. Henderson & J. W. Beers (Eds.), *Developmental and Cognitive Aspects of Learning to Spell*. Newark, Del.: International Reading Association, 1980, 112-119.

Getzel, J., & Jackson, P. *Creativity and Intelligence*. New York: John Wiley, 1962.

Geyer, J. J. Models of perceptual processes in reading. In H. Singer & R. B. Ruddell (Eds.), *Theoretical Models and Processes of Reading*. Newark, Del.: International Reading Association, 1970.

Gillet, J. W., & Gentry, J. R. Bridges between nonstandard and standard English with extension of dictated stories. *The Reading Teacher*, 1983, 36:4, 360-364.

Glass, G. G. *Teaching Decoding as Separate from Reading*. Garden City, N.Y.: Adelphi University Press, 1973.

Golinkoff, R. M. A comparison of reading comprehension processes in good and poor comprehenders. *Reading Research Quarterly*, 1975-1976, 11, 4.

Good, T. L., & Stipek, D. J. Individual differences in the classroom: A psychological perspective. In the 82nd Yearbook of NSSE, Part I, *Individual Differences and the Common Curriculum*. Chicago: University of Chicago Press, 1983, 9-43.

Goodman, K. S. Miscues: Windows on the reading process. In K. S. Goodman (Ed.), *Miscue Analysis*. Urbana, Ill.: Educational Resources Information Center, 1973.

Goodman, K. S. Behind the eye: What happens in reading. In H. Singer & R. B. Ruddell (Eds.), *Theoretical Models and Processes of Reading* (2nd ed.). Newark, Del.: International Reading Association, 1976, 470-496.

Goodman, Y., & Burke, C. *Reading Strategies: Focus on Comprehension*. New York: Holt, Rinehart & Winston, 1980.

Gough, P. B. One second of reading. In J. F. Kavanagh & I. G. Mattingly (Eds.), *Language by Ear and by Eye*. Cambridge, Mass.: MIT Press, 1972, 331-358.

Gough, P. B., & Cosky, M. J. One second of reading again. In N. Castellan, Jr., P. John, B. David, & G. R. Potts (Eds.), *Cognitive Theory* (vol. 2). Hillsdale, N.J.: Lawrence Erlbaum Associates, 1977.

References

Gradisnik, A. Bilingual education. In the 79th Yearbook of NSSE, Part II, Learn a Second Language. Chicago: University of Chicago Press, 1980, 104-127.

Graesser, A. C. Prose Comprehension: Beyond the Word. New York: Springer-Verlag, 1981.

Grant, L., & Rothenberg, J. Charting educational futures: Interaction patterns in first and second grade reading groups. Paper presented at annual meeting of the American Educational Research Association, Los Angeles, April 1981.

Graves, F. P. Great Educators of Three Centuries. New York: Macmillan, 1912.

Graves, M. F., Cooke, C. L., & Laberge, M. J. Effects of previewing difficult short stories on low ability junior high school students' comprehension, recall and attitudes. Reading Research Quarterly, 1983, 18:3, 262-276.

Graves, M. F., & Palmer, R. J. Validating previewing as a method of improving fifth and sixth grade students' comprehension of short stories. Michigan Reading Journal, 1981, 15, 1-3.

Gray, W. S. A decade of process. In the 36th Yearbook of NSSE, Part I, The Teaching of Reading: A Second Report. Bloomington, Ill.: Public School Publishing, 1937.

Gray, L. Teaching Children to Read (3rd ed.). New York: Ronald Press, 1963.

Gray, W. S. (Chair). Report of the National Committee on Reading. In the 24th Yearbook of NSSE, Part I, The Teaching of Reading. Bloomington, Ill.: Public School Publishing, 1925.

Groff, P. The topsy turvy world of sight words. The Reading Teacher, 1974, 27, 572-578.

Groff, P. Research in brief: Shapes as cues to word recognition. Visible Language, 1975, 9, 67-71.

Gunning, T. G. Wrong level test: Wrong information. The Reading Teacher, 1982, 35:8, 902-905.

Guszak, F. J. Diagnostic Reading Instruction in the Elementary School. New York: Harper & Row, 1978.

Guthrie, F. M., & Cunningham, P. M. Teaching decoding skills to educable mentally handicapped children. The Reading Teacher, 1982, 35:5, 554-559.

Guthrie, J. T. Reading interests. The Reading Teacher, 1981, 34:8, 984-986.

Guthrie, J. T. Teacher effectiveness: The quest for refinement. The Reading Teacher, 1982, 35:5, 636-638.

Guthrie, J. T. Equilibrium of literacy. Journal of Reading, 1983, 26:7, 668-670. (a)

Guthrie, J. T. Questions as teaching tools. Journal of Reading, 1983, 26:5, 478-479. (b)

Guthrie, J. T. When reading is not reading. Journal of Reading, 1983, 26:4, 382-384. (c)

Haber, L. R., Haber, R. N., & Furlin, K. R. Word length and word shape as sources of information in reading. Reading Research Quarterly, 1983, 18:2, 165-189.

Haber, R. N., & Haber, L. R. The shape of a word can specify its meaning. Reading Research Quarterly, 1981, 16:3, 334-345.

Hacker, C. J. From schema theory to classroom practice. Language Arts, 1980, 57, 866-871.
Hall, M. A., Moretz, S. A., & Statom, J. Writing before grade one--A study of early writers. Language Arts, May 1976, 53, 582-585.
Hardyck, C. D., & Petrinovich, L. F. Subvocal speech and comprehension level of reading material. Journal of Verbal Learning and Verbal Behavior, 1970, 9, 647-652.
Harris, A. J. How to Increase Reading Ability (4th ed.). New York: David McKay, 1961.
Harris, L. A., & Smith, C. B. Reading Instruction Diagnostic Teaching in the Classroom (3rd ed.). New York: Holt, Rinehart & Winston, 1980.
Harris, T. L., & Hodges, R. E. A Dictionary of Reading and Related Terms. Newark, Del.: International Reading Association, 1981.
Harrison, M. L. Reading Readiness (rev. ed.). Boston: Houghton Mifflin, 1939.
Harste, J., Burke, C. L., & Woodward, V. A. Children's language and world: Initial encounter with print. Unpublished manuscript. Indiana University, Bloomington, Ind., March 1979.
Hart, L. A. Human Brain and Human Learning. New York: Longman, 1983.
Hayes, D. A., & Tierney, R. J. Developing readers' knowledge through analogy. Reading Research Quarterly, 1982, 17:2, 256-280.
Heathington, B. S., & Koskinen, P. S. Interest inventory for adult beginning readers. Journal of reading, 1982, 26:3, 252-256.
Helfeldt, J. P. Future trends of diagnosis and instruction in the primary grades. Paper presented Thirty-fourth Annual Meeting of the Conference on Reading, Cullowkee, N.C., 1981.
Hennings, D. G. Communication in Action: Teaching the Language Arts (2nd ed.). Boston: Houghton Mifflin, 1982.
Herrick, V. E., Anderson, D., & Pierstorff, L. Basal instructional materials in reading. In the 60th Yearbook of NSSE, Part I, Development in and through Reading. Chicago: University of Chicago Press, 1961.
Hiebert, E. H. Developmental patterns and interrelationships of preschool children's print awareness. Reading Research Quarterly, 1981, 16:2, 236-260.
Hiebert, E. H. An examination of ability grouping for reading instruction. Reading Research Quarterly, 1983, 18:2, 231-255.
Hillerich, R. L. A diagnostic approach to early identification of language skills. The Reading Teacher, 1978, 31:4, 357-364.
Hittleman, D. R. Developmental Reading, K-8 Teaching from a Psycholinguistic Perspective (2nd ed.). Boston: Houghton Mifflin, 1983.
Holland, R. P. Learner characteristics and learner performance: Implications for instructional placement decisions. Journal of Special Education, Spring 1982, 16, 7-20. EJ 261 649.

References

Holmes, D. L. The independence of letter, word, and meaning identification in reading. In F. Smith (Ed.), *Psycholinguistics and Reading*. New York: Holt, Rinehart & Winston, 1973.

Holmes, J. A. The substrata-factor theory of reading. In J. L. Frost (Ed.), *Issues and Innovations in the Teaching of Reading*. Glenview, Ill.: Scott, Foresman, 1967.

Huey, E. B. *The Psychology and Pedagogy of Reading*. New York: Macmillan, 1908, 1922.

Hunt, D. E. Learning style and the interdependence of practice and theory. *Phi Delta Kappan*, 1981, 62:9, 647.

Ilg, F. L., & Ames, L. B. *The Gesell Institute's Child Behavior*. New York: Dell Publishing, 1955.

Jalongo, M. R. Bibliotherapy: Literature to promote socio-emotional growth. *The Reading Teacher*, 1983, 36:8, 796-803.

Jenkins, J. R., & Pany, D. Instructional variables in reading comprehension. In J. T. Guthrie (Ed.), *Comprehension and Teaching: Research Reviews*. Newark, Del.: International Reading Association, 1981.

Johnson, M. S., & Kress, R. A. *Informal Reading Inventories*. Newark, Del.: International Reading Association, 1965.

Juel, C., & Holmes, B. Oral and silent reading of sentences. *Reading Research Quarterly*, 1981, 16:4, 545-568.

Justiz, M. J. NAEP will help diagnose problems of the schools. *NAEP Newsletter*, Fall 1983, 16:3.

Kameenui, E. L., & Carnine, D. W. An investigation of fourth-graders' comprehension of pronoun constructions in ecologically valid tests. *Reading Research Quarterly*, 1982, 17:4, 556-580.

Kempf, W. F., & Lehrke, M. Evaluation reflections: Subject-matter directed motivation and its evaluation by means of questionnaires. *Studies in Educational Evaluation*, 1975, 1:2, 65.

Killgallon, P. A. A study of relationships among certain pupil adjustments in reading situations. Unpublished doctoral dissertation, Pennsylvania State College, 1942.

King, E. M. Prereading programs: Direct versus incidental teaching. *The Reading Teacher*, 1978, 31:5, 504-509.

Kitagawa, M. M. Improving discussions, or how to get the students to ask the questions. *The Reading Teacher*, 1982, 36:1, 42-45.

Knight, E. N. Readiness for beginning reading. In J. E. Alexander (Ed.), *Teaching Reading* (2nd ed.). Boston: Little, Brown, 1983, 25-46.

Kolers, P. A. Experiment in reading. *Scientific American*, 1972, 227, 84-91.

Kolers, P. A. Three stages of reading. In F. Smith (Ed.), *Psycholinguistics and Reading* New York: Holt, Rinehart & Winston, 1973, 28-49.

Kolker, B. Processing print. In J. E. Alexander (Ed.), *Teaching Reading* (2nd ed.). Boston: Little, Brown, 1983, 3-23.

Krashen, S. The input hypothesis. In J. E. Alatis (Ed.), *Current Issues in Bilingual Education*. Georgetown University Round Table on Language and Linguistics,

1980. Washington, D.C.: Georgetown University Press, 1980.

LaBerge, D., & Samuels, S. J. Toward a theory of automatic processing in reading. In H. Singer & R. B. Ruddell (Eds.), Theoretical Models and Processes of Reading (2nd ed.). Newark, Del.: International Reading Association, 1976, 548-579.

Labov, W. The logic of nonstandard English. In F. Williams (Ed.), Language and Poverty. Chicago: Rand McNally, 1973, 153-189.

Lamb, P., & Arnold, R. Teaching Reading Foundations and Strategies (2nd ed.). Belmont, Calif.: Wadsworth, 1980.

Lambert, W. E. The two faces of bilingual education. Focus, 1980, no. 3:1-4.

Lambert, W. E., & Tucker, G. R. Bilingual Education of Children: The St. Lambert Experiment. Rowley, Mass.: Newbury House, 1972.

Lass, B. Portrait of my son as an early reader. The Reading Teacher, 1982, 36:1, 20-28.

Lass, B. Portrait of my son as an early reader, II. The Reading Teacher, 1983, 36:6, 508-515.

Lawton, J. T. Introduction to Child Development. Dubuque, Iowa: Wm. C. Brown, 1982.

Leavitt, S. E. The teaching of Spanish in the United States. In Leavitt (Ed.), Report of Surveys and Studies in the Teaching of Modern Foreign Languages. New York: Modern Language Association, 1959-1961.

Lehr, F. Integrating reading and writing instruction. The Reading Teacher, 1981, 34:8, 958-961.

Lerner, J. W. Learning Disabilities (3rd ed.). Boston: Houghton Mifflin, 1981.

Linden, M., & Wittrock, M. C. The teaching of reading comprehension according to the model of generative learning. Reading Research Quarterly, 1981, 17:1, 44-57.

Logan, J. W. Cognitive style and reading. The Reading Teacher, 1983, 36:7, 704-707.

MacGinitie, W. H. The power of uncertainty. Journal of Reading, 1983, 26:8, 677-683.

Mackworth, J. F. Some models of the reading process: Learners and skilled readers. In F. B. Davis (Ed.), The Literature of Research in Reading, with Emphasis on Models. New Brunswick, N.J.: Rutgers--The State University, 1971.

Malicky, G. V. The effect of deletion produced structures on word identification and comprehension of beginning readers (abstract). Reading Research Quarterly, 1975-1976, 11:2, 212-216.

Mangrum, G. T. II, & Forgan, H. W. Developing Competencies in Teaching Reading. Columbus, Ohio: Charles E. Merrill, 1979.

Mann, L., & Goodman, L. Perceptual training: A critical retrospect. In E. Schopler & R. J. Reichler (Eds.), Psychopathology and Child Development: Research and Treatment. New York: Plenum, 1976.

References

Manzo, A. V. The ReQuest procedure. *Journal of Reading*, 1969, 13:2, 123-126, 163.

Manzo, A. V. Guided reading procedure. *Journal of Reading*, 1975, 18:4, 287-291.

Marchbanks, G., & Levin, H. Cues by which children recognize words. *Journal of Educational Psychology*, 1965, 56, 57-61.

Marksheffel, N. D. *Better Reading in the Secondary School*. New York: Ronald Press, 1966.

Martin, J. *Mastering Education*. Boston: Allyn & Bacon, 1983.

Mason, M. When do children begin to read: An exploration of four-year-old children's letter and word reading competencies. *Reading Research Quarterly*, 1980, 15:2, 203-227.

Mass, L. N. Developing concepts of literacy in young children. *The Reading Teacher*, 1982, 35:6, 670-675.

Mateja, J. Musical cloze: Background, purpose, and sample. *The Reading Teacher*, 1982, 35:4. 444-448.

Mathewson, G. C. The function of attitude in the reading process. In H. Singer & R. B. Ruddell (Eds.), *Theoretical Models and Processes of Reading* (2nd ed.). Newark, Del.: International Reading Association, 1976, 655-676.

May, F. B. *Reading as Communication*. Columbus, Ohio: Charles E. Merrill, 1982.

Maxim, G. W. *The Very Young: Guiding Children from Infancy through the Early Years*. Belmont, Calif.: Wadsworth Publishing, 1980.

McGuffey, *Fifth Eclectic Reader* (rev. ed.). New York: American Book Company, 1879, 1896, 1907, & 1920.

McGuffey, *Sixth Eclectic Reader* (rev. ed.). New York: American Book Company, 1879, 1896, 1907, & 1921.

McGuffey, *Eclectic Primer* (rev. ed.). New York: American Book Company, 1881, 1909.

McKenna, M. C. Informal reading inventories: A review of the issues. *The Reading Teacher*, 1983, 36:7, 670-679.

McLeod, K. A. Multiculturalism and multicultural education. In the 8th Yearbook of CSSE, *Education and Canadian Multiculturalism: Some Problems and Some Solutions*, D. Dorotich (Ed.). Saskatoon, Sask.: Canadian Society for the Study of Education, 1981.

McNeil, J. D. False prerequisites in the teaching of reading. *Journal of Reading Behavior*, 1974, 6:4, 421-427.

McNeil, J. D., Donant, L., & Alkin, M. C. *How to Teach Reading Successfully*. Boston: Little, Brown, 1980.

Mehan, H., Cazden, C. B., Cotes, L., Fisher, S., & Maroules, N. *The Social Organization of Classroom Lessons*. La Jolla, Calif.: The Center for Human Information Processing, 1976.

Micklos, J., Jr. A look at reading achievement in the United States: The latest data. *Journal of Reading*, 1982, 25:8, 760-762.

Mikulecky, L. Job literacy: The relationship between

school preparation and workplace actuality. Reading Research Quarterly, 1982, 17:3, 400-419.

Modolfsky, P. B. Teaching students to determine the central story problem: A practical application of schema theory. The Reading Teacher, 1983, 36:8, 740-745.

Moffett, J., & Wagner, B. J. Student-Centered Language Arts and Reading, K-13: Handbook for Teachers (3rd ed.). Boston: Houghton Mifflin, 1983.

Montessori, M. The Montessori Method. Translated by A. E. George. New York: Schocken Books, 1964.

Montessori, M. From Childhood to Adolescence (2nd ed.). Translated by the Montessori Educational Research Center. New York: Schocken Books, 1976.

Morphett, M. N., & Washburne, C. When should children begin to read? Elementary School Journal, March 1931, 31, 496-503.

Morrison, B. S. One route to improved reading comprehension. In C. Pennock (Ed.), Reading Comprehension at Four Linguistic Levels. Newark, Del.: International Reading Association, 1979, 34-43.

Munby, H. Discovery teaching and discovery learning: A comment on Stewart. Canadian Journal of Education, 1980, 5:3, 87-93.

Munby, H., & Russell, T. A common curriculum for the natural sciences. In the 82nd Yearbook of NSSE, Part I, Individual Differences and the Common Curriculum. Chicago: University of Chicago Press, 1983.

Murrey, F. B., Sharp, H. R., & Pikulski, J. (Eds.). The Acquisition of Reading. Baltimore: University Park Press, 1978.

Neville, M. H., & Pugh, A. K. Context in reading and listening: Variations in approach to cloze task. Reading Research Quarterly, 1976-1977, 12:1, 13-31.

Nolen, P. Sound reasoning in spelling. The Reading Teacher, 1980, 33:5, 538-543.

O'Donnell, H. The use of illustrations in textbooks. The Reading Teacher, 1983, 36:4, 462-464.

Ohnmacht, F. W., & Fleming, J. T. Cloze and closure: A second analysis. In the 21st Yearbook of the NRC, Investigations Relating to Mature Reading, F. P. Greene (Ed.). Milwaukee, Wis.: The National Reading Conference, 1972, 35-44.

Ortiz, R. K. Generating interest in reading. Journal of Reading, 1983, 27:2, 113-119.

Otto, J. The new debate in reading. The Reading Teacher, 1982, 36:1, 14-18.

Patterson, C. H. Foundation for a Theory of Instruction and Educational Psychology. New York: Harper & Row, 1977.

Pearson, P. D., & Camperell, K. Comprehension of text structures. In J. T. Guthrie (Ed.), Comprehension and Teaching: Research Reviews. Newark, Del.: International Reading Association, 1981, 27-55.

Pertz, D. L., & Putnam, L. R. An examination of the relationship between nutrition and learning. The Reading Teacher, 1982, 35:6, 702-706.

Piaget, J. The Language and Thought of the Child. New York: Meridian Books, 1960.
Piaget, J., & Inhelder, B. The Psychology of the Child. Translated by H. Weaver. New York: Basic Books, 1969.
Pikulski, J. A critical review: Informal reading inventories. The Reading Teacher, 1974, 28:2, 141-151.
Pikulski, J., & Kirsch, I. S. Organization for instruction. In R. C. Calfee & P. A. Drum (Eds.), Compensatory Reading Survey. Newark, Del.: International Reading Association, 1979.
Postman, N. Teaching as a Conserving Activity. New York: Delacorte Press, 1979.
Powell, W. Validity of the I.R.I. reading levels. Elementary English, 1971, 48:637-642.
Power, E. J. Philosophy of Education. Englewood Cliffs, N.J.: Prentice-Hall, 1982.
Propst, I. K., Jr., & Baldauf, R. B., Jr. Use matching cloze tests for elementary ESL students. The Reading Teacher, 1979, 32:6, 683-690.
Radebough, M. R. Critically speaking, a book review. The Reading Teacher, 1983, 36:6, 600-601.
Random House Dictionary, College Edition. New York: Random House, 1968.
Rankin, E. F. Uses of cloze procedure in the reading clinic. In J. A. Figurel (Ed.), IRA Proceedings, 1959, 4: 228-232.
Rankin, E. F. The cloze procedure--A survey of research. In the 14th Yearbook of the NRC, The Philosophical and Sociological Bases of Reading. Milwaukee, Wis.: The National Reading Conference, 1965, 133-150.
Rankin, E. F., & Culhane, J. W. Comparable cloze and multiple-choice test scores. Journal of Reading, 1969, 13:3, 193-198.
Ransom, G. A. Preparing to Teach Reading. Boston: Little, Brown, 1978.
Rayner, K. Developmental changes in word recognition strategies. Journal of Educational Psychology, 1976, 68, 323-329.
Read, D., & Smith, H. M. Teaching visual literacy through wordless picture books. The Reading Teacher, 1982, 35:8, 928-933.
Reynolds, R. E., Taylor, M. A., Steffenson, M. S., Shiren, L. L., & Anderson, R. C. Cultural schemata and reading comprehension. Reading Research Quarterly, 1982, 17:3, 353-366.
Richek, M. A. Readiness skills that predict initial word learning using two different methods of instruction. Reading Research Quarterly, 1977-1978, 13:2, 200-222.
Richek, M. A., List, L. K., & Lerner, J. W. Reading Problems: Diagnosis and Remediation. Englewood Cliffs, N.J.: Prentice-Hall, 1983.
Rickards, J. P. Processing effects of advance organizers interspersed in text. Reading Research Quarterly, 1975-1976, 11:4, 599-622.
Robinett, B. W. The domain of TESOL. TESOL Quarterly, September 1972, 6, 202.

Robinson, F. P. Phonetics or phonics. The Reading Teacher, 1955, 9:2, 84-88.
Robinson, F. P. Effective Study (rev. ed.). New York: Harper & Row, 1961.
Robinson, H. A. Meeting Individual Differences in Reading. Supplementary Educational Monograph, No. 94, Chicago: University of Chicago Press, 1964, v-vi.
Robinson, H. A. Teaching Reading, Writing, and Study Strategies: The Content Areas (3rd ed.). Boston: Allyn & Bacon, 1983.
Rubin, D. A Practical Approach to Teaching Reading. New York: Holt, Rinehart & Winston, 1982.
Rumelhart, D. E. Toward an interactive model of reading. In S. Dornic (Ed.), Attention and Performance VI. Hillsdale, N.J.: Lawrence Erlbaum Associates, 1977, 573-603.
Rumelhart, D. E. Schemata: The building blocks of cognition. In J. T. Guthrie (Ed.), Comprehension and Teaching: Research Reviews. Newark, Del.: International Reading Association, 1981, 3-26.
Rumelhart, D. E., & Ortony, A. The representation of knowledge in memory. In R. C. Anderson, R. J. Spiro, & W. E. Montague (Eds.), Schooling and the Acquisition of Knowledge. Hillsdale, N.J.: Lawrence Erlbaum Associates, 1977.
Rupley, W. H., & Blair, T. R. Teacher effectiveness in reading instruction. The Reading Teacher, 1978, 31:8, 970-973.
Samuels, S. J. Hierarchical subskills in the reading acquisition process. In J. T. Guthrie (Ed.), Aspects of Reading Acquisition. Baltimore: Johns Hopkins University Press, 1976.
Samuels, S. J. Introduction to theoretical models of reading. In W. Otto, C. Peters, & N. Peters (Eds.), Reading Problems: A Multidisciplinary Perspective. Reading, Mass.: Addison-Wesley, 1977.
Sanders, N. M. Classroom Questions: What Kinds? New York: Harper & Row, 1966.
Schallert, D. L., Kleiman, G. M., & Rubin, A. D. Analysis of differences between oral and written language. Technical report no. 29. Urbana, Ill.: University of Illinois, Center for the Study of Reading, April 1977.
Scheflen, A. Body Language and Social Order. Englewood Cliffs, N.J.: Prentice-Hall, 1972.
Schneyer, J. W. Use of the cloze procedure for improving reading comprehension. The Reading Teacher, 1965, 19:3, 174-179.
Schubert, D. G., & Torgerson, T. L. Readings in Reading: Practice Theory Research. New York: Thomas Y. Crowell, 1968, 47-57.
Scott, E., & Annesley, F. R. Some implications of cognitive style for reading achievement and curriculum design. Paper presented at the International Reading Association World Congress, Singapore, 1976. (ERIC Document Reproduction Service No. ED 200 192)
Seaver, J. T., & Botel, M. A first-grade teacher teaches

References

reading, writing and oral communication across the curriculum. The Reading Teacher, 1983, 36:7.

Sheffensen, M. S., Joag-Dev, C., & Anderson, R. C. A cross-cultural perspective on reading comprehension. Reading Research Quarterly, 1979, 15:1, 10-29.

Shimron, J., & Navon, D. The dependence on graphemes and on their translation to phonemes in reading: A developmental perspective. Reading Research Quarterly, 1982, 17:2, 210-228.

Shuy, R. W. The sociolinguists and urban language problems. In F. Williams (Ed.), Language and Poverty. Chicago: Rand McNally, 1973, 335-350.

Silvaroli, N. J. Classroom Reading Inventory. Dubuque, Iowa: Wm. C. Brown, 1982.

Singer, H. Active comprehension: From answering to asking questions. The Reading Teacher, 1978, 31:8, 901-908.

Singer, H., & Donlan, D. Reading and Learning from Text. Boston: Little, Brown, 1980.

Singer, H., & Donlan, D. Active comprehension: Problem solving schema with question generation for comprehension of complex short stories. Reading Research Quarterly, 1982, 17:2, 166-186.

Smale, M. Teaching secondary students about reading to children. Journal of Reading, 1982, 26:3, 208-210.

Smith, E. B., Goodman, K. S., & Meredith, R. Language and Thinking in School (2nd ed.). New York: Holt, Rinehart & Winston, 1976.

Smith, E. E., & Kleiman, G. M. Word recognition: Theoretical issues and instructional hints. In L. B. Resnick & P. A. Weaver (Eds.), Theory and Practice of Early Reading (vol. 2). Hillsdale, N.J.: Lawrence Erlbaum Associates, 1979.

Smith, F. Psycholinguistics and Reading. New York: Holt, Rinehart & Winston, 1973.

Smith, F. Understanding Reading (3rd ed.). New York: Holt, Rinehart & Winston, 1982.

Smith, F. R. Alec in reading land: Some reactions to and implications of the Durkin findings. Reading Research Quarterly, 1978-1979, 14:4, 534-538.

Smith, H. P., & Dechant, E. V. Psychology in Teaching Reading. Englewood Cliffs, N.J.: Prentice-Hall, 1961.

Smith, L. L., Johns, J. L., Ganschow, L., & Masztal, N. B Using grade level vs. out-of-level reading tests with remedial students. The Reading Teacher, 1983, 36:6, 550-553.

Smith, M. S. Semantics, Concepts, and Culture. Washington, D.C.: National Institute of Education, 1975. Educational Resources Information Center No. ED 0113376.

Smith, N. B. American Reading Instruction. Newark, Del.: International Reading Association, 1965.

Smith, R. J., & Johnson, D. D. Teaching Children to Read (2nd ed.). Menlo Park, Calif.: Addison-Wesley, 1980.

Spache, G. D., & Spache, E. B. Reading in the Elementary School (4th ed.). Boston: Allyn & Bacon, 1977.

Spenser, F. SQ3R: Several queries regarding relevant research. Research on Reading in the Secondary Schools, 1978, 2, 23-38.

Spiegel, D. L. Six alternatives to the Directed Reading Activity. The Reading Teacher, 1981, 34:8, 914-920.
Spilich, G. J., Vesonder, G. T., Chiesi, H. L., & Voss, J. F. Text processing of domain-related information for individuals with high and low domain knowledge. Journal of Verbal Learning and Verbal Behavior, 1979, 18, 275-290.
Stanovich, K. E. Toward an interactive-compensatory model of individual differences in the development of reading fluency. Reading Research Quarterly, 1980, 16:1, 32-71.
Stauffer, R. G. Directing Reading Maturity as a Cognitive Process. New York: Harper & Row, 1969. (a)
Stauffer, R. G. Teaching Reading as a Thinking Process. New York: Harper & Row, 1969. (b)
Stewart, J. D. Teaching strategies: Is discovery one of them? Canadian Journal of Education, 1979, 4:2, 55-65.
Stewart, J. D. A response and an addendum to Munby. Canadian Journal of Education, 1980, 5:3, 94-98.
Stewart, O., & Tei, E. Some implications of metacognition for reading instruction. Journal of Reading, 1983, 27:1, 36-43.
Stewart, W. A. Urben Negro speech: Sociolinguistic factors affecting English teaching. In R. W. Shuy (Ed.), Social Dialect and Language Learning. Champaign, Ill.: National Conference of Teachers of English, 1965.
Stewart, W. A. Toward a history of American Negro dialect. In F. Williams (Ed.), Language and Poverty. Chicago: Rand McNally, 1973, 351-379.
Strickland, D. Parent involvement: Where do we go from here? News for Parents, International Reading Association, April 1982, 4, 1.
Sucher, F., & Allred, R. A. Screening Students for Placement in Reading. Provo, Utah: Brigham Young University Press, 1971.
Taba, H. Curriculum Development, Theory and Practice. New York: Harcourt Brace Jovanovich, 1962.
Taba, H. The teaching of thinking. Elementary English, May 1965, 42, 534-542.
Taschow, H. G. A junior college reading program in action. In P. C. Berg & J. E. George (Eds.), Highlights of Pre-Convention Institute. Newark, Del.: International Reading Association, 1968, 27-33.
Taschow, H. G. Silent reading in the primary grades. It's Our Bag, 1971, 2:3, 14-22. Early Childhood Education Council, Saskatoon, Sask., Canada.
Taschow, H. G. Pathway to critical reading. Paper presented at the International Reading Association Convention, Detroit, May 1972. Educational Resources Information Center No. ED 063598. (a)
Taschow, H. G. Reading in mathematics. Improving College and University Teaching, 1972, 20:4, 312-314. (b)
Taschow, H. G. Project study: Diagnosis, prescription, and remediation of reading difficulties for classroom teachers on classroom levels. Unpublished report. University of Saskatchewan, Regina Campus, Regina, 1973.
Taschow, H. G. How to teach critical reading. In R. T. Williams (Ed.), Insights into Why and How to Read.

Newark, Del.: International Reading Association, 1976, 90-97.

Taschow, H. G. The usefulness of five basic word lists in teaching adults to read. Journal of Reading, 1977, 20: 5, 377-380.

Taschow, H. G. Socrates in adult basic education, or the art of questioning. In Learning Assistance: Charting Our Course. Proceedings of the 11th Annual Western College Reading Association Conference, 1978, 11:77-82.

Taschow, H. G. Alice in REALLAND or on becoming a thinking reader. Paper given at the 8th Plains Regional International Reading Association Conference, Bismarck, N.D., September 1980.

Taschow, H. G. Shaping and changing adult learning. Paper presented at the 10th Plains Regional International Reading Association Reading Conference, Omaha, Neb., September 30-October 2, 1982.

Taschow, H. G., & Cicansky, F. French Immersion: A Three-Year Report. University of Regina, Sask., 1982.

Taylor, W. L. Cloze procedure: A new tool for measuring readability. Journalism Quarterly, 1953, 30, 414-438.

Templeton, S. Using the spelling/meaning connection to develop word knowledge in older students. Journal of Reading, 1983, 27:1, 8-14.

Tharp, R. G. The effective instruction of comprehension: Results and description of the Kamehameha Early Education Program. Reading Research Quarterly, 1982, 17: 4, 503-527.

Thorn, E. A., & Braun, C. Teaching Language Arts: Speaking, Listening, Reading and Writing. Toronto: Gage Educational Publishing, 1974.

Thorndike, E. L. Reading as Reasoning: A Study of Mistakes in Paragraph Reading. Journal of Educational Psychology, 1917, 8, 323-332.

Thorndike, R. L. Reading Comprehension Education in Fifteen Countries. New York: John Wiley, 1973.

Tierney, R. J., & Pearson, P. D. Learning to learn from text: A framework of improving classroom practice. Reading Education Report, No. 30. Urbana, Ill.: Center for Study of Reading, 1981.

Tomatis, A. A. Education and Dyslexia. Translated by L. Guiny. Fribourg, Switzerland: Association Internationale d'Audio-Psycho-Phonologie, 1978.

Tonjes, M. J., & Zintz, M. V. Teaching Reading (Thinking) Study Skills in Content Classrooms. Dubuque, Iowa: Wm. C. Brown, 1981.

Torney, J. W. Psychological and institutional obstacles to the global perspective in education. In J. M. Becker (Ed.), Schooling for a Global Age. New York: McGraw-Hill, 1979.

Tucker, G. R. Implications for U.S. bilingual education evidence from Canadian research. Focus, February 1980, No. 2.

Tuinman, J., & Kendall, J. R. British Columbia Reading Assessment General Report. Victoria, B.C.: Ministry of Education, Learning Assessment Branch, 1980.

Turner, R. N. Questioning techniques: Probing for greater

meaning. In J. E. Alexander (Ed.), Teaching Reading (2nd ed.). Boston: Little, Brown, 1983, 199-219.
Veatch, J., & Acinapuro, P. J. Reading in the Elementary School. New York: Ronald Press, 1966.
Ventriglia, L. Conversation of Miguel and Maria. Reading, Mass.: Addison-Wesley, 1982.
Vernon, M. D. Reading and Its Difficulties. London: Cambridge University Press, 1971.
Vukelich, C. Parents are teachers: A beginning reading program. The Reading Teacher, 1978, 31:5, 524-527.
Vygotzky, L. S. Thought and Language. Translated by E. Hanfman & G. Vakar. Cambridge, Mass.: The MIT Press, 1962, 1977.
Vygotzky, L. S. The problem of age-periodization of child development. Translated by M. A. Zender & B. F. Zender. Human Development, 1974, 17, 24-40.
Waller, T. G. Think First, Read Later! Piagetian Prerequisites for Reading. Newark, Del.: International Reading Association, 1977.
Walmsley, S. A. The criterion referenced measurement of an early reading behavior. Reading Research Quarterly, 1978-1979, 14:4, 574-604.
Washburne, C. Ripeness. Progressive Education, February 1936, 13, 125-130.
Watts, G. B. The teaching of French in the United States: A history. French Review, 1963, 37:14.
Weaver, C. Psycholinguistics and Reading. Boston: Little, Brown, 1980.
Webb, M. W., II. A scale for evaluating standardized reading tests, with results for Nelson-Denny, Iowa, and Stanford. Journal of Reading, 1983, 26:5, 424-429.
Wepman, J. M. Auditory Discrimination Test. New York: Cambridge University Press, 1958.
Weinstein, R. S. Reading group membership in first grade: Teacher behavior and pupil experience over time. Journal of Educational Psychology, 1976, 68, 103-116.
Wheat, H. G. The Teaching of Reading. Boston: Ginn, 1923.
White, C. S. Learning style and reading instruction. The Reading Teacher, 1983, 36:8, 842-845.
Whitehead, A. N. The Aims of Education. New York: The New American Library, A Mentor Book, 1958.
Wiesendanger, K. D., & Wollenberg, J. P. Prequestioning inhibits third graders' reading comprehension. The Reading Teacher, 1978, 31:8, 892-895.
Wildman, D. M., & Kling, M. Semantic, syntactic, and spatial anticipation in reading. Reading Research Quarterly, 1978-1979, 14:1, 128-164.
Wilson, C. R. Teaching reading comprehension by connecting the known to the new. The Reading Teacher, 1983, 36:4, 382-390.
Wilson, R. M. Diagnostic and Remedial Reading for Classroom and Clinic (4th ed.). Columbus, Ohio: Charles E. Merrill, 1981.
Wittrock, M. C. Education and the cognitive processes of the brain. In the 77th Yearbook of NSSE, Education and

the Brain. Chicago: University of Chicago Press, 1978, 61-102.

Woods, M. L., & Moe, A. J. Analytical Reading Inventory. Columbus, Ohio: Charles E. Merrill, 1977.

Yaden, D. B., Jr. Short-term memory capacity and letter identification rate. Journal of Reading, 1982, 26:3, 235-238.

Young, W. E. The relation of reading comprehension and retention to hearing comprehension and retention. Journal of Experimental Education, September 1936, 5, 30-39.

Zintz, M. V. The Reading Process: The Teacher and the Learner (2nd ed.). Dubuque, Iowa: Wm. C. Brown, 1975.

Zintz, M. V. The Reading Process: The Teacher and the Learner (3rd ed.). Dubuque, Iowa: Wm. C. Brown, 1980.

About the Author

Horst G. Taschow is Professor of Education at the University of Regina, Regina, Saskatchewan, Canada. He received his Ph.D. from Oregon State University with a specialty in the teaching of reading. His interest in reading was developed through his own teaching experiences in Germany, Bolivia, the United States, and Canada. He has taught elementary school, where he was also a principal; high school; and undergraduate and graduate university courses. His research findings have been published in professional journals and presented at professional meetings at national and international levels.

Index

Accommodation, 32
Active cognitive style, 33–34
Addressor-addressee register, 10–11
Addressor-subject register, 10–11
Adolescent development, 55–56, 57, 58–59
Aims of Education, The (Whitehead), 61
Alphabet, 69
   identification of letters of, 82–83
   languages based on, 83
Analysis in reading, 73–74
   questions for, 116
Analytic phonics, 95
Analytic teaching, 199
Application in reading, 38, 39
   questions for, 116
Approach, instructional, 138
Articulation of phonics, 96
Assessment, 196–200
   classroom, 198–99
   individual, 197–98
   school, and beyond, 199–200
Assimilation, 32
Association, word, 35–36
Attention span, 50
Attitudes
   toward language, 188–89
   toward reading, 26–27
Auditory processing, 47
   discrimination in, 92
Autistic thinking, 113

Background experiences, 29–30
   direct, 30
   Directed Reading Activity Method and, 141–42
   semantics and, 103–4
   vicarious, 30
Basal Reader Approach to Reading, The (Auckerman), 122

Basal readers, 119–25
   as basis for literature reading, 136–37
   changes in, 120–22
   defined, 119
   development of, 119–20
   Directed Reading Activity Method for, 138–49
   purposes of, 122–23
   textbooks compared to, 124–25
Basic Interpersonal Communicative Skills (BICS), 191
Becoming, 51
Bibliotherapy, 51
Bidialectism, 184
Bilingualism, 185–92
   additive, 186–87
   differences among second-language learners, 188–89
   instructing second-language learners, 189–91
   subtractive, 187–88
Bottom-up processing, 106–8
Bound morphemes, 21
British Columbia Reading Assessment (Tuinman and Kendall), 199
Bruner, Jerome S., 53, 59–60

Categorical thinking, 112
Certainty in reading, 34–35
Chalkboards, 151–53
Childhood development, 55, 56, 58, 59–60
Chronological age (CA), 64
Classroom Questions: What Kinds (Sanders), 114
Cloze junctures, 93, 94
Cloze procedure, 204–7
   preparation, administration, scoring, and interpretation of, 205–6
   as a teaching device, 206–7

Cognition, 31–34, 52–61
   metacognition, 170–72
   reading understanding in, 31–32
   stages in development of, 53–61
   style of, 32–34, 172.
   See also Thinking
Cognitive/Academic Language Proficiency (CALP), 191
Comenius, 82
Communication
   kinds of, 3–4, 6–11
   nature of, 3–4
   response and feedback in, 16–18
   sender-message-receiver in, 4–5
   special needs in, 18.
   See also Language development
Comprehension, 127–31
   advance organizers for, 129
   assimilation and accommodation in, 32
   defined, 23
   discussion and, 144
   equilibration in, 32
   generative learning and, 111–12, 130–31
   in informal reading inventories, 210–12
   kinds of thinking and, 112–13
   methods of information processing in, 106–10
   perceptual training in, 48–49
   prequestioning for, 128
   previewing for, 129–30
   qualitative measures of, 31
   quantitative measures of, 31
   questions and, 31, 113–18, 130, 144–45
   reading speed and, 36
   rereading to aid, 145–46
   textbook, 134–37
   vocabulary and, 131–33
Computer-assisted instruction, 175–77
Concentration, 171
Concepts, 104
Connotation, 136
Consonant clusters, 91-92
Consonant digraphs, 92
Consonants, 90–91
   letter-sound combinations with, 91–92
Content reading, 28–29, 126–27
Content words, 21, 25
Convergent thinking, 112–13
Copying, 15
Criterion-referenced tests, 201–2
Cultural deprivation, 180, 181

Cultural schemata, 192–93
CVC trigrams, 74–75, 149

Deep structure, 36, 100, 103
Denotation, 136
Derived scores, 201
Diachronic linguistics, 136
Diagnostic teaching, 198
Diphthongs, 90
Directed Reading Activity Method, 138–49
   outline of, 140–41
   describing and interpreting, 141–47
   instructional practices derived from, 147–48
Directed Reading-Thinking Activity (DRTA), 147
Directing Reading Maturity as a Cognitive Process (Stauffer), 147
Discussion, 144
Divergent thinking, 113
Dolch Basic Sight Vocabulary, 98

Eclectic approaches, 155–58
   example of, 157
   reading ranges and, 156–57
Educational television, 65
Emotion, 24–30
Encouragement, 61–62
Equilibration, 32
Evaluation, 196–213
   assessment methods for, 196–200
   defined, 196
   formal testing for, 200–3
   informal testing for, 203–13
   self-, 154
Evaluation questions, 116–17
Experience-Text-Relationship Method, 148
Exploring, 38, 39
Eyes
   movement of, 43–45, 46, 88, 166
   visual discrimination and, 88
   visual processing and, 45–46, 47

Field-dependent students, 172
Field-independent students, 172
Filmstrips, 28, 30
Fixation pauses, 44
Fluency in reading, 35–36
Formal testing, 200–3
Formative evaluation, 197
Free morphemes, 21–22

Index

Fricatives, 91
Frustration level, 206
Fry's List of Instant Words, 98
Function words, 21, 25, 101

Generative learning, 111-12, 130-31
Ginn and Company, 120, 121, 122
Glides, 91
Grammar, 22-23
Graphemes, 74
 translation of, to phonemes, 83-85
Graphic information, 81-83
 constituents of, 86-89
 letter identification in, 82-83, 86-87
 patterns of patterns in, 93-94
 word identification in, 81-82, 87.
 See also Written communication
Graphophonological information, 81-86
 described, 81.
 See also Phonics; Phonological information
Grouping of students, 161-62
Guided Reading Procedure (GRP), 147-48

Habits, 170
Head Start, 181
Holophrases, 12
Homonyms, 92
Hornbook, 82-83

Imitation, 12
Immediate word recognition, 97-98
Impulsive cognitive style, 33
Indentation, 102
Independent reading, 161-77
 correlates of using knowledge and, 170-77
 grouping and, 161-62
 level of, 205
 oral versus silent reading and, 162-66
 reading interest and, 24-30
 study techniques to encourage, 167-70
Individual assessment, 197-98
Individualized reading, 153-55
Inflection, 9-10
 sentence patterns and, 101
Informal reading inventory (IRI), 207-13
 interpretation of, 211-13
 isolated word recognition in, 208-9
 listening comprehension in, 211
 oral reading in, 210-11
 preparation of, 209-10
 silent reading and oral rereading in, 211

Informal testing, 203-13
 cloze procedure in, 204-7
 informal reading inventory in, 207-13
Information
 processing of, 106-10
 semantic, 102-6
 syntactic, 100-2
Instruction
 in basal readers, 138-49
 bilingualism and, 185-92
 computer-assisted, 175-77
 eclectic approaches to, 155-58
 individualized reading, 153-55
 Language Experience Approach to, 150-53, 184
 in linguistic readers, 149-50
 procedures for, 138.
 See also Teachers
Instructional reading level, 205-6
Intelligence quotient (IQ), 64
Interactive processing, 109-10
International Phonetic Alphabet (IPA), 94
International Reading Association, 114-15
Interpersonal communication, 16-17
Interpretation questions, 115-16
Intonation, 9-10, 93
Intrapersonal communication, 17-18
Investigating, 38, 39

Junctures in speech, 93-94

Kamehameha Early Education Program (KEEP), 193
Kinesic behavior, 4, 6-7
Kinesthetic processing, 47
Kucera-Francis Corpus, 98

Language development, 11-15
 bidialectism and, 184
 bilingualism and, 185-92
 individual differences in, 179-83
 integrating reading and writing in, 13
 language teaming in, 14-15
 movement from listening to speaking in, 12
 pluralism in monolingual instruction and, 192-94
 rhythm of education in, 54
 speech refinement in, 12-13
 vocabulary in, 13-14.
 See also Communication

Language Experience Approach (LEA), 150–53, 184
Language teaming, 14–15
Learning styles, 172–73
  language, 189
Learning to read, 50
Letters
  identification of, 82–83, 86–87
  visual discrimination of, 88
Linguistic readers, 149–50
Lippincott Basic Reading series, 149
Listening
  in informal reading inventories, 211
  movement from, to speaking, 12
  as sensory processing, 47
  speech refinement through, 12–13
  spelling and, 15
  vocabulary development through, 13–14
Literature, 136–37

Mastery learning, 70
Mathematics, 134–35, 169
McGuffy's Eclectic Readers, 119–20, 121, 122, 163
Meaning in communication, 8–9
Mediated word recognition, 97, 98
Memory questions, 115
Mental age (MA), 64
Mental Measurements Yearbooks (Buros), 200
Merrill Linguistic Reading Program, 149
Metacognition, 170–72
  concentration and self-discipline in, 171
  perseverance in, 171–72
Metacommunication, 4, 6–7
Method, instructional, 138
Montessori, Maria, 53, 54–56
Morphemes, 21–22
Motivation to read, 27–29
  extrinsic, 27–28
  intrinsic, 28
  subject-matter-directed, 28–29
Movement as communication, 7, 9, 47

Nasals, 91
New England Primer, 83
Noncategorical thinking, 112
Nonverbal communication, 4, 6–7
  background experiences through, 29–30
  metacommunication, 4, 6–7
  movement as, 7, 9

visuals in, 7, 9
wordless reading as, 7
Norm-referenced tests, 201
Norms, 201
Nutrition, 50

Open junctures, 93, 94
Oral communication, 3–4, 8
  auditory processing in, 47, 92
  intonation in, 9–10, 93
  meaning in, 8–9
  psychomotor abilities and, 34–37
  registers in, 10–11
  visual processing in, 45–46, 47.
  See also Language development; Phonological information
Oral reading, 163–64
  importance of, 83–84
  informal reading inventories and, 210–11
  movement from, to silent reading, 165–66
Orbis Pictus (Comenius), 82
Organizers, advance, 129
Overview, Key ideas, Read, Record, Recite, Review, Reflect (OK5R) method, 169

Paralinguistic communication, 4, 6–7
Parents, reading readiness and, 65, 67–69
Passive cognitive style, 33–34
Pauses in speech, 93
Perception, 48–49, 77–78
Perseverance, 171–72
Phonemes, 69, 74, 89, 97
  translation of graphemes to, 83–85
Phonetics, 94
Phonics, 89–92, 94–97
  articulation of, 96
  auditory discrimination in, 92
  consonants in, 90–92
  CVC trigrams in, 74–75, 149
  rules of, 96–97
  sounds in, 89
  synthetic and analytic, 94–95
  vowels in, 76–77, 90, 91
Phonograms, 150
Phonological information, 22, 83–85
  patterns of patterns in, 93–94.
  See also Graphophonological information; Phonics
Phrases
  identification of, 87–88
  visual discrimination of, 88

Index

Piaget, Jean, 53, 57–59
Pitch, 9–10
PLATO, 176
Plosives, 91
Prequestioning, 128
Preview, Question, Read, Summarize, Test (PQRST) method, 168–69
Previewing, 129–30
Psychological context of communication, 4–5
Psychomotor abilities, 34–37
  certainty in reading, 34–35
  eye movements as, 43–45, 46, 88, 166
  fluency in reading, 35–36
  in sensing, 45–48
  speed in reading, 36, 43–45
Punctuation, 102
Purpose, Ask questions, Read, Summarize (PARS) method, 169

Questions, 144–45
  content of, 114–18
  prequestioning, 128
  reading comprehension and, 31, 113–18, 130, 144–45
  ReQuest and, 147
  self-generated, 130
  student-directed, 113–14

Rainbow Edition (Ginn), 120, 121, 122
Raw scores, 201
Read, Encode, Annotate, Ponder (REAP) method, 169
Readers.
  See Basal readers; Linguistic readers
Reading as Reasoning (Thorndike), 164
Reading in Elementary School (Spache and Spache), 114
Reading interest, 24–30
  attitude toward reading and, 26–27
  background experiences and, 29–30
  characteristics of, 24–26
  motivation to read and, 27–29
Reading ranges, 156–57
Reading readiness, 63–71, 141
  advanced reading instruction and, 74–77
  basic factors in, 65–67
  beginning reading instruction and, 72–74
  partnerships in, 67–71
  sources of, 63–65
Reading tests and Reviews (Buros, ed.), 200
Reflection, 33, 38, 39, 113

Registers, 10–11
REIVA processing, 37–40
  components of, 37–39
  development of, 37
  thinking and, 49
  uses of, 40
Report of the National Committee on Reading (Gray), 63, 64, 178
ReQuest, 147
Rereading, 145–146
  in informal reading inventories, 211
Research, 146
Rhyming, 95
Rhythm of education, 54

Saccadic movements, 44
Schemata, 104–5
  cultural, 192–93
  interaction of, 109
Science, 135–36, 168
Scott, Foresman and Company, 120
Second language. *See* Bilingualism
Self-discipline, 171
Self-evaluating, 154
Self-generated questions, 130
Self-pacing, 154
Self-seeking, 154
Self-selecting, 154
Semantics, 22, 23, 102–6
  concepts and schemata in, 104–5
  experience and, 103–4
  vocabulary in, 105
Semantic webbing, 148
Semivowels, 91
Sensing, 45–48
  hearing, 47
  moving, 47
  seeing, 45–46
  touching, 48
Sentences
  free morphemes in, 22
  identification of, 87–88
  markers in, 101–2
  patterns of, 101–2
  summary, 111–12
  transformations of, 102
Sight words, 95
Sign-gesture language, 3–4
Silent communication, 8
Silent reading, 164–65
  importance of, 143

Silent reading *(continued)*
  in informal reading inventories, 211
  movement from oral reading to, 105–6
  teacher observation of, 143–44
Skill, reading, 51–52
Social studies, 135
Sounding out, 8
Sounds, 89
Speed of reading, 36
  eye movements and, 43–45
Spelling, 173–75
  language teaming in, 15
  linguistic readers and, 149–50
Stage theories of development, 53–61
  of Bruner, 59–60
  of Montessori, 54–56
  of Piaget, 57–59
  queries on, 60–61
  of Vygotzky, 56–57
  of Whitehead, 54
Standardized reading tests, 200–3
  criterion-referenced, 201–2
  norm-referenced, 201
  use of, 202–3
Strategy, instructional, 138
Stresses in speech, 93
Subvocalization, 166
Summary sentences, 111–12
Summative assessment, 196
Surface structure, 36, 100, 103
  bilingualism and, 185–86
Survey, Question, Read, Question, Compute, Question (SQRQCQ) method, 169
Survey, Question, Read, Recite, Review (SQ3R) method
  described, 167–69
  research results from, 169
Syntax, 22–23, 100–2
  pattern markers in, 101–2
  sentence patterns in, 101–2
  sentence transformations in, 102
Synthesis, 73, 74
  questions for, 116
Synthetic phonics, 94–95

Tactile processing, 48
Teachers
  observation of silent reading by, 143–44
  questions posed by, 113–14
  reading readiness and, 65, 69–71, 71–77.
  See also Instruction
Teaching English as a Foreign Language (TEFL), 189
Teaching English as a Second Language (TESL), 189
Teaching English to Speakers of Other Languages (TESOL), 189–90
Teams, 146
Technique, instructional, 138
Television, educational, 65
Terminal speech junctures, 93, 94
Testing, 196
  formal, 200–3
  informal, 203–13
Textbooks, 134–37
  basal readers compared to, 124–25
  defined, 123–24
  literature, 136–37
  mathematics, 134
  science, 135–36
  social studies, 135
Thinking, 49–50, 110–18, 142
  generative learning and, 111–12, 130–31
  kinds of, 112–13
  question strategies in, 113–18.
  See also Cognition
Thinking Goes to School (Furth and Wachs), 112
Thorndike, E.L., 110–11
Top-down processing, 106, 108–9
Transformation, sentence, 102
Translation questions, 115

VAK procedure, 47–48
VAKT procedure, 48
Verbal communication, 3–4, 7–11
  meaning in, 8–9
  silent, 8
  stresses in, 93.
  See also Language development; Oral communication; Written communication
Verbal deprivation, 180–83
Veridicality, 78
Verification, 38, 39, 145
Visual aids, 7, 9
Visual literacy, 7

Index

Visual processing, 45–46, 47
Vocabulary, 131–33, 142, 174
  aptitude hypothesis for acquiring, 132–33
  development of, 13–14
  instrumentalist hypothesis for acquiring, 132
  knowledge hypothesis for acquiring, 133
  linguistic readers and, 149–50
  semantics and, 105
Vowel clusters, 90
Vowel controllers, 90
Vowel digraphs, 90
Vowels, 76–77, 90
  semi-, 91
Vygotzky, Leo S., 53, 56–57

Whitehead, Alfred North, 53, 54, 61
Wisconsin Design for Reading Skill Development, 202
Wishful thinking, 113
Worcester, Samuel, 82
Word-calling, 8, 84, 89
Wordless reading, 7
Word lists, 98–99
Word recognition, 97–99, 107
  in informal reading inventories, 208–9
  in Language Experience Approach, 151
  word lists in, 98–99.
  See also Words
Words
  associations with, 35–36
  content, 21, 25
  function, 21, 25, 101
  function of, 20–21
  identification of, 81–82, 87
  as language symbols, 8
  as morphemes, 21–22
  sight, 95
  visual discrimination of, 88.
  See also Word recognition
Workbooks, 121–22
Written communication, 3–4
  integration of reading with, 13
  language teaming and, 14–15
  meaning in, 8–9
  movement and, 47
  psychomotor abilities and, 34–37, 43–48, 88, 166
  registers in, 10–11
  vocabulary development and, 13–14.
  See also Graphic information